Strategic Environmental Assessment in Transport and Land Use Planning

Meinen Eltern

Strategic Environmental Assessment in Transport and Land Use Planning

Thomas B Fischer

Earthscan Publications Ltd
London • Sterling, VA

First published in the UK and USA in 2002
by Earthscan Publications Ltd

ISBN: 1 85383 812 8 paperback
         1 85383 811 X hardback

Typesetting by Composition and Design Services (www.cdsca.com)
Printed and bound in the UK by Creative Print & Design Wales, Ebbw Vale
Cover design by Danny Gillespie

For a full list of publications please contact:

Earthscan Publications Ltd
120 Pentonville Road, London, N1 9JN, UK
tel: +44 (0)20 7278 0433
fax: +44 (0)20 7278 1142
email: earthinfo@earthscan.co.uk
web: **www.earthscan.co.uk**

22883 Quicksilver Drive, Sterling, VA 20166-2012, USA

Earthscan is an editorially independent subsidiary of Kogan Page Ltd and publishes in
association with WWF-UK and the International Institute for Environment and
Development

A catalogue record for this book is available from the British Library

Library of Congress Cataloging-in-Publication Data

Fischer, Thomas B., 1965–.
Strategic environmental assessment in transport and land use planning / Thomas B.
Fischer.
p. cm.
Includes bibliographical references and index.
ISBN 1-85383-811-X (cloth) — ISBN 1-85383-812-8 (pbk.)
1. Transportation—Environmental aspects—Europe. 2. Land use—Planning—
Environmental aspects—Europe. 3. Environmental impact analysis—Europe. 4. Strategic
planning—Europe. I. Title

333.7'2–dc21   2001002399

Contents

Dedication   *ii*
List of tables, figures and boxes   *viii*
Preface   *xiii*
Acnowledgements   *xv*
Acronyms and abbreviations   *xvi*

Part 1 – Background

Introduction to Part 1   **3**

1   Introduction   **4**
      SEA background   4
      Potential benefits of SEA application   9
      SEA effectiveness   13
      SEA research   14
      Aim, research questions and objectives   16
      Structure of the book   17

2   How to systematically conduct strategic environmental assessment
      research   **19**
      Choice of sample regions   19
      Problems in transnational comparative research on SEA   22
      Establishing the context for SEA application 25
      Framework for comparing SEA practice   26
      Data collection   34

Part 2 – Planning Context

Introduction to Part 2   **39**

3   Organization of planning   **40**
      Political and administrative context   40
      Planning systems   42
      Planning instruments   50
      Legislation and guidance   53
      Cross-regional characteristics   57

4   Policies, plans and programmes   **58**
      Selection of PPPs   58

PPP relevance   67
PPP accountability   71
PPP inter-modality   77
PPP procedure   78
Cross-regional characteristics   80

Part 3 – Strategic Environmental Assessment: Empirical Research Results

Introduction to Part 3   **85**

5   SEA practice   **86**
Extent of SEA application   86
Types of SEA   87
Context variables and SEA presentation aspects   93
Procedural aspects of SEA application   95
Impact coverage   102
Other methodological aspects   115
SEA preparation times   122
Summary   123

6   Opinions and attitudes of authorities   **126**
Overall picture   126
Opinions on current SEA   128
Attitudes of authorities towards formalized SEA   136
Summary   148

7   The Consideration of Sustainability Aspects   **149**
Overall picture   149
Sustainability objectives   152
Sustainability targets   161
Measures for sustainability   170
Overall evaluation of sustainability objectives, targets and measures   177
Summary   180

8   Potential benefits from SEA application   **182**
Overall picture   182
Wider consideration of impacts and alternatives   184
Proactive assessment: SEA as a supporting tool for PPP formulation for
sustainable development   188
Strengthening project EIA: Increasing the efficiency of tiered decision
making   191
Systematic and effective consideration of the environment at higher
tiers of decision making   194
Consultation and participation on SEA-related issues   197
Overall evaluation of the potential SEA benefits   201
Requirements of the EC SEA Directive   202
Summary   206

Part 4 – Summary and Conclusions

Introduction to Part 4   **211**

9   Overview and synthesis   **212**
       Overall results   212
       Evaluation of individual SEAs   218
       Correlation analysis of SEA aspects   219
       Interpretation of the results   224

10   Conclusions   **228**
       Extent of SEA application and SEA classification   228
       Authorities' opinions on current SEA and their attitudes towards
       formalized SEA   230
       Consideration of sustainability objectives, targets and measures and
       the role of SEA   232
       Extent to which assessments result in the five potential SEA benefits   234
       Suggestions for improving current practice   235

Appendix 1 Main source documentation used in the analysis   242
Appendix 2 Statutes and statutory instruments   246
Appendix 3 List of all the SEAs in the three regions   249
*Appendix 4 Conformity of case study SEAs with the requirements
       of the EC SEA Directive proposal*   254
*Appendix 5 Comparison of targets of the Fifth Environmental Action
       Programme with national sustainable development strategies*   256
Notes   258
References   264
Index   278

List of tables, figures and boxes

TABLES

2.1	SEA in the transport sector in EU member states	20
2.2	Baseline data on the three sample regions	22
2.3	Administrative structure, area and population sizes of sample regions	35
3.1	Landscape planning and spatial planning in Germany	49
3.2	Main features of transport and spatial/land use planning	56
4.1	PPPs in North West England	59
4.2	PPPs in Noord-Holland	60
4.3	PPPs in EVR Brandenburg-Berlin	62
4.4	PPPs selected for analysis	64
4.5	Policy and project orientation of PPPs	67
4.6	PPP relevance in North West England	70
4.7	PPP relevance in Noord-Holland	72
4.8	PPP relevance in EVR Brandenburg-Berlin	74
4.9	Overall context variable scores	81
5.1	SEA types and their characteristics in the sample regions	88
5.2	SEAs undertaken at different administrative levels in the three sample regions	92
5.3	Procedural coverage in 25 SEAs	95
5.4	Types of environmental impacts assessed in SEA	103
5.5	Types of socio-economic impacts assessed in SEA	104
5.6	Extent of impacts assessed in SEA	113
5.7	Methods in documentation for the three SEA types	117
5.8	Techniques in documentation for the three SEA types	119
5.9	Overall evaluation of the use of methods and techniques for all SEAs	120
5.10	SEA variables scores	124
6.1	Overall evaluation of opinions on current SEA	134
6.2	Overall evaluation of attitudes towards the application of formalized SEA	144
7.1	Reduction targets of the Fifth Environmental Action Programme considered in PPPs	168
7.2	Implicit consideration of targets from the Fifth Environmental Action Programme	169
7.3	Overall ranking and evaluation for all PPPs	179
8.1	SEA-specific evaluation of the potential SEA benefit 1, 'wider consideration of impacts and alternatives'	185

8.2 SEA-specific evaluation of the potential SEA benefit 2, 'proactive assessment: SEA as a supporting tool for PPP formulation for sustainable development'   189

8.3 SEA-specific evaluation of the potential SEA benefit 3, 'strengthening project EIA, increasing efficiency of tiered decision making'   192

8.4 SEA-specific evaluation for the potential SEA benefit 4, 'systematic and effective consideration of the environment at higher tiers of decision making'   195

8.5 SEA-specific evaluation of the potential SEA benefit 3, 'consultation and participation on SEA-related issues'   199

8.6 Overall evaluation of the potential SEA benefits for the individual SEAs   202

9.1 Results for the seven main comparative aspects for individual SEA and the identification of good practice cases   220

9.2 Correlation of context and SEA variables and the other SEA aspects   223

10.1 Current SEA type practice for the transport and spatial/land use sectors at national, regional and local levels in the three sample regions   237

10.2 Improving current SEA instruments   240

FIGURES

1.1 Integrated procedure in support of sustainable development   11

1.2 Objectives and outline of the book   18

2.1 The sample regions and administrative boundaries of authorities responsible for local land use PPPs   23

3.1 Spatial/land use planning in England and Wales   43

3.2 Trunk roads planning process in the UK   44

3.3 Spatial/land use planning in The Netherlands   45

3.4 National transport infrastructure planning process in The Netherlands   46

3.5 Spatial/land use planning in Germany   47

3.6 Federal transport infrastructure planning process in Germany   48

5.1 SEA presentation aspects and context variables   94

5.2 Overall coverage of SEA procedural stages   97

5.3 SEA procedural stages considered in the three sample regions   99

5.4 SEA procedural stages considered in the three SEA types   101

5.5 SEA procedural stages considered in the two sectors   101

5.6 Extent of procedural stages covered in SEA and the associated PPP   102

5.7 Environmental and socio-economic impacts considered in all SEAs   107

5.8 Consideration of environmental impacts in the three sample regions   108

5.9 Consideration of socio-economic impacts in the three sample regions   109

5.10 Consideration of environmental impacts in the three SEA types   110

5.11 Consideration of socio-economic impacts in the three SEA types   110

5.12 Consideration of environmental impacts in the two sectors   111

5.13 Consideration of socio-economic aspects in the two sectors   113

5.14 Overall scores for impact coverage for the regions, SEA types and sectors   115

5.15 Methods used in SEA documentation   116
5.16 Methods used in SEA documentation for the two sectors   117
5.17 Techniques used in SEA documentation   118
5.18 Techniques used in SEA documentation for the two sectors   119
5.19 Overall scores for the regions, SEA types and sectors   122
5.20 SEA preparation times for the three sample regions   123
6.1   Opinions and attitudes on current SEA and formalized SEA   127
6.2   Opinions of authorities on current SEA and attitudes towards
      formalized SEA representing the cross-section of 36 PPPs by region   128
6.3   Views about the influence of current SEA in PPP formulation by region   129
6.4   Views about the influence of current SEA in PPP formulation by
      SEA type   129
6.5   Views of local authorities in North West England and EVR
      Brandenburg-Berlin on the influence of current SEA   130
6.6   Views on the quality of current SEA by region   131
6.7   Views on the quality of current SEAs by SEA type   132
6.8   Views on the quality of current SEA by sector   132
6.9   Views of local authorities on the quality of current SEA in EVR
      Brandenburg-Berlin and North West England   133
6.10 Opinions on current SEAs by region, SEA type and sector   136
6.11 Views on the possibility of integrating formalized SEA into the PPP
      process   137
6.12 Views on a possible delay of PPP preparation through formalized SEA   139
6.13 Expectations of local authorities for formalized SEA to delay PPP
      preparation   140
6.14 Views on the possibility of accelerating project preparation through
      formalized SEA   141
6.15 Views of local authorities on the possibility of accelerating project
      preparation through formalized SEA   142
6.16 Views on the possibility of formalized SEA leading to a better
      consideration of environmental concerns   143
6.17 Views of local authorities on the possibility of formalized SEA leading to a
      better consideration of environmental concerns   144
6.18 Overall scores for attitudes towards formalized SEA by region, SEA type,
      sector, and PPPs with and without SEA   147
7.1   Sustainability aspects in the cross-section of PPPs   150
7.2   Sustainability aspects in local land use PPPs with and without SEA   150
7.3   Explicit objectives, explicit targets and measures by region   151
7.4   Objectives, targets and measures in local land use PPPs   152
7.5   Sustainability objectives considered in the individual PPP   153
7.6   The consideration of sustainability objectives in the three sample regions   154
7.7   Sustainability objectives considered in the two sectors   155
7.8   Sustainability objectives and SEA application   156
7.9   Sustainability objectives and SEA application per sample region   156
7.10 Objectives considered in the two sectors and SEA application   157
7.11 SEA types and the consideration of sustainability objectives   158
7.12 Sustainability objectives considered in local land use PPPs   160

7.13 SEA application and the consideration of sustainability objectives in local land use PPPs 161
7.14 Sustainability targets considered in the individual PPP 162
7.15 The consideration of sustainability targets by region 163
7.16 Sustainability targets in the two sectors 164
7.17 Sustainability targets and SEA application 164
7.18 Sustainability targets and SEA application for the regions 165
7.19 Sustainability targets in the two sectors and SEA application 166
7.20 Sustainability targets and SEA types 167
7.21 Sustainability targets considered in local land use PPPs 169
7.22 SEA application and the consideration of sustainability targets in local land use PPPs 170
7.23 Sustainability measures considered in the individual PPP 171
7.24 The consideration of sustainability measures in the cross-section of PPPs 172
7.25 Sustainability measures by sector 173
7.26 Sustainability measures and SEA application 173
7.27 The impact of SEA on the consideration of sustainability measures 174
7.28 The impact of SEA on the consideration of sustainability measures by sector 174
7.29 Measures considered in the three SEA types and in PPPs without SEA 175
7.30 Measures considered in local land use PPPs 176
7.31 SEA and the consideration of sustainability measures in local land use PPPs 176
7.32 Sustainability scores for the individual PPP 178
7.33 Overall average scores for the regions, SEA types, sectors and PPPs with and without SEA 181
8.1 Extent to which SEAs for the cross-section of PPPs result in the potential SEA benefits 183
8.2 Regional average scores by potential SEA benefit 183
8.3 SEA-type evaluation for the potential SEA benefit 1, 'wider consideration of impacts and alternatives' 187
8.4 Sector-specific evaluation for the potential SEA benefit 1, 'wider consideration of impacts and alternatives' 187
8.5 SEA-type evaluation for the potential SEA benefit 2, 'proactive assessment: SEA as a supporting tool for PPP formulation for sustainable development' 191
8.6 SEA-type evaluation for the potential SEA benefit 3, 'strengthening project EIA: increasing the efficiency of tiered decision making' 194
8.7 SEA-type evaluation for the potential SEA benefit 4, 'systematic and effective consideration of the environment at higher tiers of decision making' 197
8.8 SEA-type evaluation for the potential SEA benefit 5, 'consultation and participation on SEA-related issues' 200
8.9 Sector-specific evaluation for the potential SEA benefit 5, 'consultation and participation on SEA-related issues' 201
8.10 Average potential SEA benefit scores for the regions, SEA types and sectors 203

8.11 Extent to which individual SEAs meet the requirements of the EC SEA
     Directive proposal   204
8.12 Extent to which the criteria of the EC SEA Directive proposal are
     considered   205
8.13 Average scores for the SEA Directive proposal requirements by region,
     SEA type and sector   207
9.1 Results for seven SEA aspects by region   213
9.2 Results for seven SEA aspects by SEA type   215
9.3 Results for seven SEA aspects by sector   216
9.4 Sustainability aspects and attitudes in PPPs with and without SEA   216
9.5 Regional overall scores for local land use PPPs   217
10.1 Status and tasks of SEA types   236

BOXES

1.1 Components of NEPA-based assessment   5
1.2 Potential benefits of SEA application   10
1.3 Aim of the book   16
1.4 Research questions   16
1.5 Objectives of the book   17
2.1 Design of analytical framework for comparing SEA practice   26
2.2 Framework for comparing the consideration of sustainability aspects   28
2.3 SEA benefits, principles and evaluation criteria   30
2.4 Requirements of the EC SEA Directive (1999 draft)   33
5.1 Policy and project orientation and SEA-type application   91

Preface

Strategic environmental assessment (SEA) has been interpreted in many different ways. Currently, it is mostly portrayed as a process for assessing environmental impacts in strategic decision making above the project level. Increasingly, socio-economic impacts are also included. While different suggestions have been made on the form that SEA should take, due to a lack of empirical research the extent to which different aspects are considered in current practice has largely remained unclear. An important and yet unanswered question is whether every SEA needs to fulfil the same requirements or whether there are methodological differences regarding, for example, the planning level or the sector of its application. In this context there is a need to acknowledge the increasing criticism of traditional planning approaches that are portrayed as being rather ineffective and overly complex.

This book covers most of the issues addressed in recent SEA debates and is based on a systematic analysis of 80 assessments in the UK, The Netherlands and Germany in transport and spatial/land use planning. Assessments include those likely to be the basis for formal SEA following the requirements of the European SEA Directive and are therefore referred to as SEA. This book goes beyond the simple analysis of procedures, methods and techniques, and also considers the underlying political and planning systems. Based on the evidence provided by the empirical analysis, it is suggested that SEA can take different forms, depending on the level of its application. Three main SEA types are introduced, with distinct methodological requirements. For convenience and in order not to confuse the SEA debate any further, these three SEA types are called policy-SEA, plan-SEA and programme-SEA. It is suggested that only a tiered system using all three SEA types is able to meet the requirements formulated in the SEA literature.

To date, most international comparative SEA research studies have applied a case study approach without systematically comparing different assessments. It has therefore remained impossible to clearly identify good practice cases. In order to remedy this shortcoming, the book systematically compares practice based on a common set of factors and variables. Good practice examples are identified and suggestions for improving current assessments are made.

This book is written for a broad audience; planners, assessment practitioners, politicians and academics. It refers to the two sectors that are frequently portrayed as having the most excessive SEA experience: transport and land use planning. It is intended to serve as both a basis for better SEA application and a model for more systematic comparative SEA research. It concludes that a more consistent and systematic approach to SEA is needed and that there are certain rules for conducting SEA, depending mainly on the decision making level. It does not only give guidance on how SEA should be conducted, but also explains why certain aspects are of particular importance for overall SEA success. It therefore touches on new territory and goes far beyond the scope of most of the existing studies on SEA.

Acknowledgements

This book is based to a large extent on the findings of research undertaken for a PhD at the EIA Centre, the University of Manchester. First and foremost, I therefore wish to thank Chris Wood and Carys Jones, the supervisors of my PhD dissertation. I am also most grateful for the valuable support provided by the EIA Centre at the School of Planning and Landscape, particularly by Norman Lee. I am grateful for the cooperation which I have received from everyone, particularly the officers who agreed to be interviewed and who returned my questionnaires. Thanks to my examiners John Glasson and Chris Banister for their critical comments and to Dieter Wagner (Stadt- und Regionalplanung, Dr Paul G Jansen).

I would also like to thank Ted Kitchen (Sheffield Hallam University, Sheffield), Mathias Lade (Berlin), Claudia Riehl (Technical University of Berlin) and Luc Kapoen (University of Amsterdam) for their comments on pilot questionnaires, as well as Robert Hull (European Commission (EC), DG XI) for his comments on the framework depicting transport-related sustainability objectives, targets and measures of the EC Fifth Environmental Action Programme. Thanks to Roel, who helped me with the Dutch translations and who was a great host during my stays in The Netherlands. Thanks also to Clive George (University of Manchester), Adam Barker (University of Aberdeen), Simon Marsden (formerly University of Tasmania), Cecilia Wong (Liverpool University), Paul Scott (formerly University of Manchester) and Stephanie Hevecker (Eberswalde) for always interesting discussions and support.

Finally, I would like to thank my whole family and all my friends for their enduring support without which I would have never been able to complete this book.

I gratefully acknowledge the financial support of the University of Manchester and the Brian Large Bursary Fund.

Acronyms and abbreviations

BauGB	Construction Statute Book (*Baugesetzbuch*) (German statute on construction law)
BfRBS	Federal Ministry for Spatial Organization, Construction and City Development (*Bundesministerium für Raumordnung, Bauwesen und Städtebau*) (Germany)
BMU	Federal Environment Ministry (*Bundesministerium für Umvelt, Naturschutz und Reaktorsicherheit*) (Germany)
BMVBW	Federal Ministry for Transport, Construction and Settlements (*Bundesministerium für Verkehr, Bau- und Wohnungswesen*; formerly BfRBS and BMV) (Germany)
BoN	regional level administration (*besturen op niveau-regio*) (The Netherlands)
BVWP	Federal Transport Infrastructure Plan (*Bundesverkehrswegeplan*) (Germany)
CBA	cost–benefit analysis
CEAA	Canadian Environment Assessment Agency
CEARC	Canadian Environmental Assessment Research Council
CEQA	California Environmental Quality Act
CO_2	carbon dioxide
DB	national railways (*Deutsche Bahn*) (Germany)
dB(A)	decibel
DETR	Department of the Environment, Transport and the Regions (formerly DoE and DoT) (UK)
DG XI	*former* Directorate-General for Environment, Consumer Protection and Nuclear Security; *now* Environment Directorate-General (EC)
DoE	Department of the Environment (UK)
DoT	Department of Transport (UK)
DTLR	Department for Transport, Local Government and the Regions (formerly DETR) (UK)
EC	European Commission
ECMT	European Conference of Ministers of Transport
EEA	European Environment Agency
EIA	environmental impact assessment
EU	European Union
EVR	Berlin-Brandenburg Planning Region
FNP	statutory local land use plan (Germany)

GL	Common Land Planning Authority (Berlin and Brandenburg)
GOR	government office for the regions (UK)
IAIA	International Association for Impact Assessment
IEEP	Institute for European Environmental Policy
IIED	International Institute for Environment and Development
INVERNO	Integrated Transport Vision for the Northern Wing of the Randstad (The Netherlands)
IPVR	Inter-Provincial Urbanization Vision for the Randstad (The Netherlands)
IVP	integrated transport plan Brandenburg (Germany)
LBBW	Authority for Construction, Construction Techniques and Settlements (*Landesamt für Bauen, Bautechnik und Wohnen*) (*Land* Brandenburg, Germany)
LEP	regional development plan (Germany)
LEPeV	regional development plan Berlin-Brandenburg (Germany)
LEPro	land development programme (Germany)
LP	local plan
MCA	multi-criteria analysis
MIT	long-range infrastructure and transport programme (*Meerjarenprogramma Infrastructuur en Transport*) (The Netherlands)
MURL	Ministry for the Environment, Nature Protection, Agriculture and Consumer Protection (*Ministerium für Umwelt und Naturschutz, Landwirtschaft und Verbraucherschutz*) (*Land* Northrhine-Westfalia, Germany)
MVA	group consultancy
MVW	Ministry of Transport, Public Works and Water Management (*Ministerie van Verkeer en Waterstaat*) (The Netherlands)
NATO	North Atlantic Treaty Organization
NEPA	National Environmental Policy Act (US)
NIMBY	not in my back yard
NMP	National Environmental Policy Plan (*Nationaal Milieubeleidsplan*) (The Netherlands)
NO_x	nitrous oxides
NS	national railways (*Nationale Spoorwegen*) (The Netherlands)
PPG	planning policy guidance
PPPs	policies, plans and programmes
RDA	regional development agency
ROA	Regional Body of Amsterdam
ROPOrient	Federal Spatial Orientation Framework (*Raumordnungspolitischer Orientierungsrahmen*) (Germany)
RPG	regional planning guidance (UK)
RVVP	integrated transport plan (*regionaale verkeers– en vervoersplannen*) (The Netherlands)
SEA	strategic environmental assessment
SO_2	sulphur dioxide
StEP	integrated city development plan Berlin (Germany)

SVV	Transport Structure Plan (*Structuurschema Verkeer en Vervoer*) (The Netherlands)
SVVII	Second Transport Structure Plan (The Netherlands)
TPP	transport policy *or* programme (UK)
UDP	unitary development plan (UK)
UK	United Kingdom
UNECE	United Nations Economic Commission for Europe
US	United States of America
UVP	*Umweltverträglichkeitsprüfung* (environmental impact assessment)
VINEX	National Spatial Plan (The Netherlands)
VOC	volatile organic compound
VROM	Minstry of Housing, Spatial Planning and the Environment (*Ministerie van Volkshuisvesting, Ruimtelijke Ordening en Milieubeheer*) (The Netherlands)

Background

Introduction to Part 1

Part 1 of the book consists of Chapters 1 and 2, which include an introduction to the topic and a presentation of the framework used for analysing and comparing strategic environmental assessment (SEA) practice in England, The Netherlands and Germany.

Chapter 1 portrays current understanding of SEA, and depicts the potential benefits that should result from SEA application. The aim, questions and objectives of the book are also outlined. Chapter 2 explains the choice of three sample regions to be included in research underlying the book and the problems faced when undertaking transnational, comparative research on SEA. Finally, the development of the analytical framework for comparing SEA practice in the three countries and the data collection are explained.

Chapter 1

Introduction

Chapter 1 is divided into six main sections. The first portrays the background to strategic environmental assessment (SEA). This is followed by a section identifying the potential benefits of SEA application, as proposed in the SEA literature. In order to achieve the potential benefits, SEA needs to be applied effectively, and the third section therefore identifies aspects for effective SEA application. The fourth section describes previous SEA research, based on which research problems and needs are determined, while the fifth section sets out the aims and objectives. The final section outlines the structure of the book.

SEA BACKGROUND

Rationale

Strategic environmental assessment (SEA) is a rapidly emerging area of professional and general interest and practice. It aims at ensuring that environmental aspects are addressed and incorporated at decision making levels prior to, or above, the project level (Elling and Nielsen, 1996, p9), ie at strategic decision making levels, which are also frequently referred to in terms of policies, plans and programmes, (PPPs) (Sadler and Verheem, 1996b, pp55–57).[1] SEA helps to improve the quality of decision making by providing policy, plan or programme (PPP) makers with the information necessary to conduct informed choices, thus reducing the potential harm done to the environment. SEA is usually understood to be an iterative and adaptive process with an opportunity for external control and public involvement (Elling and Nielsen, 1996, p4). The usefulness of SEA has been widely discussed (see, for example, Sadler and Verheem, 1996a; Glasson, 1995b; Wood and Djeddour, 1992), and is reflected in the potential benefits that should result from SEA application. Potential SEA benefits are discussed in the next section.

Origins and definition of SEA

The foundations of SEA were laid in 1969 by the National Environmental Policy Act (NEPA) in the US. NEPA did not distinguish between PPPs and projects, but generally referred to actions, ie no distinction was made between strategic and project levels of decision making. Many countries followed NEPA's example and established provisions for environmental assessment, although typically these were aimed only at projects and not at policies, plans and programmes.

When the actual term 'strategic environmental assessment' was coined in 1989 in the UK, an understanding of the concept was derived from that of project-based environmental impact assessment (EIA).[2] The principles of SEA and EIA were perceived to be the same (Wood, 1997, p5; Lee and Walsh, 1992, p131; United Nations Economic Commission for Europe (UNECE) 1992, p1). This understanding may be illustrated by the US NEPA-based process (see Box 1.1; for a further discussion of project EIA, see, for example, Petts, 1999, and Glasson et al, 1995).

Before the start of the assessment process, objectives and goals and possible development alternatives are identified. The SEA process itself starts with the screening stage which determines the need for assessment. It does so by assessing whether the impacts[3] of a PPP are potentially in conflict with previously identified objectives and targets. Screening is followed by scoping, which creates the terms of reference for assessment (Lee and Hughes, 1995, p4). Scoping allows key environmental issues that are potentially significantly affected by the PPP to be identified, and determines the issues to be addressed in the assessment. The assessment report is prepared in order to provide authorities with factual information and comprises the analysis of environmental impacts and consequences (Sadler, 1996, p159). Review is of importance in order to check the quality and adequacy of the assessment report. Due to the uncertainties of predictions it is necessary to monitor the actual effects, which include post PPP analysis and post auditing (Dipper et al, 1998). Based on the findings of monitoring, action can be taken to mitigate any significant non-predicted impacts (Marr, 1997, p192). Consultation and participation are

---

BOX 1.1: COMPONENTS OF NEPA-BASED ASSESSMENT

A. Consideration of possibilities for development, eg, *alternative means* for achieving objectives and goals (scenarios may also help to address uncertainties).
B. *Designing* development *proposals.*
C. Determining whether an assessment is necessary for a particular proposal (*screening*).
D. Deciding on the topics to be covered in SEA (*scoping*).
E. Preparing an *assessment report* (ie, inter alia, describing (A) the proposal and (B) the environment affected by it, assessing the *magnitude* and *significance* of *impacts*).
F. *Reviewing* the assessment report to check its adequacy.
G. *Deciding* on the proposal, using the assessment report, and opinions expressed about it.
H. *Monitoring* the impacts of the proposal if it is implemented.

Source: adapted from Wood, 1995, p5

considered to be of fundamental importance in the assessment process and their use results in one of the potential benefits of SEA.

More recently, the range of interpretation of SEA has become much wider and the term is also used for other assessment types apart from those based on project EIA principles. A current, widely used, definition of SEA was given by Thérivel et al (1992, pp19–20). They described SEA as a formalized, systematic and comprehensive process that evaluates the environmental impacts of PPPs, considers alternatives, includes a written report on the findings of the evaluation and uses these findings in publicly accountable decision making. Even though this definition does not contradict more traditional approaches, certain EIA process-based principles are not mentioned (for example, screening, scoping and review). More recent definitions describe SEA in a less stringent manner (for example, Sadler and Verheem, 1996a, p27) and it has also been proposed that the term SEA be used for any form of assessment of the environmental impacts of PPPs (Steer Davies Gleave, 1996, p24). There are so many different SEA descriptions and interpretations that it was suggested that the 'lack of knowledge and standardised terminology, both as regards "SEA" and "PPPs", often confuses discussion on the issue' (Environment Australia, 1997, Chapter 6).

Recent developments

A number of authors have suggested that SEA should develop more independently of project EIA (for example, Niekerk and Voogd, 1996, para 3; Sadler and Verheem, 1996a, p22; Thérivel and Partidário, 1996b, p53). Furthermore, in line with the findings of empirical research on PPP processes, the need to apply SEA processes in a flexible manner was recognized (see, for example, Partidário, 2000, and Koernov, 1999). Thus, it was suggested that PPP making might not follow a hierarchical and logical sequence of predetermined steps (Bregha et al, 1990; O'Riordan, 1986; Wildavsky, 1979), but rather a continuous interaction and negotiation process by different parties (Thissen, 1997, p24; Innes, 1994, p41). Higher tiers (ie those applied early in the planning cycle) in particular, were identified as political activities that need to consider and balance the perceptions and interests of individual actors (Gordon et al, 1993, p7). It was, however, recognized that outcomes of decisions are influenced by the information available to authorities (Minogue, 1993, p17), and that factual information can influence decision making (Innes, 1994, p31).[4]

Many authors have stressed the desirability for SEA processes to be fully integrated into policy, plan or programme processes (Sadler and Verheem, 1996a, p80; Thérivel, 1996, p30; Institute for European Environmental Policy (IEEP), 1994, p5)[5]. It was also suggested that SEA 'is only a temporary instrument and is not necessary when environment is fully integrated in economic planning' (Verheyen 1996, p199).

Even though integrative forms of impact assessment were proposed by various authors, for example, adaptive environmental management by Holling (1978) or policy assessment by Boothroyd (1994), to date it has remained unclear what form SEA should take if fully integrated into the PPP process. It has also remained unclear whether the potential SEA benefits could still be achieved. Basic SEA principles are therefore usually still portrayed as being NEPA or EIA process based[6] (European Commission (EC), 1997a, p3; Sadler and Verheem, 1996a, p79, p173; Elling and Nielsen, 1996, p8; Lee and Hughes, 1995, p4; University of Manchester, 1995a; UNECE, 1992).

SEA categorization to date

While a number of possibilities for the categorization of SEA have been proposed, to date research activities have failed to deliver a clearer understanding of how different SEA categories compare. Therefore, the different forms of SEA categorization suggested to date are portrayed.

A common approach for categorizing SEA relates to the sector of application, such as transport and spatial/land use. Sectoral categorization of SEA is frequently undertaken, for example, by Goodland (1997), Sheate (1995), Pinfield (1992), Lee and Wood (1978). To date, it has largely remained unclear what the differences of SEA application for different sectors are.

Another possibility for the categorization of SEA refers to the level in the planning process of its application, ie to PPPs (Lee and Wood, 1978). In order to distinguish between the three terms, Wood and Djeddour (1992, p6) suggested that:

> *'a policy may ... be considered as the inspiration and guidance for action, a plan as a set of co-ordinated and timed objectives for the implementation of the policy, and a programme as a set of projects in a particular area'.*

Referring to local land use plans in Germany, Hübler et al (1995) distinguished two main stages in environmental assessment. The first stage deals with different development scenarios and can be regarded as being policy oriented. The second stage deals with concrete land use changes and is therefore project oriented. More recently, the European Commission (1999a) referred to network and corridor SEAs in the transport sector. While the former deals with entire transport networks and is more policy oriented, the latter deals with transport corridors and is more project oriented.

As environmental assessment is first and foremost a procedural 'instrument', SEA can also be categorized according to procedural aspects. The Institute for European Environment Policy (IEEP, 1994), distinguished 'full' EIA-process-based SEA from other SEA types. More recently, Gosling (1999) distinguished four SEA types, depending on the degree to which SEA is integrated into the PPP and the stage in the planning cycle of its application. English Nature (1996) distinguished three SEA types according to their integration into the PPP process, namely 'consent related', 'integrated' and 'objectives-led' SEA. Whereas 'consent related' SEA was said to join the process at one particular point, 'integrated' SEA was said to be fully integrated into the process. 'Objectives-led' SEA was seen as an extension of 'integrated' SEA, defining environmental objectives and goals.

Following the perception that SEA should be a supporting tool for PPP making for sustainable development (Lawrence, 1997; Lee and Walsh, 1992; Jacobs and Sadler, 1989), impact coverage has become the basis for SEA categorization. SEA that only considers aspects of the physical environment can thus be distinguished from SEA that considers environmental and socioeconomic aspects. Whereas the former is unsuitable for sustainable development assessment, the latter can potentially be developed to become a tool that supports decision making for sustainable development.

It is suggested that SEA categorization can lead to a more efficient and effective use of SEA. Thus, if SEA 'type specific' application rules could be identified, resulting SEA tasks could be clearly outlined. Based on a clear set of criteria, Chapter 5 categorizes the SEAs found in the three sample regions into three main SEA types. For convenience and in order not to confuse discussion on SEA any further, existing terminology is used and the three SEA types are called policy-SEA, plan-SEA and programme-SEA. Each of these SEA types fulfils certain distinguishable tasks.

SEA in the European Union

Even before the SEA Directive was officially adopted in 2001, a number of European Commission (EC) documents had stressed the need to apply SEA (EC, 1993a; EC, 1992; see also the EC Habitats Directive, 92/43/EEC). To date, mandatory provisions for assessing environmental impacts have only referred to the project level and were introduced in 1988 following the EIA Directive (85/337/EEC)[7] and subsequently amended (97/11/EC).

Despite the lack of formal European Union (EU) wide requirements, informal provisions and guidance for taking environmental aspects into account in PPP making were found in many EU countries, mostly at regional and local levels, particularly for land use plans. According to Lee and Hughes (1995, Table 3), by 1995 only Luxembourg and Greece did not have any SEA-type provisions. This was later confirmed by a number of other sources (EC, 1998b; Thérivel and Partidário, 1996a; Wood, 1995; Gilpin, 1995; Thérivel et al, 1992).

SEA research studies have been conducted in many countries. Examples of informal SEA practice in the EU include:

- **European Commission:** an SEA for the European High Speed Train Network was conducted in 1993 (EC, 1993b). In 2000, the EC was preparing an SEA for the Trans-European-Networks (see also EC, 1998a; European Environment Agency, 1998). Furthermore, environmental appraisal of regional plans is conducted in the context of the structural funds (Bradley, 1998).
- **Denmark:** an administrative order identifies requirements for environmental assessments of bills and other government proposals (Ministry of Environment and Energy, 1995a and 1995b).
- **Germany:** the landscape planning systems cover certain elements of SEA (Wagner, 1990) and a number of voluntary SEAs were conducted for local land use plans (Ministerium für Umwelt, Raumordnung und Landwirtschaft,

MURL, 1997; Jacoby, 1996). Since 1975, there have also been provisions for assessing the impacts of public measures of the Federation (Grundsätze für die Prüfung der Umweltverträglichkeit öffentlicher Maßnahmen des Bundes). Furthermore, it was suggested that there is SEA experience in the transport sector (Wagner, 1994).

- **The Netherlands:** an environment test (e-test, *milieutoets*) is applied to certain policy guidance and regulations (de Vries and Tonk, 1997; Ministerie van VROM, 1996b; Verheem, 1992). Furthermore, formal project EIA principles are applied in The Netherlands to certain spatial/land use plans following the amended Environment Act of 1994 (Ministerie van VROM, 1994a).
- **Sweden:** informal SEA is conducted for local land use plans (Bonde, 1998; EC, 1997a, p24). More recently, a major transport corridor SEA was undertaken (Vägverket, 1998).
- **France:** Since 1990, the French government have attempted to introduce SEA (Falque, 1995) and environmental impacts are currently to some extent considered in land use planning (Ministère de l'Environnement, 1995). Furthermore, an SEA was conducted for the Rhône transport corridor between Lyon and Marseille (Ministère de l'Equipement, 1992).
- **UK:** a checklist approach ('policy impact matrix') to 'environmental appraisal' (more recently referred to as 'sustainability appraisal' is applied to development plans (Thérivel, 1995; Department of the Environment (DoE), 1993). Furthermore, government policies are appraised, following the guide *Policy Appraisal and the Environment* (DoE, 1991; Department of the Environment, Transport and the Regions (DETR), 1998c). An evaluation of practice up to 1998 was provided by the DETR (1998g).

All EU countries that had some SEA-related experience in the transport sector in 1996 (the time when the empirical research underlying the book was started) are identified in Chapter 2.

POTENTIAL BENEFITS OF SEA APPLICATION

A number of potential benefits that should result from SEA application were suggested by Sheate (1996), Lee and Walsh (1992), Thérivel et al (1992), UNECE (1992) and Wood and Djeddour (1992). These can be described by five main themes which are summarized in Box 1.2 and discussed below. The potential benefits are used for evaluating SEA practice in the three sample regions (see Chapter 8).

Benefit 1: Wider consideration of impacts and alternatives

The first potential SEA benefit results from the consideration of a wider range of impacts and alternatives than usually made in project EIA. For transport-related assessment, Eriksson (1994, p1) suggested that:

BOX 1.2: POTENTIAL BENEFITS OF SEA APPLICATION

1. Wider consideration of impacts and alternatives.
2. Pro-active assessment – SEA as a supporting tool for PPP formulation for sustainable development.
3. Strengthening project EIA – increasing the efficiency of tiered decision making.
4. Systematic and effective consideration of the environment at higher tiers of decision making.
5. Consultation and participation on SEA-related issues.

'the strategic approach to environmental assessment is necessary for considering eg impacts on the global environment and including intermodal aspects in the development of efficient transport.'

Impacts to be considered include indirect and induced impacts (resulting from the stimulation of other developments), synergistic impacts (where the impacts of several projects may exceed the sum of individual impacts), long-range, delayed and global impacts (for example, greenhouse gas emissions). The SEA scope should therefore be commensurate with the scope of the PPP (Sadler and Verheem, 1996a, p79). General cumulative impacts should also be considered (Sadler and Verheem, 1996a, p32).[8]

The use of SEA allows for the consideration of alternatives that are often not considered at the project level (for example, alternative sites and modes). The development and comparison of alternative PPPs:

'allow the decision-maker to determine which PPP is the best option: which achieves the objective(s) at the lowest cost or greatest benefit to the environment or sustainability, or which achieves the best balance between contradictory objectives' (Thérivel, 1996, p33).

An evaluation of the potential impacts of different alternatives, based on clear underlying objectives and targets allows the impact significance to be determined. Furthermore, a wider consideration of impacts and alternatives also includes the use of scenarios, allowing ranges of uncertainty to be identified. Finally, SEA is able to widen the range of impacts and alternatives by dealing with small-scale projects or non-project actions, for which no project EIAs are conducted (Lee and Walsh, 1992, p129).

Benefit 2: Proactive assessment – SEA as a supporting tool for PPP formulation for sustainable development[9]

The second potential SEA benefit results from its application as a proactive tool in PPP making that, in line with the demands of the precautionary principle, addresses the causes of environmental impacts rather than simply treating the symptoms of environmental deterioration (Sadler and Verheem, 1996b, p55). SEA may thus enhance the credibility and acceptability of decisions (Goodland and Tillman, 1995, Chapter 3) and structure and shape PPP processes (Abaza, 1996, p218; Riehl and Winkler–Kühlken, 1995, p3). Being proactive, SEA should start as early as possible (Thérivel, 1996, p183) and accompany the whole process. Being able to potentially meet certain procedural requirements, SEA is now widely considered to be an appropriate tool for supporting PPP formulation for sustainable development (Ministry of Environment and Energy, 1995b, p3; Mikesell, 1994; Lee and Walsh, 1992, p128; Rees, 1988, p273). EC (1996a, p88) suggested that:

> '*Environmental Impact Assessments (EIAs) [comprising project EIA and SEA] are a key instrument in the implementation of the Fifth Action Programme*[10] *at both EU and member state level*'.

In order to support PPP formulation for sustainable development, SEA needs to be proactive and to consider economic, environmental and social aspects (Gardner, 1989, p41).[11] In this context, Lawrence (1997, p23) stated that sustainability can give EIA (and SEA) a clear sense of direction, provided that it is defined sufficiently, in other words its aims and objectives are clear (EC, 1997a, Box 12). Clear sustainability objectives and terms of reference are important in order to ensure:

> '*that the PPP achieves those objectives, to test whether the PPP's objectives are in line with those of higher-level PPPs, or to implement the PPP effectively*' (Thérivel, 1996, p31).

There are substantive and procedural requirements for sustainable development. Substantive requirements include the consideration of environmental and socio-economic aspects. Procedural requirements can be met by a NEPA (ie project EIA) based process (Box 1.1). SEA in support of sustainable development should be fully integrated into the PPP process and be objectives-led (English Nature, 1992; Sheate, 1992). Figure 1.1 shows the integration of SEA into a simplified process in support of sustainable development.

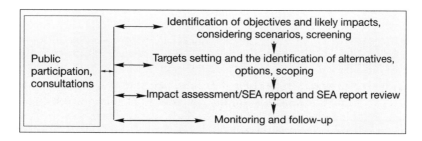

Figure 1.1: *Integrated procedure in support of sustainable development*

Benefit 3: Strengthening project EIA – increasing the efficiency of tiered decision making

The third potential benefit of SEA results from the strengthening of project EIA. SEA is needed as project EIA currently starts too late within a tiered decision making system to consider the full range of alternatives and impacts. SEA can increase the efficiency of tiered decision making by shortening and simplifying, or even making project EIAs redundant altogether (European Conference of Ministers of Transport (ECMT), 1998, p16). In this context:

> 'it is essential to recognise that a tiered approach to (environmental assessment) requires the assessment at a particular decision making level to address only those matters and at that level of detail which are appropriate to it' (Sheate, 1992, p178).

This can lead to an acceleration of subsequent projects, and to time and cost savings (EC, 1997a, p33; Commissie voor de Mer, 1996, p31; Bass and Herson, 1993, p47).[12] The streamlining of SEA/EIA processes therefore means addressing the issues appropriate to the decision making level. While strategic choices for considering alternatives are numerous at higher (more policy oriented) tiers of decision making, they are small at lower (more project oriented) tiers. Operational choices, on the other hand, are numerous at lower tiers and less at higher tiers (Niekerk and Arts, 1996, p7). Streamlining SEA/EIA also means that SEA should propose mitigation for reducing residual impacts of a PPP after alternatives have been assessed and a decision for a best option/alternative has been made. If significant impacts cannot be mitigated, compensation should be outlined.

Benefit 4: Systematic and effective consideration of the environment at higher tiers of decision making

The fourth potential benefit of SEA is the systematic consideration of the environment at policy, plan and programme levels of decision making. Wood (1995, p74) suggested that 'it is important, in the interests of certainty, that the specified system is adhered to, and that accepted procedures are not changed arbitrarily'.

Clear provisions and requirements (policy, law, regulations and guidelines) lead to environmental considerations being built consistently into all levels of decision making (Environment Australia, 1997, Chapter 6) and bring certainty into SEA systems (Partidário, 1996, p52). They show commitment towards SEA and are needed in order to apply SEA effectively (Sadler, 1996, p165). In this context, it was suggested that if SEA is well founded and based on the application of clear SEA principles, the greater the likelihood of its relevance to decision making (Sadler, 1996, p156).

In the interest of a systematic consideration of the environment, it was suggested that initiating agencies need to be made accountable, possibly through external mechanisms (Partidário, 1996, p51; Sadler and Verheem, 1996a, p76) which can increase the credibility of decision making. A review of the

SEA report (possibly external) is needed in order to check the adequacy of information collected during the SEA process and to identify uncertainties and contradictions, leading to enhanced accountability and enforceability. Where provisions for independent quality review are in place, they are 'generally regarded as adding significantly to the level of quality, objectivity, and influence of the SEA process' (Sadler, 1996, p160).

SEA report review can be conducted by various bodies, including independent external bodies with appropriate expertise, environment authorities, the public and expert committees. Authorities should provide a record of the decision making process which should include a statement on how a decision was reached and a description of how SEA results were used (UNECE, 1992, p8).

Benefit 5: Consultation and participation on SEA-related issues

The fifth potential benefit results from consultation and public participation on SEA-related issues.[13] The public, non-governmental organizations (NGOs) and other institutions should be consulted as early as possible, in order to identify possible problems at the beginning of the planning process. Delays of actions due to public opposition may thus be prevented (Sheate, 1994). Public reaction towards a policy, plan or programme depends largely on the possibility of clearly locating impacts. Thus, if impacts can be clearly located, public opposition is often strong. If, however, a clear location of the impacts is not possible, public opposition is usually weak. This has been described as the NIMBY (not in my backyard) phenomenon (Voogd, 1996; see also Popper, 1981).

Public involvement has been described as the 'litmus test' of the utility and effectiveness of SEA, which can lead to increased public acceptance of PPPs (Sadler, 1994, p11; Wood, 1995, p73). Sadler (1996, p153) stated that 'public involvement brings valuable information into the SEA and increases the credibility of the plan finally accepted'. Consultation and public involvement should take place at several stages in the planning process, at least at the initiation and the review stage of SEA.

SEA application should result in the previously described SEA benefits. In order to decide whether this is in fact happening, criteria need to be defined that are able to describe these benefits. SEA principles that can be used to describe potential SEA benefits have been introduced in the SEA literature. They are introduced in Chapter 2.

SEA EFFECTIVENESS

The term 'effectiveness' describes whether something works as intended and meets the purpose for which it is designed (Sadler, 1995, p6). To date, experience with evaluating effectiveness has been limited to project EIA (Commissie voor de Mer, 1996; EC, 1994a; Lee and Colley, 1992). SEA effectiveness, or performance, may be described in terms of substantive issues, ie by its ability to help to achieve established objectives. This is done in Chapters 7 and 8, examining the role of SEA in considering sustainability aspects and identifying the extent to which current assessments result in the potential SEA benefits. Effectiveness may also be described in procedural terms, by the choice of 'fit for purpose' processes (Sadler, 1996, p165), and by the ability to meet certain procedural provisions[14] and principles (Sadler and Verheem, 1996a, p19). Chapter 5 determines the extent to which SEA procedural stages are covered. It was suggested that clear provisions and requirements are needed (Sadler, 1996, p39) in order to ensure a high SEA effectiveness. An effective environmental assessment process requires an approach that considers environmental aspects at all tiers of decision making (EC, 1997a, p28).

A high degree of organizational support and positive attitudes towards SEA are important building blocks for an effective SEA system. In this context, Elling (1998, p14) suggested that, fundamentally, constraints for SEA are not legal, but political. Competent practitioners and a supportive political culture (Sadler, 1996, p39) determine abilities to deliver substantive effectiveness (the ability to help to achieve established objectives) and procedural effectiveness (the ability to meet procedural provisions and principles) at least cost in the minimum time possible. SEA cannot be expected to work effectively if the practitioner resists or circumvents it (Sadler, 1996, p41). An underlying assumption is that attitudes towards SEA are more positive if its application is thought to be beneficial. Opinions on the quality and influence of current SEA as well as attitudes of authorities towards formalized SEA are therefore identified in Chapter 6.

Finally, appropriate methodologies are a precondition for effective SEA (Sadler and Verheem, 1996a, p117) and the extent to which methods and techniques are currently used in SEA reports in transport and spatial/land use planning is therefore determined in Chapter 5. 'Costs' and 'benefits' might be used to describe effectiveness (Wood, 1995, Chapter 18), that is high costs and long SEA preparation times should be associated with high benefits (Sadler, 1996, p39). SEA preparation times are presented in Chapter 5.

SEA RESEARCH

Previous SEA research

In order to advance general SEA theory, there is a need to review SEA case studies (see, for example, Canter, 1996, p94; EC, 1994a, pp18–19). To date, however, there has been little systematic comparative research on SEA on an international scale to provide a sufficient basis on which to determine overall good SEA practice. Consequently, understanding of how SEAs from different systems compare has remained poor. Those few studies that compared SEA practice from different systems and countries relied on a limited number of case studies and applied only a few evaluation criteria (Partidário, 1997; EC, 1997a; EC, 1996b). More recently, a comprehensive package to review the quality of SEA reports for land use plans from two countries was developed and applied for SEA of local land use plans in the UK and Sweden (Lee et al, 1999; Bonde, 1998).

Some systematic research on SEA was conducted in the context of distinct national SEA systems, and typically these included SEA in the spatial/land use sector.[15] In a UK context, systematic research on environmental appraisal practice was conducted by Curran et al (1998), Counsell (1998), Marsh (1997) and Thérivel (1995).

Non-systematic, international comparative research on SEA has been more frequent. However, only a limited number of case studies have been mentioned or discussed in the literature, some of which have been reviewed on a number of occasions (EC, 1999a; ECMT, 1998; EC, 1997a; EC, 1996b; Steer Davies Gleave, 1996; Thérivel and Partidário, 1996a; Sadler and Verheem, 1996a; EC, 1994b; OECD, 1994). In addition, it has usually remained unclear why certain cases were chosen and what criteria were used (case studies are usually not officially called SEA). Workshops and conferences have been of particular importance for an exchange of international SEA experience (International Association for Impact Assessment (IAIA), 2000; IAIA 1999; Kleinschmidt and Wagner, 1998; EC, 1998b; DETR, 1998e; IAIA, 1998; MURL, 1997; North Atlantic Treaty Organization (NATO), 1997; IAIA, 1997; NATO, 1996; IAIA, 1996).

Research needs

In order to obtain a better knowledge of the extent to which SEA is currently applied and to establish a better understanding of how assessments of different SEA systems compare, there is a need for systematic, transnational SEA research. SEA research needs are identified, following in parts Kleinschmidt and Wagner (1998), Sadler and Verheem (1996a) and the EC (1994a).

The extent of SEA application in the EU remains unknown and it was suggested that there are only about 50 to 200 reported SEAs in the EU (EC, 1994b). It was also suggested that:

> 'extensive investigations, utilising computerised literature and Internet searches as well as professional person to person contacts, highlighted a disparity between the perception that the practice of SEA is widespread and evidence to support this assertion' (Steer Davies Gleave, 1996, p23).

Even though there are possibilities for categorizing SEA, differences between categories have not been determined. Whereas the need to identify good SEA practice was widely stressed, in practice, this has not been achieved. The main reason has been a general lack of international research as well as a lack of development of common evaluation criteria that would make a comparison possible.

The need for a supportive political and administrative culture for effectively conducting SEA has been repeatedly stressed. While attitudes of national governments in EU member states towards SEA are known to some extent through the negotiation process for the EC SEA Directive, the opinions and attitudes of regional and local authorities have largely remained unidentified.

In order to obtain a clearer picture of current SEA practice, systematic research that includes different countries and regions is required. As most SEA application in the EU have been informal, research studies need to include any assessment of the environmental impacts of a PPP. To categorize SEA and to identify different SEA types, clear comparative criteria need to be designed. An analysis of whether current SEA application results in potential benefits and the identification of the differences and similarities of different SEA types and categories can potentially help decision makers to make informed SEA choices. Finally, an examination of the extent to which sustainability aspects are considered in PPPs that involve SEA preparation and those that do not, can help to understand the current role of SEA.

AIM, RESEARCH QUESTIONS AND OBJECTIVES

This book has one main aim, presented in Box 1.3:

BOX 1.3: AIM OF THE BOOK

To report on the findings of a systematic comparative analysis of SEA in the transport and spatial/land use sectors in three EU countries; to explain the observed patterns and to suggest improvements to SEA practice.

Following the research needs laid out earlier, four main research questions are addressed. These are presented in Box 1.4:

BOX 1.4: RESEARCH QUESTIONS

1. What is the extent of SEA application, and is it possible to classify SEA types based on current practice?
2. What are authorities' opinions on current SEA, and attitudes towards formalized SEA?
3. What is the role of SEA in considering sustainability objectives, targets and measures?
4. To what extent do assessments result in the five potential SEA benefits?

In order to meet the main aim of the book and to answer the research questions, six objectives are addressed, presented in Box 1.5. In order to achieve the objectives, a clear analytical framework needs to be developed. This is further explained in Chapter 2.

BOX 1.5: OBJECTIVES OF THE BOOK

1. To establish the context of SEA application and to systematically identify and describe transport and spatial/land use PPPs in three EU regions.
2. To identify SEA application and to classify SEA types, based on sectoral and procedural characteristics, the level of their application in the planning cycle, impact coverage and other methodological characteristics.
3. To identify opinions of authorities about current SEA practice and their attitudes towards the application of formalized SEA.
4. To identify whether SEA application leads to a better consideration of sustainability objectives, targets and measures in PPP formulation.
5. To determine the extent to which SEA results in the potential SEA benefits.
6. To summarize and interpret the results of the analysis and to suggest improvements to current practice.

STRUCTURE OF THE BOOK

The book is organized into four main parts. Part 1 provides the background and consists of two chapters, this introduction and the description of how SEA research can be systematically conducted. This is of great importance in the light of the current problems with SEA research. SEA context criteria are identified and described and data collection and survey methods are explained. Furthermore, the comparative criteria used in the analysis for meeting the research objectives are introduced.

Part 2 consists of two chapters that establish the planning context in the three sample regions and identify and portray transport and spatial/land use policies, plans and programmes to be used in the further analysis of the book. A set of context 'variables' is derived, used for explaining similarities and differences in SEA practice.

Part 3 consists of four chapters, presenting the results of the analysis underlying the book. The extent of SEA application is established and SEA types are identified. Procedural characteristics, impact coverage and other methodological issues (methods and techniques) are explained in further detail. The opinions and attitudes of authorities on current SEA and towards formalized SEA are presented. The consideration of sustainability aspects in PPPs and the role of SEA are analysed. Finally, the extent to which current assessment practice results in the potential SEA benefits is determined.

Part 4 consists of two chapters. An overview and synthesis of the results are provided. Conclusions are drawn and suggestions are made for improving current practice. Figure 1.2 depicts the research objectives and relates them to the outline of the book.

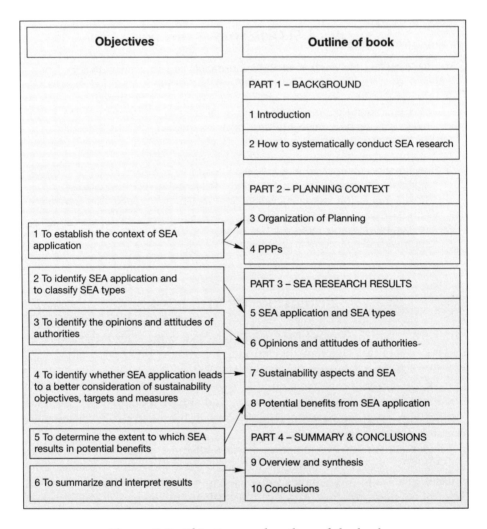

Figure 1.2: *Objectives and outline of the book*

Chapter 2

How to systematically conduct strategic environmental assessment research

One of the main reasons that there have hardly been any international systematic and comparative research studies to date are methodological problems. For this reason, Chapter 2 describes in somewhat more detail how the research underlying the book was conducted. It therefore provides a blueprint for further research activities. Firstly, it describes the choice of the sample regions. All EU countries that would have been suitable for research are identified and the three sample regions finally chosen are portrayed. This is followed by an identification of the problems of transnational research on SEA. How the context for SEA application was established is also explained. This is of great importance for explaining the patterns found in analysis. The design of the analytical framework for comparing SEA practice in the three sample regions is presented and this is followed by an examination of the data collection strategy and a description of the data evaluation process.

CHOICE OF SAMPLE REGIONS

This section firstly identifies those EU countries that would have been suitable for research on SEA for transport and spatial/land use PPPs. Secondly, the three sample regions finally included in the research are described.

Identification of suitable countries for research

Assessments that are the basis for formal SEA have been conducted in most EU member states for land use plans. Judging from previous case study reviews, SEA practice for transport PPPs (any kind of written transport document at a tier prior to the project approval stage) appeared to be more limited.

In order to identify suitable countries, experts and authorities of all EU member states were contacted and existing documents were examined. The following questions were asked:

1. Is there a national transport PPP?
2. Are there any regional transport PPPs?
3. Are environmental impacts for transport PPPs assessed or considered?
4. Is formal SEA carried out for transport PPPs?

Table 2.1 summarizes the results. Respondents did not always answer all four questions – some simply replied that there was no SEA experience at all in the transport sector. Countries with some experience of formal or informal SEA in the EU in 1996 included Austria, Denmark, Finland, France, Germany, The Netherlands, Portugal, Sweden and the UK.

Table 2.1: *SEA in the transport sector in EU member states**

Country	Existence of SEA for transport PPPs
Austria	A future national infrastructure plan will include SEA elements; some experience with environmental evaluation exists at lower administrative levels.
Belgium	No experience with SEA for regional transport plans and no national transport plan has been prepared.
Denmark	SEA for the national transport plan was conducted; some experience of decision making exists at lower administrative levels.
Finland	The SEA for the 'Nordic Triangle' was Finland's first SEA. The national transport plan also considers environmental aspects.
France	No SEA experience in the transport sector, but some environmental evaluations were undertaken for regional road plans. It is intended to prepare a national transport plan.
Germany	An environmental evaluation for the national infrastructure plan has been conducted; furthermore, environmental evaluations have been undertaken for *Länder*, regional and local transport plans.
Greece	No SEA experience in any transport related fields.
Ireland	No SEA experience in the transport sector.
Italy	No SEA experience in the transport sector.
The Netherlands	Environmental evaluations for the national transport plan and most other transport plans at the regional and local level have been conducted.
Portugal	No experience with formal SEA in the transport sector; however, environmental aspects are considered in transport planning to some extent.
Spain	No experience with SEA of transport PPPs.
Sweden	Environmental evaluation is conducted for the national transport plan and other transport plans at lower administrative levels of decision making.
UK	There are plans for a future national integrated transport plan that will consider environmental impacts; there is also environmental evaluation of transport policies and programmes (TPPs).

* No response from Luxembourg.

Key: ☐ Countries with some SEA-related experience in the transport sector in 1996.

Not all of the countries were suitable for inclusion in the research. For example, although Portugal and Finland had some experience with SEA application in the transport sector, this was limited in comparison to other EU member states. In Austria, there were plans to improve the consideration of the environment in the transport sector, particularly with regard to the national transport plan. Practice, however, was still rather limited. SEA experience in the transport sector in France appeared to be very much 'big project'-related (Ministère de l'Équipement, du Logement et des Transport, 1992) and SEA practice in the transport sector was not widespread. Five countries remained that appeared to be best suited for research, namely, Denmark, Germany, Sweden, The Netherlands and the UK.

Williams (1986, p329) suggested the restriction of comparative studies to no more than two or three study areas. Three countries were therefore chosen, including the UK, The Netherlands and Germany.

Identification of the three sample regions

In order to decide what sample regions to include in the research, aspects are needed that help to identify similar regions. Two aspects were chosen in the context of the book. Firstly administrative regions around metropolitan areas (or 'city regions') with at least 1 million inhabitants were to be compared. Secondly, sample regions were chosen that only had one regional level of decision making.[1]

In The Netherlands, only the region around the Regional Body of Amsterdam (ROA, *Regionaal Orgaan Amsterdam*), namely the *provincie* (province) of Noord-Holland meets the selection criteria. Noord-Holland is part of the Randstad, which has a voluntary planning body (RoRo: *Randstad Overleg Ruimtelijke Ordening*) of four *provincies*, namely Noord and Zuid Holland, Utrecht and Flevoland.

In Germany, it was decided to include a region from the 'new' *Länder* (former East Germany). The main reason was planning horizons for local land use plans (FNPs), which on average are between 15 and 20 years. Furthermore, once established, land use plans tend to be 'adjusted' rather than redrafted. Therefore, whereas in former West Germany where land use plans often date back to the 1970s, regions in former East Germany generally have more recently prepared land use plans. Only one region meets the selection criteria, namely the inner planning region of Brandenburg-Berlin (EVR, *engerer Verflechtungsraum*), a recently established planning region with one planning authority (*Gemeinsame Landesplanung, GL*).

In England, metropolitan areas with more than 1 million inhabitants include Greater London, the West Midlands (Birmingham), Greater Manchester, Merseyside (Liverpool), West Yorkshire (Leeds), South Yorkshire (Sheffield) and Tyne and Wear (Newcastle). It was decided to look at the region around Greater Manchester, North West England, as the adjoining counties of Lancashire and Cheshire had a good record of considering environmental aspects (Marsh, 1997; Davoudi et al, 1996). In England, regional levels of decision making were confined to a voluntary cooperation of counties and districts within regional

Table 2.2: *Baseline data on the three sample regions*

	North West England (excl. Cumbria)	Noord-Holland	EVR Brandenburg-Berlin
Area (km²)	7331	2667	5368
Per cent total national geographical area	3.0	6.4	1.5
Population (millions)	6.4	2.5	4.3
Per cent total national population	10.7	16.2	5.2
Population density in the region (inhabitants/km²)	873	937	792
Biggest 'city region'	Greater Manchester (10 districts)	Regionaal Organ Amsterdam (ROA) (16 municipalities)	City of Berlin (1 city)
– population (millions)	2.5	1.3	3.5
– area (km²)	1285	811	889

Sources: Fischer Weltalmanach (1994); Ministerium für Umwelt, Naturschutz und Raumordnung (1995b); North West Regional Association (1994); Regionaal Orgaan Amsterdam (1993); Provincie Noord-Holland (1994)

associations. In order to obtain the desired regional picture and also to have roughly comparable regions, it was decided to look only at those counties in North West England that adjoin Greater Manchester. These include Lancashire, Cheshire, Merseyside and Greater Manchester, but exclude Cumbria.

Table 2.2 presents area and population sizes of the chosen sample regions. Map 2.1 shows the sample regions in direct comparison with each other, including the boundaries of local administrative areas. The combined population of the three regions is 3.5 per cent of the total EU population and the combined area size is 0.5 per cent of the total EU area.

PROBLEMS IN TRANSNATIONAL COMPARATIVE RESEARCH ON SEA

Planning practice can be improved as a result of the stimulus provided by transnational studies (Williams, 1986, p25). There are, however, also a number of problems that can arise when conducting transnational research on SEA, which are discussed below.

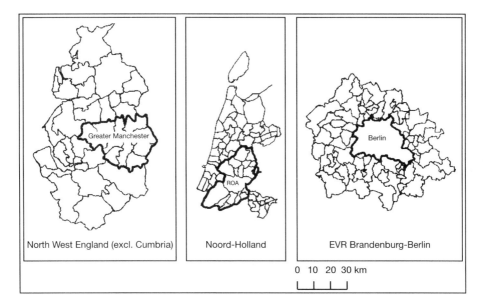

North West England (excl. Cumbria) | Noord-Holland | EVR Brandenburg-Berlin

0 10 20 30 km

Figure 2.1: *The sample regions and administrative boundaries of authorities responsible for local land use PPPs*

Data availability

Data availability in different countries might not be the same (Marr, 1997, pp13–15) and PPPs might not always be directly comparable (Flynn, 1993, p62). In the three chosen countries, transport and spatial planning systems were not organized in the same way. In the UK, there were fewer administrative levels of decision making than in The Netherlands and in Germany. Instead of comparing specific decision making levels (which might lead to an only partial coverage of SEA practice), the book therefore provides a cumulative view of a cross-section of PPPs, covering all administrative levels.

Common basis for comparison

Even though knowledge of practice in one country might encourage innovation in another country (Masser, 1984, p151), different planning traditions and political, institutional and cultural circumstances might require adaptation to different environments. Thus, it might not be possible to transfer practice from one country to another, as:

> *'the danger of proposing change in practice in the light of experience abroad is that practice may be dependent for its success upon a chain of circumstances which does not apply at home'* (Booth, 1986, p1).

These chains of circumstances depend, in particular, on political and organizational structures. The context of SEA application therefore needs to be highlighted. Once differences are explained, proposals for improving practice can be made. Chapters 3 and 4 therefore portray the planning context in the three sample regions and identify all relevant PPPs in transport and spatial/land use planning.

Data collection

Before the start of the data collection, it is often unclear whether the information to be obtained is in fact appropriate for quantitative analysis. In the research underlying the book, interviews were therefore conducted for a cross-section of PPPs, covering all administrative levels in the three sample regions. Interviews provide for flexibility to react, for example, to any misunderstandings and to add any other questions, if necessary. In order to include all of the authorities responsible for the preparation of PPPs in the three sample regions, a postal questionnaire was sent to all remaining (mostly local) authorities. Further problems might arise with terminology having different meanings in different countries. In the UK, The Netherlands and Germany, for example, there is a different understanding of 'qualitative' and 'quantitative' sustainability targets[2] and an apparently unclear understanding of the SEA procedural stages.

Language problems

The use of different languages is a potential problem when comparing practice in different EU countries. For example, the transferability of certain terms and expressions might be difficult. Translations might not be easily achieved and certain terms could have different meanings in different countries. In this context, two examples are presented, using the terms 'SEA' and 'sustainability'. Whereas the English term SEA currently affords a variety of different interpretations, the frequently used German and Dutch equivalents '*Plan- und Programm-UVP*' (EIA of plans and programmes) and '*strategische mer*' (strategic EIA) are based on an EIA procedural based understanding of the instrument.

Sustainability is translated into Dutch as '*duurzamheid*' as well as '*leefbarheid*'. While the first term describes long-term sustainability (for example, potential impacts on climate change), the second term is used to describe more short-term sustainability (for example, in terms of accessibility). In German, two terms are mostly used to describe sustainable development, namely '*Nachhaltigkeit*' and '*Zukunftsfähigkeit*'. Both appear to be used in the same way. In order to overcome problems connected with language, original as well as translated terminology was presented in interviews and questionnaires. Furthermore, those terms and notions that might not be clearly intelligible were explained.

Identification of PPPs and SEAs to be included in research

The identification of the relevant transport and spatial/land use PPPs to be included in SEA research is not straightforward, as:

- a large number of PPPs are usually relevant; and

- responsibilities are not always clearly defined and are often intertwined at different administrative levels (for example, national, regional, subregional and local levels).

A final decision on the PPPs to be included in research can therefore only be made after consultation with experts and decision makers.

Identification of SEAs needs to be done carefully, as other terminology than SEA is usually used. The fact that assessments are usually not 'officially' called SEA is one of the reasons for past confusion in SEA research. In the case of the three sample regions portrayed in the book, SEA was particularly difficult to recognize where it was fully integrated into the main PPP documentation. In other cases, it was integrated into an overall assessment, which also addressed socio-economic impacts. The problem of deciding what assessments to consider was overcome by including any type of assessment of the environmental impacts of a PPP.

ESTABLISHING THE CONTEXT FOR SEA APPLICATION

In order to identify and analyse SEA practice systematically and to explain differences and similarities, the context for SEA application needs to be established. In the context of the book, the general features of the transport and spatial/land use planning systems need to be explained. Furthermore, the relevant PPPs need to be identified. In order to explain the observed patterns, context variables need to be described. Chapters 3 and 4 will meet these tasks. They will therefore portray the organization of planning in the three sample regions and describe the different planning systems. In this context, government and other relevant publications are considered. Furthermore, political and administrative structures are portrayed and the main planning instruments as well as relevant legislation and guidance are identified. Finally, those PPPs included in the analysis are identified and described.

PPPs need to be classified according to the stage of application in the planning cycle (Lee and Walsh, 1992, p136; Thérivel and Partidário, 1996a, p5). As differences between stages are not always clear, a classification into 'policy orientation' and 'project orientation' of the PPPs is a feasible way to achieve the goal. Policy orientation means that a more general, non-site-specific information is provided with a focus on development options, scenarios and inter-modal alternatives. Project orientation means that more site-specific information is provided and specific projects are listed. The results of the research underlying the book indicate that a further distinction becomes indeed possible through SEA classification into policy-SEA, plan-SEA and programme-SEA.

Context variables need to be designed in order to be able to conduct statistical analysis for explaining the observed SEA patterns. Variables used in the research underlying the book include 'PPP relevance', 'PPP accountability', 'PPP inter-modality', and 'PPP procedural coverage'. Chapter 5 establishes these context criteria for a set of PPPs, representing all the administrative levels of decision making.

FRAMEWORK FOR COMPARING SEA PRACTICE

This section shows how to systematically compare SEA practice from different systems. In this context, a common set of comparative criteria is developed in order to be able to isolate important aspects of SEA practice from the general PPP context. This is of fundamental importance, as 'context and phenomenon are often entwined to an extent that the boundaries of the unit of study are unclear' (Yin, 1982, p84).

Following the research questions and the objectives of the book, the analytical framework for comparing SEA practice consists of four main parts. These are presented in Box 2.1.

BOX 2.1: DESIGN OF ANALYTICAL FRAMEWORK FOR COMPARING SEA PRACTICE

1. Development of criteria for classifying SEA types and the identification of SEA variables to be used in statistical analysis (including procedural stages, impact coverage, other methodological characteristics, preparation times).
2. Development of criteria for identifying the opinions and attitudes of authorities.
3. Development of criteria allowing the determination of the role of SEA in considering sustainability aspects within PPPs.
4. Development of criteria allowing the determination of the extent to which assessments result in the potential SEA benefits.

The main ingredients to the four parts of the analytical framework underlying the book are briefly presented below.

Classification of SEA types

The classification of SEA types is based on the sectoral coverage, the level of application in the planning cycle, procedural characteristics, impact coverage and other methodological characteristics. Two sectors are included in the analysis, namely transport and spatial/land use. Regarding the level of application in the planning cycle, policy orientation is distinguished from project orientation. Procedural characteristics, impact coverage and other methodological characteristics can not only be used to describe SEA types, but can also serve as SEA variables in statistical analysis with other SEA aspects (see Chapters 6 to 8):

- Procedural aspects of SEA application are further analysed in the book based on the SEA procedure in support of sustainable development laid out in Figure 1.1. Furthermore, in this context, whether SEA involves integrated and objectives-led procedures is to be determined.

- Impact coverage criteria are identified, based on the assumption that SEA is a supporting tool for sustainable development. Environmental, as well as socio-economic, aspects are therefore considered. The EC SEA Directive proposal (COM(96)511 and COM(99)073) was used to identify the environmental criteria, including fauna, flora, soil, water, air (including noise), pollution, climate, landscape and cultural heritage. As the SEA Directive proposal only requires three rather general socio-economic criteria to be assessed, namely human beings, material assets and cultural heritage, a more comprehensive list of socio-economic aspects needs to be identified, following Leistritz (1995) and Glasson (1995a). These include economic, demographic, fiscal, income and social impacts as well as housing and public services.
- Other methodological aspects include SEA methods and techniques. Methods and techniques to be used in SEA are identified in Petts (2000), the EC (1997a), Sheate (1996), Steer Davies Gleave (1996), Sadler and Verheem (1996a), Thérivel and Partidário (1996a) and Wood and Djeddour (1992). Methods include impact prediction, the evaluation of impacts, consideration of alternatives and scenarios, mitigation and compensation. Techniques include field research, simulation, mapping and overlay techniques, matrices, checklists and workshops.

Chapter 5 presents the findings of the empirical research underlying the book.

Opinions and attitudes of authorities

Several questions can be used in order to identify the opinions of decision makers on current SEA practice and attitudes towards formalized SEA.[3] Questions on current assessments include those on the quality and the influence in PPP making. Questions on attitudes towards formalized SEA include those on a possible integration of formal SEA into the PPP process, a delay of its preparation, a possible acceleration of project preparation and the possibility for a better consideration of environmental aspects. Chapter 6 presents the empirical findings on the opinions and attitudes of authorities in the three sample regions.

Sustainability aspects and the role of SEA

SEA may address environmental, social and economic aspects in an integrated manner (Lawrence, 1997; Thérivel and Partidário, 1996b, p53). It can therefore function as a 'sustainability analysis' or 'sustainability test' (Sadler and Verheem, 1996a, p36). Procedural requirements were introduced by the procedural framework in support of sustainable development outlined in Figure 1.1. Regarding substantive requirements, the sustainable development strategy of the EC, the Fifth Environmental Action Programme (EC, 1993a), is a suitable source for comparing practice in the EU,[4] combining objectives, targets and proposals for measures. As the Fifth Environmental Action Programme

BOX 2.2: FRAMEWORK FOR COMPARING THE CONSIDERATION OF SUSTAINABILITY ASPECTS

Sustainable PPP formulation framework referring to the Fifth Environmental Action Programme of the EC

Stages/tasks	Objectives, targets and measures to be considered				
1. Identification of sustainability objectives	<ul><li>Climate change</li><li>Acidification</li><li>Air quality</li><li>Nature and biodiversity</li><li>Water</li><li>Urban environment</li><li>Waste management/raw material consumption</li></ul>				
2a. Identification of types of targets based on impacts	Emission levels	Noise levels	Land-take	Waste/consumption levels	Accident levels
2b. Identification of targets (transport sector is *not* specified)	CO₂: 1990–2000: no increase, progressive reduction until 2005/2010 NOₓ: 1990–1994: no increase 1990–2000: –30% VOC: 1990–96: –10% 1990–99: –30% SO₂: 1985–2000: –35% O₃: Air quality framework directive CO: Problem identification by 1997	Never >85dB(A) >65 dB (A) to be phased out 55–65 dB(A): no increase Areas now below 55 dB(A) not over 55 dB(A) in the future	Maintenance or restoration of natural habitats Protection and enhance-ment of historical heritage of cities and towns and provisions of green spaces	Rational sustainable use of resources Halt and reverse current trend in waste generation Recycling/reuse of paper, glass and plastics of at least 50%	No targets given
3a. Identification of changes necessary to achieve targets	<ul><li>Technical changes</li><li>Behavioural changes</li><li>Infrastructural</li></ul>				
3b. Identification of instruments to achieve changes	<ul><li>Legislative instruments</li><li>Market-based instruments</li><li>Horizontal, supporting instruments (eg better data, research)</li><li>Financial support mechanisms</li></ul>				
3c. Identification of possible measures to achieve objectives and targets	<ul><li>Land use planning</li><li>Infrastructure investment</li><li>Infrastructure charging</li><li>Economic and fiscal incentives to use environmentally friendly transport means</li><li>Regulation changes</li><li>Information and education</li><li>Interactive communication infrastructures</li><li>Public transport</li></ul>				
4.	Monitoring				

does not mention socio-economic aspects, the book only compares the extent to which environmental sustainability aspects were considered in PPPs with and without SEA. Box 2.2 shows the framework for comparing the consideration of sustainability aspects. Chapter 7 presents the findings of the analysis.

Appendix 5 compares EU and national targets in the three sample regions (DoE, 1994; Ministerie van VROM, 1994b, 1989a; Bundesministerium für Umwelt (BMU), 1994). Only in The Netherlands were requirements for the transport sector further specified and were national targets stricter than EU targets. In Germany, national targets were usually stricter than EU targets, except noise levels. In the UK, however, a number of EU targets were stricter than national targets. These include carbon dioxide (CO_2), nitrous oxides (NO_x), sulphur dioxide (SO_2) and noise levels.

Whether the objectives, targets and options formulated in the Fifth Environmental Action Programme can be regarded to be sufficient for achieving sustainable development is not discussed here. In this context, reference is made to other work that can serve as the basis for evaluation, namely Milieudefensie (1996), Wuppertal Institut (1995), Friends of the Earth (1995), Milieudefensie (1992) and Karas (1991).[5] The book also does not discuss the effectiveness of measures for achieving sustainability objectives and targets, which is done, for example, by Acutt and Dodgson (1996), Goodwin and Parkhurst (1996), ECMT (1995; 1993), Rommerskirchen (1993) and Schallaböck (1991).

Potential SEA benefits

The extent to which assessments resulted in the potential SEA benefits presented earlier was determined using SEA principles. Five main potential benefits were distinguished:

1. Wider consideration of impacts and alternatives.
2. Proactive assessment – SEA as a supporting tool for PPP formulation for sustainable development.
3. Strengthening project EIA – increasing the efficiency of tiered decision making.
4. Systematic and effective consideration of the environment at higher tiers of decision making.
5. Consultation and participation on SEA-related issues.

Box 2.3 presents the principles used to describe the five potential benefits, distinguishing between framework and procedural principles, as laid out in the SEA literature. In order to identify the extent to which assessments result in the potential SEA benefits, overall scores can be calculated and approved based on these evaluation criteria. This is done in Chapter 8.

Requirements of the EC SEA Directive

Those SEA principles that will need to be met, following the adoption of the EC SEA Directive, are identified in Box 2.4. Based on this evaluation, the

Box 2.3: SEA BENEFITS, PRINCIPLES AND EVALUATION CRITERIA

SEA benefit	SEA principle (a) framework principle (b) procedural principle	SEA evaluation criteria
Wider consideration of impacts and alternatives	(a) SEA scope be commensurate with scope of PPP (b) impact prediction	• Does SEA address the same issues as the PPP at the same geographical scale? • Are environmental impacts assessed? • Are impacts of CO_2 emissions/ energy consumption considered? • Are impacts on transport generation considered? • Are general cumulative impacts of the whole PPP assessed?
	(b) evaluation of impacts	• Is the significance of impacts regarding environmental objectives and targets evaluated?
	(b) specification of alternatives	• Is the zero alternative considered? • Are intermodal/intramodal alternatives considered?
	(b) specification of scenarios	• Are scenarios considered?
Proactive assessment – SEA as a supporting tool for PPP formulation for sustainable development	(a) application of SEA as early as possible	• Did SEA start before/at beginning, during or after the PPP process? • When were environmental issues first considered?
	(a) clear objectives and terms of reference/ environmental standards	• Are environmental objectives considered? • Are economic objectives considered? • Are social objectives considered? • Are transport-specific objectives considered? • Are environmental/traffic reduction standards considered?
	(a) proactive, structuring process that also considers socio-economic impacts	• Is there a predetermined, formal PPP process? • Does SEA structure run parallel to a structured PPP process? • Are socio-economic impacts assessed?

Box 2.3: Continued

SEA benefit	SEA principle (a) framework principle (b) procedural principle	SEA evaluation criteria
	(a) sustainable development should be supported	• Is sustainable development considered? • Are sustainable development strategies considered?
	(b) screening	• Is there a documented process with consultation or a simple checklist approach?
	(b) scoping	• Is there a documented process with consultation or a simple checklist approach?
	(b) SEA report	• Is there a separate assessment report or is an assessment report integrated into PPP?
	(b) monitoring and follow-up	• Is any monitoring and follow-up provided? (eg, auditing, research)
Strengthening project EIA – increasing the efficiency of tiered decision making	(a) tiered SEA/EIA system	• Do SEA and EIA assess different issues (are different environmental impacts considered)? • Does SEA lead to an acceleration of project EIAs? • Does SEA substitute (parts of) project EIA?
	(b) mitigation	• Is mitigation provided for potentially remaining impacts at the SEA level?
Systematic consideration of the environment at higher tiers	(a) clear provisions	• What is the status of the SEA (statutory or non-statutory)? • What is the status of the PPP (statutory or non-statutory)?
	(a) clear requirements	• Is there any guidance for SEA (official, research or other studies)? • Is there any guidance for the PPP (official, research or other studies)?
	(a) accountability of initiating agencies	• Is the SEA initiating body not the approving body? • Is the PPP initiating body not the approving body?
	(b) SEA results effectively considered in PPP making	• How are SEA results considered in decision making?

BOX 2.3: CONTINUED		

SEA benefit	SEA principle (a) framework principle (b) procedural principle	SEA evaluation criteria
	(b) review	• Is there an outside review of SEA?
Consultation and participation on SEA-related issues	(b) consultation and participation process	• Is there consultation of external bodies for the SEA? • Is there consultation of external bodies for the PPP? • Is there public participation or consultation for the SEA? • Is there public participation or consultation for the PPP? • Is there public reporting of the results for the SEA? • Is there public reporting of the results for the PPP?

extent to which existing SEAs fulfil the SEA Directive's requirements can be determined (see Chapter 8). The SEA Directive only aims at plans and programmes that include information on the type, size and location of projects and set up the framework for subsequent approvals (Feldmann, 1998b, p108). Examples of those plans and programmes that are likely to be subject to formal SEA requirements are listed in the explanatory memorandum to the SEA Directive (COM (96)511 and COM(99)073). They include the following plans and programmes in the three sample regions:

- ***The UK:***
  - Structure plans and unitary development plans part one; and
  - Local plan and unitary development plan (UDP) part two.

- ***The Netherlands:***
  - National Spatial Plan VINEX
  - *Streekplannen*; and
  - *Structuurplannen.*

- ***Germany:***
  - *Landesraumordnungsprogramme/pläne*;
  - *Landesentwicklungsprogramme/pläne*;
  - *Regionalprogramme/pläne*; and
  - *Flächennutzungspläne.*

As will be shown in Chapter 5, most of these plans and programmes currently involve the preparation of informal SEA. Exceptions include the regional plans

---

BOX 2.4: REQUIREMENTS OF THE EC SEA DIRECTIVE (1999 DRAFT)

SEA principle	SEA Directive requirements	Where mentioned
SEA scope be commensurate with scope of PPP	✗	✗
Impact prediction of environmental and other impacts	✓	Article 1, Annex (e)
Evaluation of significance	⇔	Article 5
Specification of alternatives	✓	Annex (b)
Scenarios	✗	✗
Application of SEA as early as possible	⇔	Recital 1
Clear objectives and terms of reference/ environmental standards	✗	✗
Proactive, structuring process that also considers socio-economic impacts	✗	✗
Sustainable development should be supported	✓	Recital 2
Screening	⇔	Article 4b
Scoping	✗	✗
SEA report	✓	Article 2 (e)
Monitoring and follow-up	✗	✗
Tiered SEA/EIA system	✗	✗
Mitigation	✓	Annex (b)
Clear provisions	✓	whole Directive
Clear requirements	⇔	whole Directive
Accountability of initiating agencies	✗	✗
SEA results effectively considered in final decision	✓	Recital 14
Review*	⇔	Recital 11(a)
Consultation and participation process**	✓	Recital 12

✓ = yes, direct requirement; ⇔ = indirect requirement; ✗ = no requirement

* Judicial review is explicitly *excluded* (Article 10). However, the Åarhus Convention, signed by all EU member states, opens the possibility for litigation to the general public and NGOs. To date, the consequences of the convention have remained unclear.
** These include public participation, consultation of external bodies and the final reporting of the SEA results.

(*streekplannen*) in The Netherlands, which involve the preparation of formal 'big-project' SEA/EIA (however, not for the whole plan, but only for 'big projects') and the *Länder* spatial plans and programmes (*Landesraumordnungsprogramme und -pläne*) as well as the development plans and programmes (*Landesentwicklungspläne und -programme*) in Germany which do not involve SEA preparation at all. Chapter 9 will suggest that based on this distinction, the SEA Directive requirements will probably cover a larger number of plans and programmes in Germany and England than in The Netherlands.

DATA COLLECTION

The aim, research questions and objectives of the book determine the data collection strategy. Empirical information for all parts of the analytical framework need to be systematically collected for all types of PPPs in the three sample regions in order to identify all formal/informal SEAs. Subsequently, the data collection methods are described and data evaluation is explained. Furthermore, the response rates in the empirical research underlying the book are presented.

Methods of data collection

In order to systematically cover SEA practice, data collection should provide for flexibility, but should also be able to deliver the hard facts needed to systematically compare practice in different SEA systems. Data collection for the empirical research underlying the book was therefore carried out, using both interviews and postal questionnaires, as follows:

1. 'Structured interviews' (see Yin, 1994, p80) were conducted with key personnel for all existing types of PPPs and SEAs. In this context, the main documentation was studied first in order to obtain a basic understanding of the issues. It was decided to conduct interviews for the same number of PPPs in each region in order to have a good basis for a direct (regional based) comparison of the results. Preliminary interviews and existing documentation revealed that interviews on 12 PPPs in each region would allow the whole range at all administrative levels to be covered.
2. Questionnaires were sent out by mail to all those remaining authorities in the three regions that were not interviewed (178, mainly local, authorities).

Response rates and reasons for differences

All contacted authorities participated in interviews (participation rate of 100 per cent). The overall response rate of postal questionnaire participants was 55 per cent (97 out of 178). Of the 97 returned questionnaires, 78 were properly completed and could be used for further analysis. Thus, the adjusted overall response rate is 44 per cent. Total numbers of completed postal questionnaires in the three regions were similar, however, adjusted response rates for local authorities in Noord-Holland and EVR Brandenburg-Berlin (*Gemeinden*) were 32 per cent and 38 per cent respectively, but 79 per cent in North West England.

Lower rates in Noord-Holland and EVR Brandenburg-Berlin appeared to be partly related to smaller administration areas with smaller authorities (and fewer staff). Sizes and populations of administrative areas are presented in Table 2.3.

Table 2.3: *Administrative structure, area and population sizes of sample regions*

	North West England (excl. Cumbria)	Noord-Holland	EVR Brandenburg-Berlin
Administrative structure	4 counties, 37 boroughs/districts	part of voluntary cooperating body of Randstad (RoRo), 70 *gemeenten* (municipalities)	2 *Länder*, 5 (part) *Regionen* (regions), 8 (part) *Kreise* (counties), 66 *Amtsgemeinden* (municipalities)
Average size of local administrative level (excluding biggest 'city region')			
– average population	133,607 (27 local authorities)	22,167 (54 local authorities)	11,826 (66 local authorities)
– average area size (km²)	215.93	34.37	67.88

Sources: Fischer Weltalmanach (1994); Ministerium für Umwelt, Naturschutz und Raumordnung (1995b); North West Regional Association (1994); Regionaal Orgaan Amsterdam (1993); Provincie Noord-Holland (1994)

In EVR Brandenburg-Berlin, the response rates of municipalities (*Gemeinden*) with more than 10,000 inhabitants were higher (61 per cent) than the response rates of municipalities with less than 10,000 inhabitants (26 per cent). Response rates of authorities that administered only one municipality were also higher (52 per cent) than those authorities that administered more than one municipality (only 20 per cent). Of the six known local authorities that were unable to complete the questionnaire, five administered more than one municipality. Those authorities that did not complete questionnaires provided different reasons. Most of them said that plan preparation was not far enough advanced. Some also said that their municipality was not large enough and claimed that data would be irrelevant. Furthermore, the concept of sustainable development was not well known at the local level in EVR Brandenburg-Berlin, leaving authorities unable to complete questionnaires.

All the responding authorities in Noord-Holland said that their local PPPs involved no assessment of environmental impacts. This appeared to be an important reason for authorities not completing questionnaires. Thus, authorities thought that results would be irrelevant.

Data evaluation

Data evaluation in the book is threefold and consists of:

1. The description of the main results.
2. The statistical analysis of the results.
3. The explanation of the results.

Research results are described, using tables and figures. In order to identify the appropriate instruments for statistical analysis, the data/variable set was tested for normal distribution (skewness and kurtosis) and for equal/unequal variances. It was found that variances were usually unequal and that data sets were mostly not normally distributed. Non-parametric tests were therefore applied for determining differences and associations between variables. The Mann-Whitney U test was used to examine differences and Spearman's rank-order correlation test was used to examine possible associations (Cramer, 1998, pp70–71).

Results are presented in terms of significance levels of under 0.05 ($P<.05$) and of under 0.01 ($P<.01$). Differences are presented for three main presentation aspects, including the regions, the SEA types and the sectors. Furthermore, where appropriate, differences between PPPs with and without SEA are presented. Associations are presented between context variables and a range of SEA variables (see Chapters 6 to 8). The observed patterns are explained, using the results of statistical analysis. The results are also interpreted, in terms of the characteristics of the different planning systems in the three sample regions.

Planning Context

Introduction to Part 2

Part 2 of the book includes Chapters 3 and 4 and deals with the organization of planning and the transport and spatial/land use PPPs in the three sample regions. Without an identification of these planning 'instruments' a systematic comparison of SEA practice is not possible.

Chapter 3 outlines the organization of transport and spatial/land use planning within its political and administrative context. Furthermore, the main planning instruments and associated legislation and guidance are presented.

Chapter 4 identifies the 36 PPPs at all administrative levels that are the basis for the analysis of SEA case studies in the remaining chapters of the book. These 36 PPPs (cross-section of PPPs) are further portrayed in terms of four context variables, namely PPP relevance, PPP accountability, PPP intermodality and PPP procedure.

Chapter 3

Organization of planning

This chapter deals with the organization of transport and spatial/land use planning and addresses the first part of objective 1 of the book 'to establish the context of SEA application'. It is divided into five main sections. The first describes the overall political and administrative context for transport and spatial/land use planning in the UK, The Netherlands and Germany. This is followed by a section portraying general features of the planning systems. Subsequently, the main planning instruments are identified and the associated legislation and guidance are listed. Finally the cross-regional characteristics are portrayed.

POLITICAL AND ADMINISTRATIVE CONTEXT

This section describes the general political and administrative context for transport and spatial/land use planning in the three countries under consideration, referring to the main sample regions. The organization of spatial administration is also portrayed.

North West England

The UK is a unitary state with no written constitution. All power derives from legislation that is enacted in parliament and administered by central and local governments (DoE, 1989, p36). There are democratically elected bodies at either two levels (in unitary districts) or three levels (in counties), namely:

- the national level: House of Commons, with central government;
- the county level: elected councillors; and
- the shire district level or unitary district level (local level): elected councillors.

While transport PPPs are prepared at national and county levels (local level transport policies and programmes (TPPs) are combined in counties and metropolitan areas), statutory spatial/land use plans are prepared at county and local levels. In addition, central government provides guidance for the preparation of spatial/land use plans for county and local authorities, in the form of planning policy guidance (PPG) and regional planning guidance (RPG).

Guidance on the preparation of local transport plans and programmes is provided by annual government circulars.

Following the Local Government Act in 1974, up until 1986, all of England and Wales had a two-tier administrative system with 39 counties and 264 districts (Cullingworth and Nadin, 1994, p28). On 1 April 1986, metropolitan county councils were abolished and 68 unitary authorities were created instead with a single-tier system of plan making. The number of unitary authorities has increased since then with districts outside of metropolitan areas also obtaining unitary status.

The region of North West England consists of three counties (Cumbria, Lancashire and Cheshire), 19 unitary authorities and 24 local district authorities. Unitary authorities not only include those of the metropolitan areas of Greater Manchester and Merseyside (ten and five districts, respectively) but also Warrington and Halton, formerly districts within Cheshire, as well as Blackpool and Blackburn, formerly districts within Lancashire. These districts obtained unitary authority status in April 1998. Government offices for the regions (GORs) were established in 1994. Furthermore, regional development agencies (RDAs) in the eight English regions were established in 1999 in order to strengthen the regional level (DETR, 1998b), dealing with regional-specific development issues.

Noord-Holland

The Netherlands is a decentralized unitary state with a written constitution (*grondwet*). All executive power is centralized in the national government. There are democratically elected bodies at three levels (Ministerie van VROM, 1996a):

- the national level with first and second chamber of parliament (*De Staten-Generaal*) and central government (*de regering*);
- the provincial (*provincie*) level with the Provincial Council (*Provinciale Staten*) and Provincial Executive (*Gedeputeerde Staten*); and
- the local level with the Municipal Council (*Gemeenteraad*) and the Municipal Executive (*College van Burgemeester en Wethouders*).

In addition, following the skeleton law 'changing administration' (*kaderwet bestuur in verandering,* 1994), the regional level (the level between provincial and local levels) also plays a role in decision making in the form of BoN areas (BoN = *besturen op niveau-regio* – administration at the regional level). BoN areas are administered by municipalities and provinces. Transport as well as spatial/land use PPPs are prepared at all levels of democratically elected bodies. Furthermore, they are prepared at the regional (BoN area) level.

There are 12 provinces (*provincies*), 633 municipalities (*gemeenten*) and 7 regional BoN areas in The Netherlands.[1] In 1997, two BoN areas were designated city provinces (*stadsprovincies*), namely Eindhoven (SRE) and Rotterdam (SRR) (Volkskrant, 1997). The Regional Body of Amsterdam (ROA) is a BoN area that has not yet been designated a city province.

The province of Noord-Holland consists of 70 local authorities of which 16 are organized within ROA. Regional and transport planning in ROA is carried out by a group of five officials of sub-regions, which comprise Amsterdam, Waterland, Zaanstreek, Amstelland and Meerlanden.

EVR Brandenburg-Berlin

Germany is a federal state with a written constitution (*Grundgesetz*). Executive power is shared by the Federation and the states (*Länder*). There are democratically elected bodies at four levels, namely:

- the national level with the Federal Parliament (*Bundesregierung*) and government (*Bundestag*);
- the *Länder* level with *Länder* parliaments (*Landtage*) and governments (*Landesregierungen*);
- the county (*Kreis*) and city (*kreisfreie Stadt*) level with parliaments (*Kreis- und Stadttage*) and executives (*Bürgermeister*); and
- the local level (*Gemeinden/Stadtteile*) with local parliaments (*Gemeinde- und Stadtteilvertretungen*) and executives (*Bürgermeister*).

Transport and spatial/land use PPPs are prepared at all administrative levels with democratically elected bodies. In addition, regional administration is formed by cooperating *Kreise* and cities (*kreisfreie Städte*).

Germany consists of 16 *Länder*, 426 counties (*Kreise*) and 117 self-administering cities. Furthermore, there are over 16,000 municipalities (*Gemeinden*) (Fischer Weltalmanach, 1994). Several municipalities may be administered by only one authority (*Amt*).

The functional planning region (*engerer Verflechtungsraum*, EVR) Brandenburg-Berlin consists of two Länder (Berlin and Brandenburg), one self-administering city (Potsdam), five regions (*Regionen*) and eight counties (*Kreise*). 274 municipalities (*Gemeinden*) are administered by 65 authorities (*Ämter*). The functional planning region is embedded in an overall planning cooperation of both *Länder*, which is intended to lead to a common *Land* administration.

PLANNING SYSTEMS

This section portrays general features of the planning systems in the three countries, referring to the three sample regions. Spatial/land use planning is described in a general way, covering all administrative levels. Transport planning of national transport infrastructure is also portrayed. Local transport planning in the three regions is usually integrated with local land use planning. In The Netherlands and Germany, the *provincies* and the *Länder* administer their own transport networks. However, compared with the national level, *provincie* and *Land* transport networks are small.

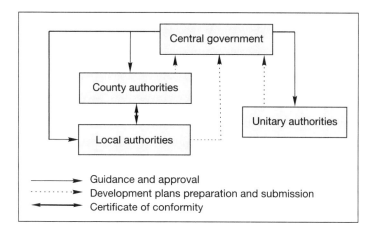

Figure 3.1: *Spatial/land use planning in England and Wales*

North West England

Spatial/land use planning

Spatial/land use planning in England and Wales is centrally guided and controlled by national government. Figure 3.1 shows the planning system in a simplified manner. Spatial/land use planning takes place within the central government dominated development plan system. While lower administrative levels are responsible for the preparation of development plans, central government provides guidance and approves the plans. Since the election of the Labour government in 1997, the devolution of certain decision making powers from national to regional and local levels has been pursued (see DETR, 1998b and DETR, 1998f).

The Department for Transport, Local Government and the Regions (DTLR) – before 1997, DoE and the Department of Transport (DoT) – has the main responsibility for planning in England and there are eight regional offices for day-to-day executive action (planning inspectorate agencies). All spatial/land use PPPs are prepared by county, unitary or local authorities and anyone refused planning permission may appeal to the Secretary of State for Transport, Local Government and the Regions (DoE, 1989, p34). Appeals are dealt with by government planning inspectors.

National policy is provided in the form of guidance for the substantive content of development plans, to which local planning authorities are not legally bound (Davoudi et al, 1996, p422). However, national government reviews all policy statements of local authorities and can seize responsibility for preparing development plans.

Transport infrastructure planning

Transport infrastructure in the UK is administered as follows:

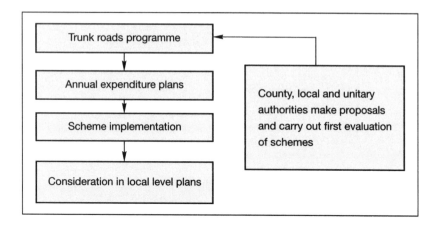

Figure 3.2: *Trunk roads planning process in the UK*

- National motorways, trunk and slip roads: since 1997 the DETR and highway agencies.[2]
- Principal roads and classified as well as unclassified roads: county councils' engineering services and highway agencies.[3]
- Railways: the railway system is privatized, the infrastructure is managed by Railtrack, services are provided by privatized companies.[4]
- Canals and other waterways: varying responsibilities.
- Airports: privatized, varying responsibilities.

National transport planning is conducted by central government. This includes mainly trunk roads planning[5], as public transport has been privatized since 1985. Figure 3.2 shows the trunk road planning process in a simplified manner. The national trunk roads programme is project oriented, and it is unclear how the projects included in the plan relate to overall transport policy.

Project proposals are made by local authorities and central government. Those proposals meeting previously defined objectives are included in the programme. If a road scheme appears in the annual expenditure plans, a clear intention for implementation is formulated.

Noord-Holland

Spatial/land use planning

Consensus-building was described as an essential element of the planning system in The Netherlands.[6] Planning therefore often involves interactive and open procedures, which provide an opportunity for widespread consultation and participation. While traditionally municipalities have much autonomy and can participate in the policy formulation of higher tiers (ie vertical administrative integration of planning), policy made at higher tiers needs to be taken into account by lower tiers when devising PPPs.[7] Public participation takes place at all administrative levels of decision making. The Dutch planning

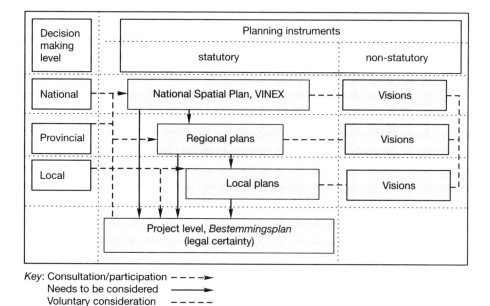

Key: Consultation/participation – – – –▶
Needs to be considered ——————▶
Voluntary consideration – – – – –

Figure 3.3: *Spatial/land use planning in The Netherlands*

system could therefore be described as being 'society consensus-led, quasi top-down'.

Figure 3.3 portrays the organization of spatial/land use planning in a simplified manner. Policies, plans and programmes are prepared at all decision making levels. The national government delegates authority to provincial and municipal governments through legislation and legal instruments that are enacted by the national parliament (DoE, 1989, p339). Current spatial/land use planning in The Netherlands uses traditional statutory instruments and, increasingly, also more non-statutory 'extra legal' instruments (visions, *visies*) at all administrative levels (EC, 1999c, p20). Visions put a higher emphasis on the integration of planning issues and compare the likely effects of different development scenarios. There is widespread participation and consultation.[8]

The only PPPs that municipalities are legally required to prepare are statutory local plans, *bestemmingsplannen* (Ministerie van VROM, 1996a, p5). These are small-scale plans (covering only parts of a municipality) that provide legal certainty. So-called *globale bestemmingsplannen* may also cover an entire urban district.

Transport infrastructure planning

Transport infrastructure in The Netherlands is administered as follows:

- National roads (*Rijkswegen*): Ministry of Transport, Public Works and Water Management (*Ministerie van Verkeer en Waterstaat*, MVW, through provincial branches, in Noord-Holland *Rijkswaterstaat Directie Noord Holland*).

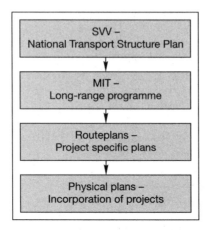

Source: adapted from Niekerk and Voogd, 1996

Figure 3.4: *National transport infrastructure planning process in The Netherlands*

- Provincial roads: *provincies* (for example, *Provincie* Noord-Holland).
- Other roads: municipalities (and regions, for example, ROA).
- National railways: *Nationale Spoorwegen* (NS), infrastructure through Ministry of Transport, Public Works and Water Management (MVW).
- Other railways: local or regional administration or private.
- Canals and rivers: varying responsibilities.
- Airports: Ministry of Transport, Public Works and Water Management (MVW).

Figure 3.4 shows the planning process of the national transport infrastructure (adapted from Niekerk and Voogd, 1996). The main steps of decision making are presented, starting with the national transport structure plan (SVV, *structuurschema verkeer en vervoer*) which outlines general policy and suggests possible projects.[9] This is followed by the long-range infrastructure and transport programme (MIT, *Meerjarenprogramma Infrastructuur en Transport*) and the route determination procedure (*Routeplan*, following the route alignment act, *tracéwet*). Finally, projects are incorporated into physical plans.

EVR Brandenburg-Berlin

Spatial/land use planning

The counter-current principle (*Gegenstromprinzip*) is often portrayed to be an important feature of the spatial/land use planning system in Germany, according to which planning is not organized in a strictly top-down, nor bottom-up manner (see, for example, EC, 1999c). Instead, higher tiers of decision making provide planning frameworks that are developed under consideration of the input of lower decision making levels. Furthermore, decisions made at lower

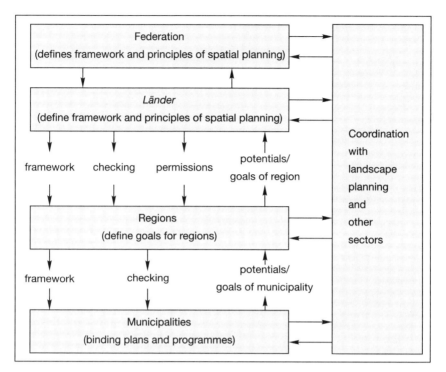

Source: adapted from Bundesministerium für Raumordnung, Bauwesen und Städtebau, 1996, p48

Figure 3.5: *Spatial/land use planning in Germany*

levels are checked by higher tier authorities. Public participation takes place mainly at the local level and the planning system could be described as having a 'public administration consensus-led, counter-current approach'.

Figure 3.5 illustrates the spatial planning system in Germany (following Bundesministerium für Raumordnung, Bauwesen und Städtebau, 1996, p9). It shows that planning is coordinated with the landscape planning system and with the planning instruments of other sectors. Landscape planning is intended to ensure that environmental aspects are considered in planning. It works as an instrument of the precautionary principle. It is further explained at the end of this section.

Transport infrastructure planning

Transport infrastructure in Germany is administered as follows:

- National roads (*Bundesautobahnen* and *Bundesstraßen*): Federal Ministry of Transport, *Bundesverkehrsministerium* (maintenance through regional branches).
- *Länder* roads (*Landstraßen*): *Länder* ministries of transport.

- Other roads (*Kreisstraßen* and *Gemeindestraßen*): *Kreise* and *kreisfreie Städte* (self-administering municipalities).
- National railways: *Deutsche Bahn* (DB, privatized), infrastructure administered by National Ministry of Transport.
- Other railways: either local or regional administration or private.
- Canals and rivers: Federal Ministry of Transport (*Bundesverkehrsministerium*).
- Airports: privatized.

Transport infrastructure planning is conducted by the bodies listed above. The *Länder* road networks in Germany are more extensive than comparable *provincie* road networks in The Netherlands (there are no similar regional transport networks in the UK).

Figure 3.6 portrays the organization of federal transport infrastructure planning. At the beginning of the process, proposals from lower-tier road planning bodies and other authorities at all decision making levels are collected. These are examined and ranked in the Federal Transport Infrastructure Plan (*Bundesverkehrswegeplan*, BVWP). Three classes of project proposals are distinguished:

1. Priority projects that had appeared in the former Federal Transport Infrastructure Plan.
2. Newly proposed priority projects.
3. Other projects.

The Federal Transport Infrastructure Plan obtains binding status through the development of the federal trunk roads and railways extension acts (*Straßen- und Schienenwegeausbaugesetze*). The five-year implementation programme lists those projects that are going to receive funding over a five-year period. Finally, object planning is conducted and projects are included in local plans.

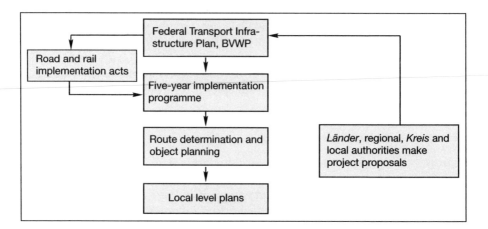

Figure 3.6: *Federal transport infrastructure planning process in Germany*

The federal transport infrastructure planning process is clearly project oriented and the connection with overall transport policy remains unclear.

Landscape planning

Landscape planning (*Landschaftsplanung*) is intended to act as an instrument of the precautionary principle and is closely connected with the spatial/land use planning system.[10] Both systems are integrated and regulated by paragraph 5 of the Federal Nature Protection Act (*Bundesnaturschutzgesetz*) and the State Nature Protection Laws (*Naturschutzgesetze der Länder*). Landscape planning is organized along the same lines as spatial/land use planning and other planning sectors, such as transportation planning. Integrated landscape plans and programmes (*Landschaftspläne und -programme*) define development goals from an environmental point of view for spatial/land use planning. Landscape planning aims at determining the capacity of natural resources and their limits and provides guidance for assessing the environmental impacts of projects and proposes compensation measures. Landscape planning attempts to make the scenic landscape and the natural ecosystem the basis for all land use considerations (Bundesministerium für Umwelt, Naturschutz und Reaktorsicherheit, 1993, p7). Table 3.1 shows that every step in the spatial/

Table 3.1: *Landscape planning and spatial planning in Germany*

Planning level	Spatial/land use planning	Landscape planning	Scale of maps
Land	*Land* spatial development plan (*Landesentwicklungs-plan/-programm*)	Landscape programme (*Landschaftspro-gramm*)	1:500,000 to 1:200,000
Region	Regional plan (*regionales Raumordnungskonzept*)	Landscape framework plan (*Landschaftsrah-menplan*)	1:50,000 to 1:25,000
Kreis	*Kreis* development plan (*Kreisentwick-lungsplan*)		
Community, city	Land use plan (*Flächennutzungsplan*, FNP, §1, BauGB)	Landscape plan (*Landschaftsplan*)	1:10,000 to 1:5,000
City district	Eg city district plan (*Bereichsentwicklungs-plan*)		Around 1:3,000
Part of the community	Master plan (B-Plan, §1, BauGB)	Open space master plan (*Grünord-nungsplan*)	1:2,500 to 1:1,000

Source: adapted from Bundesumweltministerium für Umwelt, Naturschutz und Reaktorsicherheit, 1993, p7 land use planning hierarchy can be related to different landscape planning steps.

PLANNING INSTRUMENTS

This section identifies the main transport and spatial/land use planning instruments in the three sample regions. All administrative levels of decision making and statutory as well as non-statutory instruments are covered.

North West England

At the national level, the *Trunk Roads Programme* is the most important transport infrastructure document. The only national document that currently considers all modes of transport are the annually reviewed government expenditure plans which include national roads, rail infrastructure, central government support to local authorities and the Civil Aviation Authority and London Transport. Furthermore, the DETR is working on an integrated transport strategy (DETR, 1997b). Trunk road planning is not integrated into the development control system, a situation that has been repeatedly criticized (see the Royal Commission on Environmental Pollution, 1995, paragraph 9.50). Railtrack (the company responsible for the UK rail infrastructure) prepares annual management statements on the rail infrastructure network. There is no national spatial planning document for the UK as a whole, nor are there any spatial documents for England, Scotland, Wales and Northern Ireland as separate entities.

Transport policies and programmes (TPPs) – since the beginning of 1999, TPPs are called local transport plans – are prepared annually for county and metropolitan wide areas. They:

> '*enable the government to assess local authorities proposed programmes of capital expenditure on roads and parking and to decide the way in which annual capital guidelines supplementary credit approvals and transport supplementary grant should be distributed among authorities*' (Cullingworth and Nadin, 1994, p230).

In 1994/95, for the first time, TPP bids were encouraged to cover both road and public transport investment proposals. In contrast to development plans, TPPs are neither statutory documents, nor are they subject to any formal inquiry procedures. They can, however, be regarded as quasi-mandatory instruments, as no government funding can be allocated without their preparation, on which central government publishes annual circulars. Districts of former metropolitan counties started preparing common TPP documents in 1996. These documents are generally referred to as packages. In addition to the annual TPPs, authorities have started preparing transport strategies that broadly outline transport policy for counties and districts.

While there is currently no statutory regional planning system, the regional level has become the focus of central government attention. Currently, regional planning guidance (RPG) is prepared, which is based broadly on advice given by groups of local authorities. At the county level, statutory structure plans are prepared. These are policy statements that deal with strategic land use matters (DoE, 1989, pp56–57). At the local level, statutory unitary development plans (UDPs) and in the shire districts, statutory local plans are prepared. County and local level plans are commonly referred to as development plans, which 'are prepared to assist in the regulation of the spatial distribution of activities and environments within a prescribed geographical area' (Wood, 1988, p10). All land use planning decisions have to be in accordance with these documents, unless material considerations indicate otherwise (Planning and Compensation Act 1991, section 54a). Local plans prepared by district and borough councils as well as by national park authorities set out detailed policies and specific proposals for the development and use of land.

Noord-Holland

One statutory document is prepared for each of spatial/land use and transport planning at the national level of decision making, namely the Transport Structure Plan (*structuurschema verkeer en vervoer*, SVV) and the national Spatial Planning Document (*nota ruimtelijke ordening*). The National Environmental Policy Plan (NMP – *nationaal milieubeleidsplan*) is also of importance, as the Transport Structure Plan, the National Spatial Plan and the NMP have the same underlying environmental objectives. In 1998, a long-term spatial development vision (*perspectievennota Nederland 2030,* started by *discussienota Nederland* in July 1997) was developed for the whole country (Ministerie van VROM, 1998a).

Current planning is based on the Second Transport Structure Plan (SVVII), the Fourth Spatial Planning Note (VINEX) and the Second Environmental Policy Plan (NMPII). VINEX was amended in 1997 by VINEX review. A third National Environmental Policy Plan was published in 1998 (NMPIII, Ministerie van VROM, 1998b). Furthermore, in 1998, the Dutch government underlined its intention to combine spatial planning, transport and the environment in an integrated national strategy for which the formulation process started at the beginning of 2000. The formal formulation process for a third Transport Structure Plan was started in 1999.

At the provincial level, statutory regional plans *(streekplannen)* are prepared for several parts of the *provincie*. Furthermore, non-statutory visions (*visies*) are prepared for entire provincial areas. Non-statutory, inter-provincial cooperation is conducted by the four Randstad provincies that include transport as well as spatial/land use planning. Regarding provincial transport planning, from 1989 to 1995, integrated regional transport strategies were prepared for transport regions (*vervoerregios*). These covered all transport modes as well as general transport themes, that is cycling, parking, security, public transport, roads and goods transport in a regional context. Transport regions were created following requirements formulated in the SVVII. They were abolished by the national government in 1995. However, following the VERDI agreement,[11] the Transport Planning Act (*planwet verkeer en vervoer*) was implemented, according to which *provincies* as well as municipalities need to prepare integrated transport plans (RVVPs, *regionaale verkeers- en vervoersplannen*). These RVVPs implement national policy at the provincial level and formulate specific provincial requirements.

At the local administrative level, statutory structure plans (*structuurplannen*) may be prepared. These provide a broad outline for the future land use of a municipality. Neighbouring municipalities may draw up joint structure plans. However, there are no mandatory requirements for the preparation of local/regional structure plans and non-statutory spatial/land use planning instruments have recently obtained more importance in the Dutch planning system. Non-statutory spatial/land use instruments include strategic outlook plans or visions (*structuurvisies, toekomstvisies* and *ontwikkelingsvisies*). It is assumed that these are more dynamic than traditional regulated plans and that they should help to overcome problems of the traditional regulated plans.

At the local level, the only mandatory land use plans, the *bestemmingsplannen* are prepared, which provide legal certainty. The city of Amsterdam has a special status within the planning system of The Netherlands. Urban districts (*Stadsdelen*) prepare their own local plans (*bestemmingsplannen*) that are reviewed by the city on the basis of Amsterdam's structure plan (*structuurplan*). Amsterdam's structure plan therefore has a stronger status than other structure plans in the country.

According to the Transport Planning Act (*planwet verkeer en vervoer,* 1998), local authorities will need to prepare formal local transport plans. Non-statutory plans at the local level have already been prepared in the past (see, for example, Physical Planning Department, 1993).

EVR Brandenburg-Berlin

At the national level, the Federal Transport Infrastructure Plan (*Bundesverkehrswegeplan, BVWP*) sets forth the need for adjustments and the extension of the national trunk roads and motorway system, the railway system and the waterways system. Long-term investment objectives for transport infrastructure are determined and general objectives for airports are formulated. Binding status is obtained through parliamentary implementation acts. Similar to the situation in England, national transport infrastructure planning in Germany stands outside the national planning control system. Regarding spatial/land use planning at the national level, a Spatial Action Framework (*Raumordnungspolitischer Handlungsrahmen*) is prepared by the Conference of the Ministers of Federal States (*Ministerkonferenz für Raumordnung*, MKRO). It is based on the Spatial Orientation Framework (*Raumordnungspolitischer Orientierungsrahmen*), prepared by the Federal Ministry of Spatial Planning (*Bundesministerium für Raumordnung, Bauwesen und Städtebau*, since 1999 Ministry for Transport, Construction and Dwellings, *Bundesministerium für Verkehr, Bau und Wohnungswesen*).

At the *Länder* level, spatial development plans or programmes (*Landesentwicklungspläne, -programme*) are prepared. Furthermore, *Länder* road extension programmes are prepared. County (*Kreis*) authorities prepare development plans (*Kreisentwicklungspläne*) and regional planning bodies (consisting of *Kreise* and *kreisfreie Städte*) are responsible for the definition of spatial goals in regional programmes *(regionale Raumordnungsprogramme)*. At the regional level, the main planning instruments are the regional plans (*Regionalpläne*). Non-statutory integrated *Länder* transport policies are sometimes prepared as well as other non-statutory PPPs, for example, regional railway plans.

The Construction Lead Planning system (*Bauleitplanung*) identifies the tasks of local land use planning. It consists of two instruments, namely preparatory land use plans (*Flächennutzungspläne, FNPs*) and master plans (*Bebauungspläne, B-Pläne*). Master plans are the main land use instruments of project implementation and are prepared for small areas within municipalities (*Gemeinden*). They are guided by the preparatory land use plans (FNPs) that are prepared by the municipalities. In larger municipalities, non-statutory strategic transport policies may also be prepared. Furthermore, in large cities, city district development plans are often prepared. These translate the city land use plan (FNP) to the city district.

LEGISLATION AND GUIDANCE

This section identifies important legislation and guidance for the transport and spatial/land use planning systems in the three sample regions.

North West England

Planning in England follows the Town and Country Planning Act 1990, amended by the Planning and Compensation Act 1991. Furthermore, the Town and Country Planning Regulations of 14 March 1999 are of importance. The Local Government Act of 1985 determines those development plans that need to be prepared by local authorities. Regarding transport planning, the transport acts are of particular importance. The main acts which have a bearing on county and local level TPPs are the:

- Highways Act 1980;
- Transport Act 1985 (with respect to public transport);
- Environment Act 1995 (with respect to air quality);
- Land Compensation Act 1973;
- Road Traffic Reduction Act 1997; and
- Local Authority (Capital Finance, Approved Investments) Regulations 1995.

Central government releases planning policy guidance notes (PPGs) that are to be used by local authorities when preparing development plans. PPG 1 identifies general policy and principles. PPG 12 provides guidance for the preparation of development plans and PPG 13 provides guidance for transport planning. Additional planning guidance is provided by 19 other PPGs, among which some are of particular importance for transport, such as PPG 3 (Housing), PPG 4 (Industrial and Commercial Development), PPG 6 (Town Centres and Retailing), PPG 7 (Countryside and Rural Economy), PPG 17 (Sport and Recreation) and PPG 21 (Tourism).

At present, strategic policies on spatial/land use and related planning matters at the regional level are expressed in the form of Regional Planning Guidance (RPG), issued by the Secretary of State for Transport, Local Environment and the Regions. RPG is prepared for each government office area and English regions have established (non-statutory) regional planning conferences which have had:

> *'an important function in developing policies and providing advice for the Secretary of State to consider in preparing regional planning guidance'* (Royal Commission on Environmental Pollution, 1995, paragraph 13.26).

The RPG system sets out strategic policies and guidance for land use and development (DETR, 1997c). In North West England, RPG 13 replaced the regional planning guidance note for Greater Manchester (RPG 4). However, as there are currently no overall strategic documents prepared for metropolitan areas, RPG 4 is still of importance, for example, for housing development figures.

The DETR publishes transport policy and programme circulars annually, based on which TPPs and package bids are prepared. The TPPs included in the subsequent analysis refer to either local authority circulars 2/95 (those prepared in 1996) or 2/96 (those prepared in 1997).

Noord-Holland

The organization of spatial/land use planning, as well as national transport planning in The Netherlands is based on the Spatial Planning Act with the latest amendment of 6 February 1997 (*wet op de ruimtelijke ordening*). Furthermore, at provincial and local levels, the General Administrative Act (*algemeene wet bestuursrecht*, last amended 1998) defines procedures for statutory regional plans (*streekplannen*) and statutory local land use plans in the form of structure plans (*structuurplannen*). The skeleton law Changing Administration (*kaderwet bestuur in verandering*, 1994) describes the tasks of the regional administrative level. The spatial/land use planning policy of provinces and municipalities as well as transport planning at the regional level is supervised by national government. Since 1 January 1998, transport planning is conducted according to the Transport Planning Act (*planwet verkeer en vervoer*, 1998), defining planning tasks for the national, provincial and local levels.

Guidance is primarily provided by laws (such as the Spatial Planning Act and the General Administrative Act) as well as by other PPPs. There are no planning guidance notes as such. Notes (*notas*) that are released at all administrative levels of decision making, illustrate government policy to be followed by lower tiers of decision making. *Notas* that were either mentioned during interviews or in mail questionnaires of the research underlying the book include:

- *Nota Samenwerken an Bereikbarheid* (Working Together Towards Greater Accessibility, Ministerie van Verkeer en Waterstaat, 1996a);
- *Nota transport in balans* (TiB, Transport in Balance, Ministerie van Verkeer en Waterstaat, 1996b);
- *Nota locatiebeleid* (Location Policy, Ministerie van VROM, 1991);
- *Provinciale nota locatiebeleid* (Provincial Note Location Policy, Provincie Noord-Holland, 1993);
- *Nota ruimte voor regios* (Space for Regions, Ministerie van Economische Zaken, 1995);
- *Relatienota natuurontwikkeling op landbauwgrond* (Nature Development on Agriculture Areas, Provincie Noord-Holland, 1992); and
- *Derde nota waterhuisvesting* (NW3) (Third Note Water Management, Ministerie van VROM, 1989b).

EVR Brandenburg-Berlin

Up until 1998, spatial/land use planning in Germany had been based on the Spatial Planning Act (*Raumordnungsgesetz*, ROG) and the Construction Statute Book (*Baugesetzbuch*). In 1998, a new Spatial Planning and Construction Act (*Bau- und Raumordnungsgesetz*, BauROG, 1998) was implemented by the Federal Parliament (*Bundestag*) and the parliament of the *Länder* (*Bundesrat*), amending the former two acts.

In general, spatial planning is the responsibility of the *Länder* and the Federal government has only a coordinating role. The Federal government prepares a Spatial Development Framework (*Raumordnungspolitischer Orientierungsrahmen*), which is the basis for a Spatial Action Framework (*Raumordnungspolitischer Handlungsrahmen)* to be agreed upon by the planning conference of the *Länder* ministries. Of particular importance for national transport planning are the road and rail extension acts (*Fernstraßenausbaugesetz, Schienenwegeausbaugesetz*) following the Federal Transport Infrastructure Plan (*Bundesverkehrswegeplan*, BVWP).

In the former East Germany, the planning system has radically changed following unification. A number of traditional planning instruments were simplified in order to speed up planning for extending transport infrastructure. Examples of amended legislation include the Transport Infrastructure Planning Acceleration Act (*Verkehrswegeplanungsbeschleunigungsgesetz*, 1991) and the Act of Simplification of the Provisions for and Investment in New Residential Areas (*Investitionserleichterungs- und Wohnbaulandgesetz*, 1993).

In Berlin and Brandenburg, the Land Planning Convention (*Gesetz zum Landesplanungsvertrag,* LPlV, 1995) defines the tasks of spatial planning. The Regional Planning Act (*Gesetz zur Einführung der Regionalplanung und der Braunkohle- und Sanierungsplanung*, RegBkPlG, 1993) is the basis for regional planning in the *Land* Brandenburg. *Länder*, regional and county (*Kreis*)

Table 3.2: *Main features of transport and spatial/land use planning*

	North West England	Noord-Holland	EVR Brandenburg-Berlin
Transport planning approach	While proposals for transport infrastructure projects are made by different bodies at all administrative levels, national transport infrastructure planning is organized in a top-down manner of decision making.		
Spatial/land use planning approach	centrally guided, local plan making	society consensus-led, quasi top-down approach	public administration, consensus-led, counter-current approach
Main administrative levels of policy, plan and programme making	• national • county (and region) • local	• national • *provincie* (and interprovincial cooperation) • *Regio* • *Gemeente/ Stadsdeel*	• Federal • *Land* • *region* • *Kreis/kreisfreie Stadt* • *Gemeinde/ Stadtteil*
Spatial/land use planning, main planning instruments	• guidance • structure plans at county level • local plans at local level or unitary development plans at district level	• national spatial plan (VINEX) • interprovincial vision (IPVR) • provincial vision (*visie*) • regional provincial plans (*streekplannen*) • Regional PPPs (*structuurschets, structuurplan*) • local plan (*structuurplan, visie*) • 'sub'local plan (*bestemmings-plan*)	• federal spatial frameworks (*Raumordnungs-politischer Orientierungs-und Handlungs-rahmen*) • land development programme and plan (LEPro, LEP) • regional plan (*Regionalplan*) • *Kreis* Development Plan (*Entwicklungsplan*) • preparatory land use plan (FNP) • district plan
Transport planning, main planning instruments	• Road development plan (national integrated transport plan currently being developed) • regional transport strategies • package bids, TPPs and underlying strategies	• national transport plan (SVV) + programme • provincial (formerly regional) transport plans (VVPs)	• Federal Transport Infrastructure Plan (BVWP) + Programme • *Länder* road plans and integrated transport plans • city transport plans

PPPs are usually prepared according to *Länder* legislation. Following the introduction of the Public Transport Regionalization Act (*Regionalisierungsgesetz,* 1993), public transport plans are prepared at regional levels since 1996. Brandenburg's Road Act (*Brandenburger Straßengesetz, BrbStrG*) of 1992 (last amended 1995) defines requirements for transport infrastructure planning in the *Land* Brandenburg. In Berlin, the Federal Construction Implementation Act (*AGBauGB*) translates the requirements of the Federal Construction Act (*BauGB*) to the local level.

CROSS-REGIONAL CHARACTERISTICS

Table 3.2 compares the main features of the transport and spatial/land use planning systems in England, The Netherlands and Germany, as described in the previous sections. The general planning approach, the main administrative levels and the main planning instruments are presented.

National transport planning was centrally managed by the national transport ministries in a rather top-down manner in the three regions. Spatial/land use planning involved all administrative levels of decision making and was more complex. In the UK, a centrally guided, plan-making approach was followed. In The Netherlands, a society consensus-led quasi top-down approach was applied and in Germany, a public administration, consensus-led, counter-current approach was followed.

National governments in the UK and The Netherlands were found to have had a stronger status regarding spatial planning than the federal government in Germany, where spatial planning was mainly the responsibility of the *Länder*. Other differences include the number of administrative levels. Thus, while there were five administrative levels in EVR Brandenburg-Berlin, this number decreased to four levels in Noord-Holland and to three levels in North West England. Currently, in North West England, a fourth decision making level is set up, the regional level. While both The Netherlands and Germany prepared spatial as well as transport PPPs at most decision making levels, in England, spatial/land use PPPs were prepared only at local and county levels. In England, central government was involved in spatial planning through planning guidance to local authorities (PPGs and RPGs).

Chapter 4

Policies, plans and programmes

Understanding of SEA cannot be improved if there is only limited knowledge of current planning systems. Chapter 4 therefore identifies and analyses the PPPs that are discussed in the remainder of the book. The second part of objective 1 of the book 'to systematically identify transport and spatial/land use PPPs in three EU regions' is addressed. This chapter is divided into six sections. The first lists all documents that interviewed authorities said were related to transport planning in the three sample regions. It then identifies the PPPs to be included in the analysis of Chapters 5 to 8. Overall scores for each PPP for the four context variables are identified, including PPP relevance, PPP accountability, PPP inter-modality and PPP procedure. Finally, cross-regional characteristics are summarised.

SELECTION OF PPPS

This section is divided into two sub-sections. The first presents all of the PPPs that were identified to be of importance for transport and spatial/land use planning by the authorities at all administrative levels in the three sample regions. The second section identifies the PPPs included in the analysis of the subsequent chapters.

PPPs in the three sample regions

Tables 4.1 to 4.3 list the PPPs that authorities in the three sample regions identified as being relevant for transport and spatial/land use planning. The PPPs included in further analysis are summarized later and are further examined in the remainder of this chapter. Some PPPs of other sectors were also said to be of importance. These include, in particular, those dealing with economic and agricultural issues.

A large number of PPPs in the three regions were identified, underlining the complex character of the different planning systems. The smallest number was identified in North West England, reflecting a somewhat simpler planning system.

While both Noord-Holland and EVR Brandenburg-Berlin authorities mentioned considerably more types of PPPs in the spatial/land use sector than in the transport sector, in North West England there were no clear differences between the two sectors. Generally, comparatively few statutory transport PPPs

Table 4.1: *PPPs in North West England*

Sustainability/environmental PPPs			Transport PPPs			Spatial/land use PPPs		
Non-statutory strategies	Statutory integrated PPPs & monitoring documents	Legislation/non-statutory guidelines/guidance	Legislation/non-statutory guidelines/guidance	Statutory investment plans/programmes	Non-statutory strategies/development outlook	Legislation/non-statutory guidelines/guidance	Statutory land use plans/development PPPs	Non-statutory strategies/development visions
• Sustainable development - UK strategy • Environmental action strategy North West England • Lancashire environmental action + green audit • Cheshire local Agenda 21 + state of the environment report + sustainable transport strategy • Local Agenda 21s		• National air quality strategy • Environmental Act, 1995, Section 4	• Transport circulars: DETR guidance for TPPs and package bids • Traffic Reduction Bill • White Paper Integrated Transport	• 4 TPPs/package bid documents • Roads programme	• Green Paper air quality and traffic • 3 public transport strategies • 3 integrated transport strategies • North West England transport strategy • Cycling strategy • Citizens Network (EC) • Transport – the way forward	• Former regional planning guidance 4 and Greater Manchester structure plan • RPG 13: Regional Planning Guidance 13 • PPGs (planning policy guidance), particularly PPGs 1, 6, 12, 13 • MPGs: Minerals Planning Guidance	• 2 Structure Plans • 15 UDPs (unitary development plans) • 22 local plans	• North West England economic strategy

Table 4.2: *PPPs in Noord-Holland*

Sustainability/environmental PPPs			Transport PPPs			Spatial/land use PPPs		
Non-statutory strategies	Statutory integrated PPPs & monitoring documents	Legislation/non-statutory guidelines/guidance	Statutory investment plans/programmes	Non-statutory strategies/development outlook	Legislation/non-statutory guidelines/guidance	Statutory land use plans/development PPPs	Non-statutory strategies/development visions	Legislation/non-statutory guidelines/guidance
	• NMBP + *verkenning:* National Environmental Policy Plan + Environmental Monitoring • PMBP + *verkenning:* Provincial Environmental Policy Plan + Environmental Monitoring • ROA *milieukwaliteit* + *verkenning:* ROA Environmental Policy Plan + Environmental Monitoring		• SVV 2 (+ Rail 21) + BER: Second Transport Structure Plan (+ Rail Strategy 21) + Policy Effect Report • MIT: Multi-year Programme Transport Infrastructure • RVVP NHN: Regional Transport Plan Noord-Holland Noord	• MPV IV: Fourth National Safety Programme • RISI: Randstad Investment Scheme • SWAB: Note Working Towards Greater Accessibility • Vervoer in balans: Note Transport in Balance	• WRO: Spatial Planning Act • *Wet bestuursrecht:* Administrative Management Act • *Locatienota:* Note Location Policy • *Ruimte voor regios:* Note Space for Regions • *Provinciale nota locatiebeleid:* Provincial Note Location Policy	• Structuur-schema groene ruimte: Structure Plan Green Spaces • SMT: Structure Plan Military Areas • VINEX + spatial monitoring: National Spatial plan + spatial monitoring • 5 *streek-plannen:* 5 regional plans	• NW3: Third Note Water Management • *Perspecti-vennota 2020:* Strategic Development Outlook 2020 • IPVR: Inter-Provincial Urbanisation Vision of the Randstad • *Ontwikke-lingsvisie* N-Holland: Strategic Development Outlook Noord Holland	

Table 4.2: *Continued*

Sustainability/environmental PPPs			Transport PPPs			Spatial/land use PPPs		
Non-statutory strategies	Statutory integrated PPPs & monitoring documents	Legislation/non-statutory guidelines/guidance	Legislation/non-statutory guidelines/guidance	Statutory investment plans/programmes	Non-statutory strategies/development outlook	Legislation/non-statutory guidelines/guidance	Statutory land use plans/development PPPs	Non-statutory strategies/development visions
	• Milieuplannen + verkenning: municipal environmental plans + environmental monitoring			• RVVP ROA + uitvoeringsprogramma + BER: Regional Transport Plan ROA + 2-year Programme + Policy Effect Report • Former RVVPs: regional transport plans of Haarlem/IJmond and Gooi en Vechtstreek • Uitvoeringsprogramma gemeenten: municipal programmes for transport infrastructure	• *Beleidsvisie openbaar vervoer*: Policy Vision Public Transport • Regionet rail: Note Regional Railway Network • INVERNO + BER: Transport Study of the Northern Part of the Randstad + Policy Effect Report • Vervoersplannen: municipal transport plans	• BROM: Policy Note Spatial Organisation and the Environment • Note Amsterdam Towards 2005	• Structuurplan ROA + PRV: ROA's Structure Plan and Programme Spatial Renewal • *Structuurplannen*: Municipal Structure Plans	• Economische strategie: Economic Strategy • *Ontwikkelingsvisies*: Municipal Strategic Development Outlooks

Table 4.3: *PPPs in EVR Brandenburg-Berlin*

Sustainability/environmental PPPs			Transport PPPs			Spatial/land use PPPs		
Non-statutory strategies	Legislation/ non-statutory guidelines/ guidance	Statutory integrated PPPs & monitoring documents	Legislation/ non-statutory guidelines/ guidance	Statutory investment plans/ programmes	Non-statutory strategies/ development outlook	Legislation/ non-statutory guidelines/ guidance	Statutory land use plans/ development PPPs	Non-statutory strategies/ development visions
• Berlin Climate protection strategy: *Berliner Klimaschutz-strategie*	• BNatSchG: Federal Environmental Protection Act • BrbNatSchG: Brandenburg Environmental Protection Act • BlnNatSchG: Berlin Environmental Protection Act	• LaPro Brb.: Landscape Programme Brandenburg • *8 Land-schaftsrah-menpläne*: 8 landscape framework plans • LaPro Bln.: Landscape Programme Berlin • *Land-schaftspläne*: landscape plans	• ÖPNV law: Local Public Transport Act (*Regionalisie-rungsgesetz*)	• BVWP (+FStrAbG, SchWAbG) + *5-Jahrespro-gramm*: Federal Transport Infrastructure Plan (+ extension acts for trunk roads and railways) + 5-year programme • *Straßenent-wicklungsplan*: Road Development Plan	• TENs: Trans-European Networks • *Zielnetz* 2000: Railway Network Development Outlook 2000 • *Landesver-kehrsplan*: Integrated Transport Plan • *Verkehrsent-wicklungsplan* Region Berlin: Transport Development plan for the Berlin Region	• ROG: Spatial Planning Act • BauGB: Construction Statute Book • BauNV: Construction Land Use Decree • PlaVO: Mapping Guidance • DRL: Presentation Guideline • LPIG: Land Planning Act • *Runderlaß*: Intervention Rule Decree	• LEPro: Land Development Programme • LEP1: Land Development Plan 1 • LEP Brb.: Land Development Plan for Brandenburg • LEPeVR: Land Development Plan Berlin-Brandenburg • *5 Regional-pläne*: 5 regional plans	• *Orientie-rungsrahmen*: Federal Spatial Orientation Framework • *Agrarstruktu-relle Vorplanung*: preliminary planning agriculture • *8 Entwick-lungskonzep-tionen*: 8 development concepts • STEPs Berlin: city development plans Berlin

Table 4.3: *Continued*

Sustainability/environmental PPPs			Transport PPPs			Spatial/land use PPPs		
Non-statutory strategies	Statutory integrated PPPs & monitoring documents	Legislation/ non-statutory guidelines/ guidance	Legislation/ non-statutory guidelines/guid- ance	Statutory investment plans/program- mes	Non-statutory strategies/ development outlook	Legislation/ non-statutory guidelines/ guidance	Statutory land use plans/ development PPPs	Non-statutory strategies/ development visions
					• *Nahver-kehrspläne*: local public transport plans • StEP Verkehr: City Development Plan - Transport	• RegBkPlG: Decree for Introduction of Regional Planning • LPlV: Land Planning Treaty Richtlinie • Regional-plan.: Guidance for Regional Planning • AGBauGB: Berlin Construction Statute Book • RL-FNP: Guidance for Land Use Planning • AV-BEP: City District Planning Implementation Ordinance	• FNP Berlin: Land Use Plan Berlin • *Bezirksent-wicklungs-pläne*: district development plans • 66 FNPs: 66 land use plans	

and transport legislation/guidance were mentioned by authorities in the three regions.

In Noord-Holland, the Second Transport Structure Plan (*SVVII*) and in EVR Brandenburg-Berlin the Federal Transport Infrastructure Plan (*BVWP*) were of particular importance for planning at all decision making levels. These two national plans define objectives and provide guidance on transport-related issues for all other tiers of decision making.

Regarding important sustainability/environmental planning documents in North West England, the focus of attention was on non-statutory strategies, in particular on Local Agenda 21s.[1] In the other two regions, the focus was on statutory instruments, namely landscape plans and programmes (*Landschaftspläne, -programme*) in EVR Brandenburg-Berlin and environmental policy plans (*milieubeleidsplannen*) in Noord-Holland.

PPPs included in the further analysis

Table 4.4 lists the PPPs included in the further SEA analysis, as identified in Figures 4.1 to 4.3. The number in brackets, listed with a particular PPP refers to the list of the main source documentation used in analysis after the references. All PPPs are analysed in further depth in terms of the four context variables (see Chapter 2) in the subsequent sections of Chapter 4. The choice of the 36 PPPs at all administrative levels was guided by two main aspects.

Table 4.4: *PPPs selected for analysis*

Administrative level		North West England	Noord-Holland	EVR Branden-burg-Berlin
National	Transport	• Trunk Roads Programme **[8]**	• Second Transport Structure Plan (SVVII) **[6][7]**+ Infrastructure & Transport Programme 1997-2000 **[8]**	• Federal Transport Infrastructure Plan (BVWP) + Five-year Extension Plan **[5]-[9][17]**
	Spatial/land use		• National Spatial Plan (VINEX) + VINEX review **[9]-[11]**	• Federal Spatial Planning Orientation Framework + Action Framework (*Raumordnungspolitischer Orientierungsrahmen + Handlungsrahmen*, ROP-Orient) **[4][16]**

Table 4.4: *Continued*

Administrative level		North West England	Noord-Holland	EVR Brandenburg-Berlin
Land/provincial/ sample regional	Transport	• NW Transport Strategy **[21]**	• INVERNO Transport Plan (RVVP) **[12]** • RVVP Noord-Holland Noord **[28]**	• *Land* Roads Development Plan (*Landesstraßen-bedarfsplan*, **[14]** • Provincial Integrated Transport Outline (*Integrierter Verkehrsplan*, IVP)**[15]**
	Spatial/land use	• RPG 13, Regional Planning Guidance for the North-West **[9][20]**	• Regional Plans Waterland, NH-Noord, Gooi en Vechtstreek (*Streekplannen*) **[13]-[17]** • Development Vision of Noord-Holland (*Ontwikkelings-visie*) **[18]** • Inter-provincial urbanisation vision (*Interprovinciale Verstedelingsvi-sie op de Randstad*, IPVR) **[24]-[26]**	• Land Development Programme Brandenburg-Berlin eV (*Landesentwick-lungsprogramm*, LEPro)**[11]** • Land Development Plan Brandenburg-Berlin eV (*Landesentwick-lungsplan*, LEPeV)**[10]** • Regional Plan Havelland-Fläming (*Regionalplan*) **[18]**
City-region/ *Kreis*/county	Transport	• Greater Manchester Transport Package **[10]** • Lancashire TPP **[15][16]** • Cheshire TPP **[5][6]** • Merseyside Package Bid **[18][19]**	• ROA transport plan (RVVP) + Regional Programme 95–97 **[19]-[21]** • RVVP Haarlem-IJmond **[27][5]**	• Urban Development Plan Transport Berlin (*Stadtentwick-lungsplan Verkehr*, StEP) **[19][20]**

Table 4.4: *Continued*

Administrative level		North West England	Noord-Holland	EVR Branden-burg-Berlin
	Spatial/land use	• Oldham Unitary Development Plan (UDP) **[22]**	• Structure Plan ROA (*Structuurplan*) **[22][23]**	• Land Use Plan Berlin (FNP Berlin) **[21]-[23]**
		• Salford UDP **[23]**		• County Development Plan Havelland (*Entwicklungs-konzeption,* **[12][13]**
		• Lancashire Structure Plan **[11]-[14][17]**		
		• Cheshire Structure Plan **[1]-[4][7]**		
Local	Only spatial/land use PPPs are relevant	Warrington Local Plan **[24]**	• Structure Plan Amsterdam (*Structuurplan*) **[1]-[3]**	• Land Use Plan Ketzin (FNP)**[1][2]**
			• Future Vision Hilversum (*Toekomstsvi-sie*) **[4]**	• Development Plan Charlot-tenburg (*Bereichsent-wicklungsplan*) **[3]**

Note: bold numbers in brackets refer to documentation listed after the references

Firstly, PPPs included those that were known to have an assessment of environmental impacts undertaken. Secondly, PPPs were included that decision makers identified to be of great importance for transport planning. In order to be able to compare observed patterns between the three regions, four decision making levels were distinguished, which also include the regional level in North West England. In EVR Brandenburg-Berlin, the *Länder* and regional levels were combined. Decision making levels include:

- national level;
- *Land/Provincie*/sample regional level;
- city regional/*Kreis*/county level; and
- local level.

In addition to the 36 PPPs for the cross-section of all administrative levels discussed and analysed in this chapter (based on interview results), local land use plans were also regarded (based on postal questionnaire results). This allows differences between the local level and higher tiers to be determined.

Table 4.5 indicates whether there was more of a policy orientation or a project orientation. This distinction is of importance for the identification of SEA types.

It was found that the policy or project orientation was not dependent on the tier, in other words higher tiers were not necessarily policy oriented and lower tiers were not necessarily project oriented. The Federal Transport Infrastructure Plan (BVWP), for example, consists of a compilation of projects and does not attempt to identify an optimal mix of policies and projects in order to achieve stated policy objectives. Dutch regional transport plans, on the other hand, are policy oriented, comparing impacts of different policy options (considering cumulative impacts and inter-modal alternatives) in order to identify those measures that achieve stated policy aims.

Policy orientation in North West England frequently had a different character from policy orientation in EVR Brandenburg-Berlin and Noord-Holland. Thus, in North West England, policy orientation was also present in statutory plans (structure plans and UDPs), dealing with concrete policies, such as greenbelt conservation or city area development. In Noord-Holland and EVR Brandenburg-Berlin, on the other hand, policy orientation tended to mean a focus on strategic, less concrete policy options, such as urban sprawl compared with urban concentration.

PPP RELEVANCE

This section identifies scores for the context variable PPP relevance for each of the 36 individual PPPs. PPP relevance includes the legislative status (statutory/non-statutory), provisions (mandatory/non-mandatory) and the relevance for subsequent planning (binding/non-binding) of a PPP. Resulting variable scores are used to explain the SEA patterns in Parts 3 and 4 of the book.

Table 4.5: *Policy and project orientation of PPPs*

Sector	Regions and examples
	Project orientation
Transport	(a) English PPPs
	• Cheshire TPP
	• Lancashire TPP
	• Greater Manchester Package Bid
	• Merseyside Package Bid
	• North West England Transport Strategy
	• Trunk Roads Programme
	(b) Dutch PPPs
	• no examples
	(c) German PPPs
	• Federal Transport Infrastructure Plan (BVWP)
	• Road Plan (*Landesstraßenbedarfsplan*) Brandenburg
Spatial/land use	(a) English PPPs
	• Warrington Local Plan
	(b) Dutch PPPs
	• National Spatial Plan (VINEX) review

Table 4.5: *Continued*

Sector	Regions and examples
	• Structure Plan (*structuurplan*) Amsterdam • Structure Plan (*structuurplan*) ROA • Regional Plans (*streekplannen*) Noord-Holland (c) German PPPs • Development Plan (LEP) EVR Brandenburg-Berlin • Land Use Plan (FNP) Berlin • Land Use Plan (FNP) Ketzin • District Development Plan (*Bereichsentwicklungsplan*) Charlottenburg
	Policy orientation
Transport	(a) English PPPs • Underlying strategies for TPPs and package bids (b) Dutch PPPs • Second Transport Structure Plan (SVVII) • RVVP INVERNO • RVVP Noord-Holland-Noord • RVVP ROA • RVVP Haalem-IJmond (c) German PPPs • Integrated Transport Plan (StEP) Berlin • Integrated Transport Plan (IVP) Brandenburg
Spatial/land use	(a) English PPPs • Regional Planning Guidance North West England • Lancashire Structure Plan • Cheshire Structure Plan • UDP Salford • UDP Oldham (b) Dutch PPPs • Vision (*visie*) Noord-Holland • Urbanization Vision (IPVR) Randstad • Vision (*visie*) Hilversum (c) German PPPs • Federal Spatial Orientation Framework (ROPOrient) • Land Development Programme (LEPro) Brandenburg • Regional Plan (*Regionalplan*) Havelland-Fläming • Concept (*Kreisentwicklungskonzeption*) Havelland

North West England

Tables 4.6 and 4.9 present the criteria and overall variable scores obtained by the individual PPP for the context variable PPP relevance. Statutory development plans obtained the highest scores (100 per cent). Lowest scores (under 25 per cent) were obtained by the non-statutory North West Transport Strategy and the Regional Planning Guidance RPG 13.

Six plans/programmes were statutory, including the development plans (structure plans, UDPs, local plans) and the national Trunk Roads Programme. While all regional plans and programmes were non-statutory, the package bids and TPPs were said to be quasi-statutory, as they needed to be prepared in order to secure government funding, following annual government circulars (see Chapter 3). The preparation of all statutory plans and programmes was mandatory. RPG 13 was considered to be quasi-mandatory, as central government asked for RPGs to be prepared for all English regions.

Most of the PPPs were directly binding on further planning (authorities had to take them into account in any further spatial/land use related decisions), except three cases above the county level, namely the Trunk Roads Programme, RPG 13 and the North West Transport Strategy. While the first two needed to be at least recognized in subsequent planning decisions, the North West Transport Strategy was a compendium of schemes to be implemented through other PPPs.

Noord-Holland

Tables 4.7 and 4.9 show the criteria and overall variable scores for the context variable PPP relevance in Noord-Holland. Highest scores (100 per cent) were achieved for the more traditional statutory PPPs, the National Second Transport Structure Plan and the National Spatial Plan, VINEX review, the structure plans (*structuurplannen*) and the regional plans (*streekplannen*). The lowest scores (under 25 per cent) were achieved for the new planning instruments, the spatial/land use visions (*visies*).

Most PPPs in Noord-Holland were statutory, except the three spatial visions (*visies*) Noord-Holland, IPVR and Hilversum. The Integrated Transport Plan for the northern part of the Randstad (INVERNO) was not statutory at the time of its preparation. It obtained, however, statutory status later, after the VERDI agreement in 1996 (see Chapter 3). Most of the PPPs that were statutory were also mandatory, except the structure plans (*structuurplannen*), which only needed to be prepared in case of significant changes in land use demands (only eight local *structuurplannen* were identified in Noord-Holland). All regional transport policies became binding through multi-year implementation programmes, which listed and ranked projects.[2] While the three spatial/land use visions (*visies*) Noord-Holland, IPVR and Hilversum were only partially binding for further planning, all other spatial/land use plans and programmes had to be acknowledged by authorities in further decisions.

Table 4.6: *PPP relevance in North West England*

	Relevance			Accountability					Intermodality			Stage of formulation procedures						
	Statutory/ non-statutory	Mandatory/ non-mandatory	Binding/ non-binding	Approving not preparation body	External consultation	Public participation	Elected body involved	Independent review	Public transport service	Several transport modes	Objectives for several sectors	Objective setting	Initial stage	Documentation	Review	Public participation	Consultation	Monitoring
Trunk Roads Programme	✓	✓	⇕	✗	⇕	✗	✓	⇕	✗	✗	✓	✗	✗	✓	✗	✗	⇕	⇕
North West Transport Strategy	✗	✗	✗	⇕	✓	✗	✗	⇕	✓	✓	⇕	⇕	⇕	✓	⇕	✗	✓	✗
Regional Planning Guidance RPG 13	✗	⇕	⇕	✓	✓	✗	✗	⇕	✗	✓	✓	⇕	⇕	✓	⇕	✗	✓	⇕
Lancashire Structure Plan	✓	✓	✓	✓	✓	✓	✓	✓	✗	✓	✓	⇕	⇕	✓	✓	✓	✓	⇕
Cheshire Structure Plan	✓	✓	✓	✓	✓	✓	✓	✓	✗	✓	✓	⇕	⇕	✓	✓	✓	✓	⇕
Lancashire TPP	⇕	⇕	✓	✓	✓	✗	✓	⇕	✓	✓	⇕	⇕	⇕	✓	⇕	✗	✓	⇕
Cheshire TPP	⇕	⇕	✓	✓	✓	✗	✓	⇕	✓	✓	⇕	✓	⇕	✓	⇕	✗	✓	⇕
Merseyside Package Bid	⇕	⇕	✓	✓	✓	✗	✓	⇕	✓	✓	⇕	✓	⇕	✓	⇕	⇕	✓	⇕
Greater Manchester Package Bid	⇕	⇕	✓	✓	✓	✗	✓	⇕	✓	✓	⇕	✓	⇕	✓	⇕	✗	✓	⇕
Warrington Local Plan	✓	✓	✓	✓	✓	✓	✓	✓	✗	✓	✓	✗	⇕	✓	✓	✓	✓	⇕
Oldham Unitary Development Plan	✓	✓	✓	✓	✓	✓	✓	✓	✗	✓	✓	✗	⇕	✓	✓	✓	✓	⇕
Salford Unitary Development Plan	✓	✓	✓	✓	✓	✓	✓	✓	✗	✓	✓	✗	⇕	✓	✓	✓	✓	⇕

Key: ✓ = yes. ⇔ = partially/not clearly determined. ✗ = no.   ✓ = stage fully conducted. ⇔ = partially conducted. ✗ = not conducted. ☐ informal procedure ☐ formal procedure

EVR Brandenburg-Berlin

Tables 4.8 and 4.9 show the criteria and overall variable scores for the context variable PPP relevance in EVR Brandenburg-Berlin. Highest scores (100 per cent) were obtained for a range of PPPs, including the Federal Transport Infrastructure Plan (BVWP), the Land Development Plan EVR Brandenburg-Berlin (LEPeV), the Regional Plan (*Regionalplan*) Havelland, The Land Road Development Plan (*Landesstraßenbedarfsplan*) Brandenburg and the land use plans (FNPs). Only the non-statutory Federal Spatial Orientation Framework (ROPOrient) and Integrated Transport Plan (IVP) Brandenburg obtained very low scores (under 25 per cent).

Most PPPs in EVR Brandenburg-Berlin were statutory, except the Spatial Orientation Framework (*Raumordnungspolitischer Orientierungsrahmen*) and the Integrated Transport Plan (IVP) Brandenburg. Most of the PPPs that were statutory were also mandatory, with the exception of the Development Concept (*Kreisentwicklungskonzeption*) Havelland and the Land Use Plan (FNP) Ketzin.[3] Only six policies, plans and programmes were directly binding on further planning, all of which were statutory.

PPP ACCOUNTABILITY

This section identifies individual overall scores for the context variable PPP accountability for each individual PPP. PPP accountability is determined by the following five criteria:

1. Approving body not preparation body.
2. External consultation.
3. Public participation.
4. Involvement of an elected body.
5. Review by an external body.

Resulting variable scores were used for explaining the SEA patterns in Parts 3 and 4 of the book.

North West England

Tables 4.6 and 4.9 shows the criteria and overall variable scores for the context variable PPP accountability in North West England. Highest scores (100 per cent) were obtained by the statutory development plans. Lowest scores were obtained by the National Trunk Roads Programme and the North West Transport Strategy.

Most PPP preparation bodies in North West England were not the approving bodies, except for the National Trunk Roads Programme, which was prepared and approved by the DoT (the DETR since 1997). The North West Transport Strategy was jointly prepared by county councils and the North West Regional Association. It was approved by the North West Regional Government Office. All other PPPs were prepared by county, unitary and district authorities and were approved by central government.

Table 4.7: *'PPP relevance' in Noord-Holland*

	Relevance			Accountability					Intermodality			Stage of formulation procedures						
	Statutory/ non-statutory	Mandatory/ non-mandatory	Binding/ non-binding	Approving not preparation body	External consultation	Public participation	Elected body involved	Independent review	Public transport service	Several transport modes	Objectives for several sectors	Objective setting	Initial stage	Documentation	Review	Public participation	Consultation	Monitoring
Second Transport Structure Plan (SVVII)	✓	✓	✓	✗	✓	✓	✓	⇕	⇕	✓	✓	⇕	✓	✓	⇕	✓	✓	✓
National Spatial Plan (VINEX) review	✓	✓	✓	✗	✓	✓	✓	✓	✗	✓	✓	⇕	⇕	✓	✓	✓	✓	✓
Inter-Provincial Urbanization Vision Randstad (IPVR)	✗	✗	⇕	✓	⇕	✗	✓	⇕	✗	✓	✗	✗	⇕	✓	⇕	✗	⇕	✗
Development Vision (*Ontwikkelingsvisie*) Noord-Holland	✗	✗	⇕	✗	✓	✓	✓	⇕	✗	✓	✗	✗	✓	✓	⇕	✓	✓	✗
Regional Plans (*Streekplannen*) (5 for provincie)	✓	✓	✓	✗	✓	✓	✓	✓	✓	✓	✓	⇕	⇕	✓	✓	✓	✓	✓
Integrated Transport Vision Randstad North (INVERNO)	⇕	⇕	⇕	✓	✓	✗	✓	⇕	✓	✓	✓	⇕	⇕	✓	⇕	✗	✓	✓
Transport Plan (RVVP) Noord-Holland-Noord	✓	✓	⇕	✓	✓	✗	✓	⇕	✓	✓	✓	⇕	⇕	✓	⇕	✗	✓	⇕
Structure Plan (*Structuurplan*) ROA	✓	⇕	✓	✓	✓	✓	✓	✓	✗	✓	✓	✓	✓	✓	✓	✗	✓	⇕
Transport Plan (RVVP) ROA	✓	⇕	⇕	✓	✓	⇕	✓	⇕	✓	✓	✓	⇕	⇕	✓	⇕	⇕	✓	⇕
Structure Plan (*Structuurplan*) Amsterdam	✓	✓	✓	✓	✓	✓	✓	✓	✗	✓	✓	⇕	✓	✓	✓	✓	✓	⇕

Table 4.7: *Continued*

	Relevance			Accountability					Intermodality			Stage of formulation procedures						
	Statutory/ non-statutory	Mandatory/ non-mandatory	Binding/ non-binding	Approving not preparation body	External consultation	Public participation	Elected body involved	Independent review	Public transport service	Several transport modes	Objectives for several sectors	Objective setting	Initial stage	Documentation	Review	Public participation	Consultation	Monitoring
Future Vision (*Toekomstvisie*) Hilversum	✗	✗	⇕	✗	✓	✓	✓	⇕	✗	✓	✗	✗	✓	✓	⇕	✓	✓	⇕
Transport Plan (RVVP) Haarlem-IJmond	✓	✓	⇕	✓	✓	✓	✓	⇕	✓	✓	✓	⇕	⇕	✓	⇕	✓	✓	⇕

Key: ✓ = yes. ⇔ = partially/not clearly determined. ✗ = no.   ✓ = stage fully conducted. ⇔ = partially conducted. ✗ = not conducted.   ☐ informal procedure   ☐ formal procedure

Table 4.8: 'PPP relevance' in EVR Brandenburg-Berlin

	Relevance			Accountability					Intermodality			Stage of formulation procedures						
	Statutory/ non-statutory	Mandatory/ non-mandatory	Binding/ non-binding	Approving not preparation body	External consultation	Public participation	Elected body involved	Independent review	Public transport service	Several transport modes	Objectives for several sectors	Objective setting	Initial stage	Documentation	Review	Public participation	Consultation	Monitoring
Federal Transport Infrastructure Plan (BVWP)	↘	↘	↘	✗	↕	✗	↘	↕	✗	↘	✗	↕	↕	↘	↕	✗	↕	↕
Spatial Orientation Framework (RopOrient)	✗	↕	✗	✗	↕	✗	↘	↕	✗	↘	↘	↕	↕	↘	↕	✗	↕	↕
Land Development Programme (LEPro)	↘	↘	↕	↕	↘	↕	↘	↘	↘	↘	↘	↕	↕	↘	↘	↕	↘	↕
Land Development Plan EVR Brandenb.-Berlin (LEPeV)	↘	↘	↘	✗	↘	✗	↕	↘	✗	↘	↘	↕	↕	↘	↘	✗	↘	↕
Regional Plan (Regionalplan) Havelland-Fläming	↘	↘	↘	↘	↘	✗	↕	↘	↘	↘	↘	↘	↕	↘	↘	✗	↘	↕
Development Concept (Kreisentwicklungs-konzeption) Havelland	↘	↕	✗	✗	↘	↘	↘	↘	↘	↘	↘	↘	↘	↘	↘	↘	↘	↕
Road Dev. Plan (Landesstrassen-bedarfsplan) Brandenb.	↘	↘	↘	✗	↕	✗	↕	↕	✗	✗	✗	↕	✗	↘	↕	✗	↕	↕
Integrated Transport Plan (IVP) Brandenb.	✗	✗	✗	✗	↕	✗	↕	↕	↘	↘	↘	↕	↘	↘	↕	✗	↕	↘
Land Use Plan (FNP) Berlin	↘	↘	↘	✗	↘	↘	↘	↘	✗	↘	↘	↘	↘	↘	↘	↘	↘	↕

Table 4.8: *Continued*

	Relevance			Accountability					Intermodality			Stage of formulation procedures						
	Statutory/ non-statutory	Mandatory/ non-mandatory	Binding/ non-binding	Approving not preparation body	External consultation	Public participation	Elected body involved	Independent review	Public transport service	Several transport modes	Objectives for several sectors	Objective setting	Initial stage	Documentation	Review	Public participation	Consultation	Monitoring
City Dev. Plan (StEP) Transport Berlin	✓	✓	✗	✗	✓	✓	✓	✓	✓	✓	✓	⇕	✓	✓	⇕	✓	✓	⇕
City District Dev. Plan (*Bereichsplan*) Charlottenburg	✓	✓	✗	✗	✓	✓	✓	✓	✗	✓	✓	⇕	✓	✓	✓	✓	✓	⇕
Land Use Plan (FNP) Ketzin	✓	⇕	✓	✓	✓	✓	✓	✓	✗	✓	✓	✓	✓	✓	✓	✓	✓	⇕

Key: ✓ = yes. ⇔ = partially/not clearly determined. ✗ = no. ✓ = stage fully conducted. ⇔ = partially conducted. ✗ = not conducted. ☐ informal procedure ☐ formal procedure

All of the cases involved external consultation. In the case of the Trunk Roads Programme, however, only a selected number of external bodies were contacted by the DoT. It therefore did not obtain the highest score. Public participation was only conducted for statutory development plans, that is for structure plans, local plans and UDPs. Elected bodies were directly involved in the preparation of most PPPs, except in those of the North West Transport Strategy and RPG 13. All development plans also involved review by an independent body, namely by central government.

Noord-Holland

Tables 4.7 and 4.9 show the criteria and overall scores for the context variable PPP accountability in Noord-Holland. Highest scores were achieved by the statutory structure plans (*structuurplannen*). Low scores (50 per cent to 75 per cent) were achieved by the spatial/land use visions (*visies*). Furthermore, low scores were also obtained by two regional transport plans which did not involve public participation, and by the Second Transport Structure Plan (SVVII), for which the approving and preparation bodies were identical.

Preparation of all PPPs involved consultation of external bodies. On the Inter-Provincial Urbanisation Vision (IPVR), however, only the ministries of the participating *provincies* were consulted. Most preparation procedures involved public participation, except those for the regional transport plans INVERNO and RVVP Noord-Holland-Noord and the Inter-Provincial Urbanisation Vision (IPVR). All PPPs involved the participation of elected bodies. All documentation was indirectly reviewed through general public participation and expert consultation. Review by an independent body was only conducted for the statutory structure plans (*structuurplannen*), regional plans (*streekplannen*) and the National Spatial Plan (VINEX) review.

EVR Brandenburg-Berlin

Tables 4.8 and 4.9 show the criteria and overall variable scores for the context variable PPP accountability in EVR Brandenburg-Berlin. The highest score was achieved by the Land Use Plan (FNP) Ketzin (100 per cent). Lowest scores (25 per cent to 50 per cent) were achieved by the National Federal Transport Infrastructure Plan (BVWP) and the Spatial Orientation Framework, as well as the *IVP* Brandenburg and the Road Development Plan (*Landesstraßenbedarfsplan*) Brandenburg. On average, PPP accountability was found to be higher at the local level than at higher levels of decision making.

Only 2 of the 12 cases were approved by a body other than the preparation body, namely the Regional Plan (*Regionalplan*) Havelland-Fläming and the Land Use Plan (FNP) Ketzin. All PPP processes, however, involved external consultation. In the preparation processes at the national level as well as the *Länder* transport policies and the transport programmes, however, only national ministries were consulted. Public participation was conducted only for local-level plans and for the *Kreis* Development Concept (*Kreisentwicklungskonzeption*) Havelland. In the case of the *Land* Development Programme

(*Landesentwicklungsprogramm,* LEPro), the general public was informed on the outcome of the preparation process.

Elected bodies were involved in the preparation processes of all PPPs. For the *Land* Development Plan (*Landesentwicklungsplan,* LEPeV) EVR Brandenburg-Berlin, the Regional Plan (*Regionalplan*) Havelland-Fläming and the *Land* Brandenburg transport policy and the transport programme, parliaments acknowledged their preparation, but were not actively involved in their approval. Review of the documentation took place to a certain extent (rather indirectly) for all PPPs through external consultation. A full review by an independent body took place for local-level plans and for all spatial PPPs apart from the Spatial Orientation Framework (*Raumordnungspolitischer Orientierungsrahmen*).

PPP INTER-MODALITY

This section identifies individual PPP scores for the context variable PPP inter-modality. Three criteria are used:

1. Only transport infrastructure or transport infrastructure and public transport service considered.
2. Only one transport mode or several transport modes considered.
3. Objectives for only one sector or for several sectors considered.

The overall variable scores were used in the statistical analysis in order to explain the SEA patterns described in Parts 3 and 4 of the book.

North West England

Tables 4.6 and 4.9 show the criteria and overall variable scores for the context variable PPP inter-modality. Highest scores (75 per cent to 100 per cent) were obtained by the local and county level transport TPPs and package bids.

All PPPs considered transport infrastructure. Public transport service, however, was only considered in the TPPs/package bids and the North West Transport Strategy. The lowest score (25 per cent to 50 per cent) was obtained by the Trunk Roads Programme. All PPPs in North West England considered more than one transport mode, with the exception of the national Trunk Roads Programme. While all PPPs were said to consider several sectors, the TPPs, package bids and the North West Transport Strategy considered sectors apart from transport only implicitly, referring to statutory development plans.

Noord-Holland

Tables 4.7 and 4.9 show the criteria and overall scores for the context variable PPP inter-modality. While all PPPs considered transport infrastructure, public transport service was only considered in the regional transport policies (RVVPs).

All transport and spatial/land use PPPs considered several transport modes. Furthermore, most of them had objectives for several sectors, except the non-statutory spatial/land use visions (*visies*), which were prepared in order to identify policy objectives for subsequent planning.

EVR Brandenburg-Berlin

Tables 4.8 and 4.9 show the criteria and overall scores for the context variable PPP inter-modality in EVR Brandenburg-Berlin. Highest scores (100 per cent) were achieved by three spatial/land use plans at regional and *Kreis* levels. Furthermore, highest scores were achieved by the integrated transport policies, IVP Brandenburg and StEP Berlin. Low scores (under 25 per cent and 25 per cent to 50 per cent), were achieved by the two transport programmes that considered the national transport system and the road system in the *Land* Brandenburg, namely the Federal Transport Infrastructure Plan (BVWP) and the Road Development Plan (*Landesstraßenbedarfsplan*) Brandenburg.

While all PPPs considered transport infrastructure, public transport service was considered in only five of them, namely the IVP Brandenburg and StEP Berlin, the Land Development Programme (LEPro) Brandenburg, the Regional Plan (*Regionalplan*) Havelland-Fläming and the *Kreis* Development Concept (*Kreisentwicklungskonzept*) Havelland. Furthermore, all PPPs in EVR Brandenburg-Berlin considered several transport modes, except the Road Development Plan (*Landesstraßenbedarfsplan*) Brandenburg, which only considered *Länder* roads. All of the cases also had objectives for several sectors, except the Federal Transport Infrastructure Plan (BVWP) and the Road Development Plan (*Landesstraßenbedarfsplan*) Brandenburg, both of which only had economical-led transport objectives.

PPP PROCEDURE

This section identifies the extent to which the individual PPP covered the SEA procedural stages (objective setting, initial stage, documentation, review, public participation, consultation and monitoring). Besides the identification of PPP procedure variable scores, this exercise also allowed us to determine the extent to which current procedures are suitable for SEA integration.

North West England

Table 4.6 shows the procedural stages covered by the PPPs in North West England. On average, formal procedures covered stages more fully than informal procedures (67 per cent compared with 39 per cent). Furthermore, those PPPs that were statutory covered stages more fully than those that were non statutory (70 per cent compared with 58 per cent). Formal procedures of the development plans followed those laid out in PPG 12. TPPs and package bids were prepared, according to annual guidance notes.

Two stages were fully covered in all PPPs, including the preparation of the main documentation and the consultation of external bodies. The Trunk Roads Programme was considered to only partly involve consultation with external bodies, as only a limited number of selected bodies were involved. Public participation and review by an external body (not the preparation body) was conducted for only the statutory development plans, namely the structure plans, local plans and UDPs.

At the objective setting stage, a number of PPPs referred to general, non-policy, plan or programme specific documents. For some of these, however, the influence was not entirely clear, including the Regional Economic Strategy for the North West Transport Strategy, the Lancashire Environment Action Strategy and the Cheshire Local Agenda 21. Monitoring was conducted by most PPPs in an ongoing manner, except for the North West Transport Strategy. However, usually no monitoring-specific documentation was prepared. Statutory development plans covered the procedural stages to the largest extent, followed by the quasi-statutory transport package bids and the TPPs.

Noord-Holland

Table 4.7 shows the stages covered in PPP procedures in Noord-Holland. Table 4.9 shows the overall scores. On average, stages were more fully covered in formal than in informal procedures (83 per cent compared with 62 per cent). PPPs that were statutory covered stages more fully than those that were non-statutory (77 per cent compared with 58 per cent). Procedural stages were most fully covered by the statutory National Spatial Plan (VINEX) review and the structure plans (*structuurplannen*) ROA and Amsterdam. They were least fully covered by the non-statutory Inter-Provincial Urbanization Vision (IPVR).

Three stages were met fully by at least 10 of the 12 PPPs. These include the preparation of documentation (all cases), external consultation (all cases except the Inter-Provincial Urbanization Vision, IPVR, which only involved consultation of provincial ministries) and the review stage (all cases, except the Second Transport Structure Plan, SVVII and the Inter-Provincial Urbanization Vision, IPVR). There was full public participation in 8 of the 12 PPPs.

In the case of the Regional Transport Plan (RVVP) ROA, public participation only took place after it was prepared. The regional transport plans (RVVPs) Noord-Holland-Noord and INVERNO and the Inter-Provincial Urbanization Vision (IPVR) did not involve any public participation. Statutory regional plans (*streekplannen*) and local structure plans (*structuurplannen*) followed formal procedures according to the Spatial Planning Act (*wet op de ruimtelijke ordening*), articles 4a and 7 as well as the General Administrative Act (*algemene wet bestuursrecht*). The national SVVII and VINEX followed the formal pkb (*plan-kern-beslissing*) procedure according to article 2a of the Spatial Planning Act.

PPP-specific monitoring was conducted at the national level and for the regional transport plans INVERNO and RVVP ROA. A number of cases involved general, ongoing monitoring without preparing monitoring-specific documentation. While none of the PPPs covered the objective setting stage fully, most did so partially by referring to the environmental policy plans (*milieubeleidsplannen*) and, in the case of the regional transport policies to the Second Transport Infrastructure Plan (SVVII). No objective setting stage was covered by the three visions (*visies*), as their main task was to define objectives for further planning.

EVR Brandenburg-Berlin

Table 4.8 portrays the stages covered in PPP procedures in EVR Brandenburg-Berlin. Table 4.9 shows the overall scores. On average, formal procedures covered stages more fully than informal procedures (81 per cent as compared with 51 per cent of the total score) and PPPs that were statutory covered stages more fully than those that were non-statutory (74 per cent compared with 50 per cent of the total score). The Land Development Plan (*Landesentwicklungsplan*) EVR Brandenburg-Berlin, the Land Development Programme (*Landesentwicklungsprogramm*) Brandenburg and the Regional Plan (*Regionalplan*) Havelland-Fläming followed similar formal procedures. These were laid out in the Land Planning Convention Act (*Landesplanungsvertrag, LPlVG*), articles 7 and 8 the *Brandenburger Landesplanunggesetz*, BgbLPlG), the Regional Planning Act (*Gesetz zur Einführung der Regionalplanung und der Braunkohlen- und Sanierungsplanung*, RegBkPlG) and the Federal Construction Act (*Baugesetzbuch*, BauGB), paragraph 5 (in Berlin implemented through the Implementation Act to the Federal Construction Act, AGBauGB).

Only one stage was fully met by all PPPs, namely the main documentation stage. Two stages were fully met by 8 of the 12 PPPs, including the review and consultation stages. Public participation was conducted for all cases at the local level and the *Kreis* Development Plan (*Kreisentwicklungskonzeption*) Havelland. In the case of the *Land* Development Programme (*Landesentwicklungsprogramm*, LEPro) Brandenburg, public information meetings were conducted. All other PPPs above the local level did not involve any public participation.

The objective setting stage was fully met through the preparation of landscape plans and programmes in land use plans (FNPs) as well as in the Regional Plan (*Regionalplan*) Havelland-Fläming and the *Kreis* Development Concept (*Kreisentwicklungskonzept*) Havelland. Most other PPPs acknowledged objectives set by other documentation.

CROSS-REGIONAL CHARACTERISTICS

Table 4.9 summarizes the overall scores for the four context variables per individual PPP in the three sample regions. While the variable PPP inter-modality scored similarly in the three regions (between 71 per cent and 72 per cent), differences were observed for the other variables. Thus, scores for the average PPP relevance in Noord-Holland were somewhat smaller than in the other two regions (69 per cent as opposed to 72 per cent and 74 per

Table 4.9 *Overall context variable scores*

PPPs	Relevance	Accountability	Intermodal	Procedure
Trunk Roads Programme	●	○	○	○
North West Transport Strategy	□	○	●	◉
Regional Planning Guidance RPG 13	○	◉	◉	◉
Lancashire Structure Plan	■	■	◉	●
Cheshire Structure Plan	■	■	◉	●
Lancashire TPP	◉	◉	●	◉
Cheshire TPP	◉	◉	●	◉
Merseyside Package Bid	◉	◉	●	◉
Greater Manchester Package Bid	◉	◉	●	◉
Warrington Local Plan	■	■	◉	◉
Oldham Unitary Development Plan	■	■	◉	◉
Salford Unitary Development Plan	■	■	◉	◉
Average scores PPPs North West England	**74%**	**76%**	**71%**	**63%**
Second Transport Structure Plan (SVVII)	■	◉	●	●
National Spatial Plan (VINEX) – review	■	●	◉	●
Inter-Provincial Urbanization Vision (IPVR)	□	◉	○	○
Development Vision (*Ontwikkelingsvisie*) Noord Holland	□	◉	○	◉
Regional Plans (*Streekplannen*)	■	●	◉	●
Integrated Transport Vision Randstad North (INVERNO)	◉	◉	■	◉
Transport Plan (RVVP) Noord-Holland-Nord	●	◉	■	◉
Structure Plan (*Structuurplan*) ROA	●	■	◉	●
Transport Plan (RVVP) ROA	●	●	■	◉
Structure Plan (*Structuurplan*) Amsterdam	■	■	◉	●
Future Vision (*Toekomstvisie*) Hilversum	□	◉	○	◉
Transport Plan (RVVP) Haarlem-IJmond	●	●	■	◉
Average scores PPPs Noord-Holland	**69%**	**78%**	**71%**	**72%**
Federal Transport Infrastructure Plan (BVWP)	■	○	◔	◉
Spatial Orientation Framework (RopOrient)	□	○	◉	◉
Land Development Programme (LEPro)	◉	●	■	◉
Land Development Plan EVR Brb (LEPeV)	■	◉	◉	◉
Regional Plan (*Regionalplan*) Havelland-Fläming	■	◉	■	◉
Development Concept (*Kreisentwicklungskonzept*) Havelland	◉	●	■	●
Road Development Plan (*Landesstraßenplan*) Brandenburg	■	○	□	○
Integrated Transport Plan (IVP) Brandenburg	□	○	■	◉
Local Land Use Plan (FNP) Berlin	■	●	◉	●
City Development Plan (StEP) Transport Berlin	◉	●	■	●
District Development Plan (*Bereichsplan*) Charlottenburg	◉	●	◉	●
Local Land Use Plans (FNPs) Ketzin	●	■	◉	●
Average scores PPPs EVR Brandenburg-Berlin	**72%**	**63%**	**72%**	**71%**

Key: ■ =100%; ● = 75–99%; ◉ = 50–74%; ○ = 25–49%; □ = 0–24%

cent). This is explained by the higher proportion of policy-related, non-statutory cases in Noord-Holland, including particularly the visions (*visies*). The lowest average score for the variable PPP accountability was obtained by EVR Brandenburg-Berlin's PPPs (63 per cent as opposed to 76 per cent and 78 per cent in the other two regions). This was caused by a lack of public participation at levels above the local level. Finally, North West England PPPs on average covered procedural stages less fully than those in the other two regions (62 per cent as opposed to 70 per cent and 71 per cent). This was caused by low scores at the national and regional level, at which there was no public participation at all.

Those PPPs that were statutory and had formal procedures covered procedural stages more fully than those that were non-statutory, having informal procedures (74 per cent and 77 per cent compared with 55 per cent and 51 per cent), supporting the widespread call for formal requirements.

Some PPPs that obtained a high overall score for PPP relevance had a low PPP accountability. Important decisions were therefore taken with comparatively little external input. This is regarded as being problematic and as a consequence, public opposition can be expected to be stronger at the project implementation stage. Examples include the transport programmes that list and rank projects, namely the Trunk Roads Programme, the Federal Transport Infrastructure Plan (BVWP) and the Road Development Plan (*Landesstraßen-bedarfsplan*) Brandenburg.

PART 3

Strategic Environmental Assessment: Empirical Research Results

Introduction to Part 3

Part 3 of the book presents the results of the analysis on SEA practice in the three sample regions. The findings are based on the examination of existing SEA documentation and on interviews for the core set of 36 PPPs (cross-section of PPPs), representing all administrative levels of decision making (see Chapter 4). In addition, postal questionnaire results from the remaining local authorities in the three sample regions are presented. A rather broad understanding of SEA is applied, considering any assessment of the environmental impacts of a PPP. Empirical findings are evaluated, analysed and explained, using figures and tables. In this context, reference is usually made to three presentation aspects, namely the three sample regions, the three SEA types (to be identified in Chapter 5) and the two sectors. Furthermore, in some instances results for PPPs with SEA and those without SEA are compared. Statistical analysis was applied in order to determine whether there were any significant differences (Mann-Whitney U test) or association (Spearman's rank-order test) between the context variables, defined in Chapter 4 and the SEA variables, defined in Chapter 5. Significance levels of $P<.05$ and $P<.01$ are shown. Throughout Part 3, the following symbols are used for evaluating SEA criteria:

✓ = criteria fully met
⇔ = criteria met to a reasonable extent
(⇔) = criteria only marginally met
✗ = criteria not met

Overall scores for the different SEA aspects (for example, SEA procedure or potential SEA benefits) are expressed by the following set of symbols:

- ■ = SEA meets requirements fully (all criteria obtain highest scores = 100 per cent)
- ● = SEA meets requirements to a large extent (75 per cent to under 100 per cent)
- ◉ = SEA meets requirements to a moderate extent (50 per cent to under 75 per cent)
- ○ = SEA meets requirements to a poor extent (25 per cent to under 50 per cent)
- ▫ = SEA meets requirements to a very poor extent (0 per cent to under 25 per cent)

SEA practice

Chapter 5 refers to objective 2 of the book and identifies SEA application and classifies SEA types. The basic features of SEA practice for transport and spatial/land use PPPs in the three sample regions are described, evaluated and analysed. Chapter 5 is divided into eight sections. The first determines the extent of SEA application, the second classifies SEA types, referring to the planning level, sectoral coverage, procedural and other methodological characteristics and impact coverage. The scores of the context variables for the SEA presentation aspects are identified and the procedural characteristics, impact coverage and other methodological characteristics are analysed and evaluated in further detail. SEA preparation times are show and the main results of the chapter are summarized.

EXTENT OF SEA APPLICATION

Twenty-five SEAs (broadly defined as any environmental assessment) were conducted for the 36 PPPs, representing all planning levels (see Chapter 4). These include seven SEAs in North West England, nine SEAs in Noord-Holland and nine SEAs in EVR Brandenburg-Berlin. Ten SEAs were integrated into the PPP, in other words there was no separate SEA documentation. Three cases involved the preparation of two SEAs, namely the Federal Transport Infrastructure Plan (BVWP) (SEA in the form of a cost–benefit analysis and an ecological risk assessment), the Merseyside Package Bid (SEA in the form of a multi-criteria analysis and an integrated transport strategy) and the Land Use Plan (FNP) Berlin (SEA in the form of a Landscape Programme, *Landschaftsprogramm* and an Ecological Conflict Assessment, *ökologische Konfliktanalyse*). Furthermore, the Landscape Framework Plan (*Landschafts-rahmenplan*) Havelland represents an SEA that was undertaken for two related plans, namely the Regional Plan (*Regionalplan*) Havelland-Fläming and the *Kreis* Development Concept (*Kreisentwicklungskonzeption*) Havelland.

Taking postal questionnaire results of all the remaining, mainly local authorities in the sample regions into account, an additional number of SEAs was identified:

- 14 environmental appraisals in North West England.
- Policy-SEAs for four visions (*visie*) and one regional transport plan in Noord-Holland.

- 22 landscape plans (*Landschaftspläne*) for local land use plans and two landscape framework plans (*Landschaftsrahmenpläne*) for regional plans (*Regionalpläne*) in EVR Brandenburg-Berlin.

There were also at least eight big-project SEAs/EIAs for Dutch regional plans (*streekplannen*). These were, however, not included in the analysis, as the plan as a whole was not assessed, but only large-scale projects, following the Dutch EIA Decree of 1994. Two recently undertaken SEAs could not be considered, as information became available only after data collection, namely the New Approach to Trunk Roads Planning (Price, 1998) and the National Spatial Vision of The Netherlands (Ministerie van VROM, 1998a). In addition, two SEA transport research studies were identified (MVA et al, 1999; Ministerium für Wohnungswesen, Städtebau und Verkehr, 1995). In conclusion, this research identified a minimum number of 80 SEAs in the three sample regions, 23 in North West England, 23 in Noord-Holland and 34 in EVR Brandenburg-Berlin. Appendix 3 lists all of the SEAs.

Types of SEA

Identification of SEA types

SEA can be classified into three types according to the stage of PPP formulation in the planning cycle, sectoral and procedural characteristics, impact coverage and other methodological characteristics. Using existing terminology in order not to confuse discussion any further, these SEA types are named according to existing terminology; policy-, plan-, and programme-SEA.

It needs to be stressed that regardless of terminology, the classification provided in the book is new in its methodological content, as, to date, there has not been a clear distinction between different decision making tiers and terms are used interchangeably. For that reason, terminology that is used differently from the classification introduced in the book will subsequently be marked. Table 5.1 lists the 25 SEAs for the cross-section of 36 PPPs at all administrative levels in terms of the three SEA types.

SEA application in terms of policy and project orientation

Box 5.1 shows the extent of SEA application in PPPs according to whether these were policy or project oriented. It refers to the cross-section of 36 PPPs at all administrative levels. While those cases that were transport policy oriented used policy-SEA and those that were transport project-oriented used programme-SEA, the situation in the spatial/land use sector was more complex. Several SEA types were used, including plan-SEA and policy-SEA for policy-oriented spatial/land use cases and plan-SEA, programme-SEA and big-project SEA/EIA for project-oriented spatial/land use cases.

Table 5.1: *SEA types and their characteristics in the sample regions*

SEA type	Formulation level	Sectoral coverage	Impact coverage	Procedural characteristics	Other methodological characteristics	Examples in sample regions
1. Policy-SEA Usually non-mandatory (except the Dutch SVVII) (No separate SEA document)	Policy oriented	Transport	environmental and socio-economic impacts	Integrated into the PPP process, may or may not include public participation; on average, roughly ²/₃ of SEA stages are covered	⇒ different transport modes (inter-modal alternatives)/development alternatives) ⇒ scenarios ⇒ overall cumulative impacts ⇒ general impacts on transport	(a) Dutch transport SEAs/PPPs: • Second Transport Structure Plan, SVVII • Transport Plan North Wing Randstad, INVERNO • Transport Plan, RVVP Noord-Holland-Noord • Transport Plan, RVVP + environment map (*verkeersmilieukaart*) Haarlem/IJmond • Transport Plan, RVVP + environment map ROA (b) German transport SEAs/PPPs: • Integrated Transport Plan, StEP *Verkehr* Berlin • Integrated Transport Plan, IVP Brandenburg (c) English transport strategies: • Merseyside Package Bid underlying strategy (d) Dutch development visions (SEAs/PPPs): • *Ontwikkelingsvisie* Noord-Holland • *Toekomstvisie* Hilversum
		Spatial/land use			⇒ impacts of different development scenarios on future transport infrastructure are mapped	

Table 5.1: *Continued*

SEA type	Formula-tion level	Sec-toral cover-age	Impact coverage	Procedural characteristics	Other methodological characteristics	Examples in sample regions
2. Plan-SEA Mandatory (German SEAs) or non-mandatory (English and Dutch SEAs) (separate SEA document)	Policy or project oriented	Spatial/ land use (poten-tially also trans-port)	Environ-mental impacts	SEA is started before or runs parallel to PPP process; assists in formulating environmental objectives; public participation; on average, roughly $^2/_3$ of SEA stages are covered	⇒ spatial alternatives (except environmental appraisals in North West England) ⇒ no scenarios ⇒ no overall cumulative impacts ⇒ usually no impacts on transport	(a) SEAs in the form of landscape plans and programmes, assessing environmental impacts: • Landscape Plan, *Landschaftsplan* Ketzin (b) SEAs in the form of Landscape Plans/Programmes, not assessing environmental impacts: • Landscape Framework Plan, *Landschaftsrahmenplan* Havelland • Landscape Programme, *Landschaftsprogramm* Berlin (c) Environment Matrix, *milieumatrix* Amsterdam (d) Environmental appraisal in North West England: • Cheshire Structure Plan's Appraisal • Lancashire Structure Plan's Appraisal • Warrington Local Plan's Appraisal • Oldham UDP's Appraisal
			Environ-mental & increas-ingly socio-economic impacts	Joins the PPP process at one or at several points, usually no public participation; on average, roughly $^1/_3$ of SEA stages are covered		

Table 5.1: *Continued*

SEA type	Formulation level	Sectoral coverage	Impact coverage	Procedural characteristics	Other methodological characteristics	Examples in sample regions
3. Programme-SEA Quasi-mandatory (transport SEAs) or non-mandatory (spatial/land use SEAs)	Project oriented	Transport	Environmental and socio-economic impacts	Joins the PPP process at one point, no public participation; on average, roughly $1/4$ of all SEA stages are covered	⇒ no alternatives ⇒ no scenarios ⇒ no overall cumulative impacts ⇒ no impacts on transport ⇒ hierarchies of projects are determined through cost-benefit analysis and multi-criteria analysis	(a) SEAs in the form of German transport plans (using cost-benefit analysis): • Federal Transport Infrastructure Plan, BWWP • Road Plan, *Landesstraßenbedarfsplan* Brandenburg (b) SEAs in the form of English transport investment plans (using multi-criteria analysis): • Cheshire TPP • Merseyside Package Bid (c) Assessments of projects within PPPs: • Federal Transport Infrastructure Plan, BWWP Ecological Risk Assessment
(separate SEA document/project sheets)		Spatial/ land use	environmental impacts or environmental and socio-economic impacts	EIA process principles based, joins PPP process at one point, may or may not include public participation, on average, roughly 60% of all SEA stages are covered	⇒ alternatives ⇒ no scenarios ⇒ no overall cumulative effects ⇒ may or may not consider impacts on transport ⇒ hierarchies of projects are determined through cost-benefit analysis and multi-criteria analysis	(d) Dutch spatial planning PPPs: • National Spatial Plan, VINEX review (e) German land use plans: • Ecological Conflict Assessment (*ökologische Konfliktanalyse*) for FNP Berlin

---

Box 5.1: Policy and project orientation and SEA-type
application

1. Policy oriented transport: All 7 cases (100 per cent) involved the preparation of policy-SEA.
2. Policy oriented spatial/land use: 7 of the 12 cases (58 per cent) involved SEA preparation, for 5 cases plan-SEAs were undertaken and for 2 cases policy-SEAs were undertaken.
3. Project-oriented transport: 4 of the 8 cases (50 per cent) involved SEA preparation, all of which were programme-SEAs. In addition, for 1 case an underlying strategy was prepared, which involved policy-SEA.
4. Project oriented spatial/land use: 6 of the 9 cases (67 per cent) involved SEA preparation, for 4 cases plan-SEAs were undertaken and for 2 cases programme-SEAs were undertaken. Big project SEA/EIA was undertaken for Noord-Holland's regional plans (*streekplannen*).

SEA application at different administrative levels

Table 5.2 shows the extent to which the SEA types were applied at different administrative levels in the three sample regions. All three SEA types were applied at all decision making levels, that is no SEA type is specific to a certain administrative level of decision making. Tiering between different administrative levels took the form of policies that were defined at higher tiers and considered and implemented at lower tiers. A clear inter-administrative tiering structure, however, was very difficult to establish. Only a few SEAs were tiered at a certain administrative level. Examples include the Transport Strategy Merseyside, MerITS (policy-SEA) and the Merseyside Package Bid (programme-SEA). Furthermore, they include the Integrated Transport Plan (IVP) Brandenburg (policy-SEA) with the Road Development Plan (*Landesstraßenbedarfsplan*) Brandenburg (programme-SEA). There are also examples where tiering is potentially possible, including the provincial spatial/land use Vision (*visie*) Noord-Holland (policy-SEA) with the regional plans (*streekplannen*), currently involving the preparation of big-project SEA/EIA.

The lack of tiering at the same administrative level is most likely explained by the only recent development and application of policy-SEA. Furthermore, in EVR Brandenburg-Berlin, a quick installation of the West German planning system in the new *Länder* was perceived to be necessary in order to modernize the transport infrastructure and to achieve equal living conditions.[1] The focus was therefore particularly on the preparation of traditional statutory instruments, required according to national legislation.

While the application of policy-SEA was comparatively widespread in The Netherlands, in both North West England and EVR Brandenburg-Berlin, mostly plan-SEAs were undertaken for traditional statutory plans. It is therefore indicated that policy-SEA suits the consensus-led, quasi-top-down planning approach in The Netherlands particularly well (Chapter 3). Thus, policy-SEA

Table 5.2: SEAs undertaken at different administrative levels in the three sample regions

Administrative level	SEA type	North West England		Noord-Holland		EVR Brandenburg-Berlin	
		Transport	Spatial/land use	Transport	Spatial/land use	Transport	Spatial/land use
National	Policy	✗	▨	✓	«✓»	▨	✗
	Plan	▨	▨	✗	✗	«✓»	
	Programme	«✓»		✗	✓	✓ (2)	
Sample region (including *Provincie/Land*)	Policy	«✓»		✓ (2)	«✓»	✓	
	Plan	«✓»	✗ (*)	✗	✗	✗	✓ (3)
	Programme	✗	✗	✗	✗	✓	✗
	Big-project	✗	✗	✗	«✓» (8)	✗	✗
City-region (including county/*Kreis*)	Policy	✓		✓ (3)	✗	✓	✓
	Plan	✗	✓ (2)	✗	✗	✗	✓
	Programme	✓ (2)	✗	✗	✗	✗	
Local	Policy	▨	▨	?	✓ (5)	?	
	Plan	▨	✓ (16)	?	✓	?	✓ (23)
	Programme	▨	✗	?	✗	?	✗

▨ = no PPP prepared

✓ = SEA application (number in brackets refers to the number of SEAs in the sample regions, if more than one)

«✓» = SEA application which is not included in research: big-project-SEAs/EIAs for Noord-Holland's regional plans (*streekplannen*), national level SEAs in North West England and Noord-Holland (SEAs accessible only after data collection); research transport SEAs in North West England and in EVR Brandenburg-Berlin

✗ = no SEA application

? = PPPs to be prepared under new legislation, scope unclear

(*) = DETR (1998a) explores the possibility to apply 'sustainability appraisal' to Regional Planning Guidance

allows examination of the impacts on certain policy objectives that were identified at higher tiers and involving open discussion of different policy options
with widespread consultation and participation.

The predominant use of plan-SEA in North West England and in EVR
Brandenburg-Berlin was related to the fact that an open SEA process with
widespread consultation and participation was usually only applied at lower
administrative tiers. Public administration appeared to be reluctant to consult
the public at higher decision making levels and policy-SEA application was
therefore rare. In EVR Brandenburg-Berlin, authorities often said that the current system of a representative democracy with elected bodies at four decision
making levels considered public opinions to a sufficiently large extent (see
Chapter 3). Furthermore, it was said that nothing would be gained from involving the general public in policy decisions at higher tiers. For the UK,
important policy decisions are traditionally taken by central government without involving the public to any large extent (Dalal-Clayton et al, 1994, p29).

CONTEXT VARIABLES AND SEA PRESENTATION ASPECTS

Figure 5.1 identifies the scores of the four context variables (see Chapter 4)
for the sample regions, SEA types and sectors and for the cross-section of 36
PPPs at all administrative levels with and without SEA. These scores are identified in order to have a basis for the interpretation of the observed SEA patterns
in the subsequent analysis.

Regions

PPPs with SEA in North West England and EVR Brandenburg-Berlin obtained
higher scores on the PPP relevance than those in Noord-Holland. This was
related to the larger extent of plan-SEA application in North West England and
EVR Brandenburg-Berlin, and the more extensive use of policy-SEA in Noord-
Holland. PPP accountability was smallest in EVR Brandenburg-Berlin, which
was particularly caused by a lack of public participation at higher tiers above
the local and *Kreis* levels. While EVR Brandenburg-Berlin obtained low scores
for the PPP inter-modality, Noord-Holland obtained high scores, mainly due to
the large number of policy-SEAs. The three regions obtained similar scores on
the PPP procedure.

SEA types

The PPP relevance was particularly low for policy-SEAs that were undertaken
for non-statutory policies. It was high for plan-SEAs, which were mostly undertaken for statutory plans. The PPP accountability was lowest for programme-SEA,
which was particularly caused by its application to the transport sector, involving no public participation and only limited external consultation. A reluctance
of transport authorities to involve third parties in the decision on how to rank
proposed projects is therefore indicated, most likely for a fear of NIMBYism.

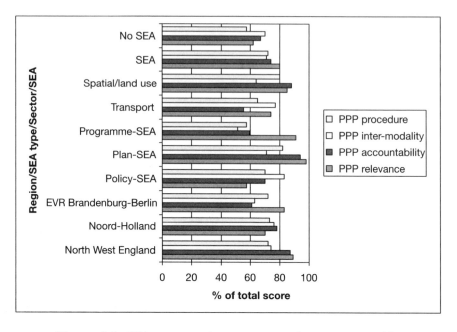

Figure 5.1: *SEA presentation aspects and context variables*

Programme-SEA obtained the lowest score on the PPP inter-modality, as all transport programme-SEAs ranked projects in a uni-modal manner, without considering alternatives. As expected, policy-SEA scored highest, having an inherently inter-modal character. For the PPP procedure, plan-SEA obtained high scores, as the plans to which plan-SEA was applied were usually statutory instruments with extensive preparation procedures.

Sectors

On average, differences between the two sectors were not as large as the differences between the regions and the SEA types. While the spatial/land use sector obtained slightly higher scores on the PPP relevance, the PPP accountability and the PPP procedure, the transport sector obtained slightly higher scores on the PPP inter-modality. This was caused by the more extensive and open preparation procedures of spatial/land use PPPs. In particular, project oriented transport plans and programmes did not involve any public participation or consultation, which is most likely explained by a fear of NIMBYism.

Differences between PPPs with and without SEA

PPPs involving SEA obtained higher scores on all context variables than those not involving SEA. SEA was applied less to PPPs with a low PPP relevance. This was, in particular, due to a large number of regional spatial/land use PPPs (including *Land* and *Provincie* levels), which did not involve SEA and only sometimes involved public participation and external consultation.

PROCEDURAL ASPECTS OF SEA APPLICATION

Table 5.3 shows the extent to which the 25 SEAs for the cross-section of the 36 PPPs at all administrative levels in the sample regions covered the different procedural stages. A scoring system from 0 (not considered) to 3 (fully considered) was applied. Subsequently, general, regional, SEA type and sector specific patterns are analysed.

Table 5.3: *Procedural coverage in 25 SEAs*

SEA	Prior to the PPP process	SEA initiation	During PPP formulation	Review	Monitoring	Public participation	External consultation	Overall evaluation
Environmental Appraisal Lancashire Structure Plan	(⇔)	(⇔)	✓	✗	(⇔)	✗	✗	○
Environmental Appraisal Cheshire Structure Plan	(⇔)	(⇔)	✓	✗	(⇔)	✓	⇔	◉
Transport Plan Cheshire TPP	⇔	(⇔)	✓	⇔	✗	✗	✗	○
Merseyside Package Bid	⇔	(⇔)	✓	⇔	✗	✗	✗	○
Merseyside Package Bid underlying strategy	✓	✗	✗	⇔	✗	✓	✓	◉
Environmental Appraisal Warrington Local Plan	✗	(⇔)	✓	✗	(⇔)	✗	(⇔)	○
Environmental Appraisal Oldham UDP	(⇔)	(⇔)	✓	✗	(⇔)	✓	(⇔)	○
Second Transport Structure Plan (SVVII)	⇔	✓	✓	(⇔)	✓	✓	✓	●
National Spatial Plan (VINEX) review	⇔	✓	✓	✓	(⇔)	✓	✓	●
Vision (*visie*) Noord-Holland	✗	✓	✓	(⇔)	✗	✓	✓	◉
Transport Plan (RVVP) INVERNO	⇔	⇔	✓	(⇔)	✓	✗	✓	◉
Transport Plan (RVVP) Noord-Holland-Noord	⇔	⇔	✓	(⇔)	✗	✗	✓	◉
Transport Plan (RVVP) ROA	⇔	⇔	✓	(⇔)	✓	✗	✓	◉
Environment Matrix (*milieumatrix*) A'dam	✗	✗	✗	✗	(⇔)	✗	✗	□

Table 5.3: *Continued*

SEA	Prior to the PPP process	SEA initiation	During PPP formulation	Review	Monitoring	Public participation	External consultation	Overall evaluation
Vision (*visie*) Hilversum	✗	✓	✓	(⇔)	(⇔)	✓	✓	◉
Transport Plan (RVVP) Haarlem-IJmond	⇔	⇔	✓	(⇔)	✗	✓	✓	◉
Federal Transport Plan (BVWP) ecological risk	✗	✗	✓	✗	(⇔)	✗	(⇔)	▫
Federal Transport Plan (BVWP)	✗	(⇔)	✓	✗	(⇔)	✗	(⇔)	O
Landscape Framework Plan Havelland	✓	✓	✗	✓	(⇔)	✗	✓	◉
Road Plan (*Landesstrassenbedarfsplan*) Brandenb.	✗	✗	✓	✗	✗	✗	(⇔)	▫
Integrated Transport Plan (IVP) Brandenburg	(⇔)	(⇔)	✓	(⇔)	✓	✗	✓	◉
Land Use Plan (FNP) Berlin, ecological assessment	✗	✓	✓	✗	(⇔)	✗	✗	O
Land Use Plan (FNP) Berlin, Landscape Programme	✓	✓	✗	✗	(⇔)	✓	✓	◉
Integrated Transport Plan (StEP) Berlin	(⇔)	✓	✓	(⇔)	(⇔)	✓	✓	◉
Land Use Plan (FNP) Ketzin, Landscape Plan	✓	(⇔)	✓	✓	(⇔)	✓	✓	●

▨ policy-SEA ☐ plan-SEA ☐ programme-SEA

Evaluation of procedural stages:

✓ = public document prepared/participation and consultation on the basis of a public document (scores 3)

⇔ = non-SEA specific document with a clear impact on SEA/identification of clear SEA objectives (scores 2)

(⇔) = general guidance/documentation with uncertain relationship to SEA/ongoing monitoring/review mainly through general consultation/external consultation only of selected bodies, results not open to public (scores 1)

✗ = no consideration (scores 0)

Overall evaluation (on the basis of criteria scores):   ◉ = met 50–74%   O = met 25–49%
                                                          ■ = met 100%   O = met 25–49%
                                                           ● = met 75–99%   ▫ = met 0–24%

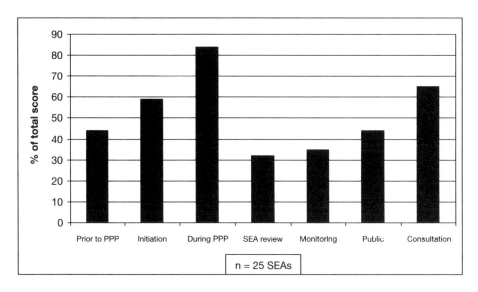

Figure 5.2: *Overall coverage of SEA procedural stages*

General findings

Figure 5.2 shows that only three SEA stages obtained over 50 per cent of the overall score, namely the initiation stage, the PPP preparation stage and the external consultation stage. The lowest overall score was obtained by the SEA report review and monitoring stages. Subsequently, the consideration of the seven SEA stages are described in further detail.

Prior to the policy, plan and programme process (screening)

Four SEAs were used to formulate objectives for the associated PPP, including a policy-SEA (the underlying strategy of the Merseyside Package Bid, MerITS) and three plan-SEAs (the landscape plans and programmes, *Landschaftspläne und -programme*). Eight SEAs (seven of which were in the transport sector) considered objectives provided by other sources, including either transport strategies or environmental policy plans (*milieubeleidsplannen*) in Noord-Holland.

Initiation of SEA (scoping)

Highest scores for the initiation stage were obtained by four SEAs in each of Noord-Holland and EVR Brandenburg-Berlin, all of which involved the preparation of scoping documents that were subject to consultation and public participation. While in Noord-Holland, higher tier SEAs were included (national and *Provincie* levels), in EVR Brandenburg-Berlin only lower tier SEAs were included (mostly local and *Kreis* levels), thus reflecting the different planning approaches in the two regions, as outlined in Chapter 3. All Dutch integrated transport SEAs/PPPs considered the themes of the Second Transport Structure

Plan (SVVII). In North West England, all SEAs except for the underlying strategy of the Merseyside Package Bid followed central government guidance, reflecting the centrally guided plan-making approach (DoE, 1993; DoT, 1995). In EVR Brandenburg-Berlin, guidance was also followed by the plan-SEA (*Landschaftsplan*) for the Land Use Plan (FNP) Ketzin (*Ministerium für Umwelt, Naturschutz und Raumordnung*, 1995a) and general research studies led to a definition of assessment tasks for the Federal Transport Infrastructure Plan (BVWP).

During PPP formulation

Of the 25 SEAs, 21 involved the preparation of public documentation during PPP formulation and directly assessed environmental impacts, all of which obtained the highest score for the during PPP formulation stage. The four remaining SEAs included three plan-SEAs and one policy-SEA. For the Environment Matrix (*milieumatrix*) Amsterdam, SEA documentation was prepared only after plan formulation. In the cases of the Landscape Framework Plan (*Landschaftsrahmenplan*) Havelland and the Landscape Programme (*Landschaftsprogramm*) Berlin, SEA documentation was prepared before PPP formulation, defining land suitability and reflecting the precautionary approach to environmental planning, based on the landscape planning system (see Chapter 3). Finally, the underlying transport strategy for the Merseyside Package Bid was prepared before programme formulation.

SEA report review

Three SEAs involved SEA report review by an external body, including the programme-SEA for the National Spatial Plan (VINEX) review (by the national EIA Commission) and the plan-SEAs, Landscape Framework Plan (*Landschaftsrahmenplan*) Havelland and Landscape Plan (*Landschaftsplan*) Ketzin (both reviewed by the *Land* Authority for Construction, Building Techniques and Settlements, LBBW). North West England TPPs and package bids were reviewed in the process of the plan approval by the DETR and the regional transport plans (RVVPs) in Noord-Holland were checked by the national Ministry of Transport (MVW). Five policy-SEAs were indirectly reviewed through general external consultation.

Monitoring

Monitoring was conducted for only four SEAs, all of which were policy-SEAs. These include the Second Transport Structure Plan (SVVII) (monitoring in the form of the national 'to measure is to know' programme, *meten=weten*), the regional transport plans (RVVP) ROA (regional monitoring), INVERNO (SEA specific monitoring planned) and the Integrated Transport Plan (IVP) Brandenburg (SEA specific monitoring planned). Non-SEA specific, general PPP monitoring was more common and was conducted for all statutory land use plans that involved the preparation of plan-SEA and the Federal Transport Infrastructure Plan (BVWP) and the National Spatial Plan (VINEX) review.

Opportunities for public participation

Public participation was conducted in three SEAs in each of North West England and EVR Brandenburg-Berlin and in five SEAs in Noord-Holland. While there was public participation for SEAs at all administrative levels in Noord-Holland, public participation in SEA in North West England and in EVR Brandenburg-Berlin was confined to the local level and in North West England also to the county level.[2] This reflects the different planning approaches in the three regions (see Chapter 3). In most cases, public participation in the SEA took place once or twice. Exceptions were the Dutch visions (*visies*), involving public participation at each step of the process (up to four times).

External consultation

External consultation was most comprehensive in Noord-Holland and EVR Brandenburg-Berlin. All SEAs in Noord-Holland, except the Environment Matrix (*milieumatrix*) Amsterdam, involved external consultation. Furthermore, five of the nine SEAs in EVR Brandenburg-Berlin, but only one of the seven SEAs in North West England involved external consultation. In addition, all 23 landscape plans (*Landschaftspläne*) for the local land use plans (FNPs) in EVR Brandenburg-Berlin involved external consultation. External consultation in the Environmental Appraisal for the Cheshire Structure Plan, the Warrington Local Plan and the Oldham UDP was limited to the DoE.

Regional comparisons

Figure 5.3 shows the extent to which procedural stages were covered in the three sample regions. Differences were significant for only two stages, namely

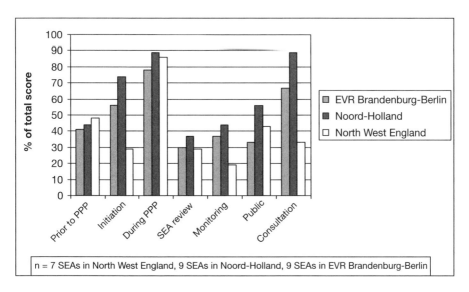

Figure 5.3: *SEA procedural stages considered in the three sample regions*

the initiation and external consultation stages, both of which were significantly more frequently considered in Noord-Holland than in North West England (P<.01). The differences are mainly explained by the larger extent of policy-SEA application in Noord-Holland. SEA-type patterns are further examined below.

Comparisons between SEA types

Figure 5.4 shows the extent to which procedural stages were considered in the three SEA types. Differences were statistically significant for most stages, except that prior to the PPP process, and SEA initiation stages. Procedural stages were usually most extensively covered by policy-SEA and least extensively covered by programme-SEA (P<.05 for monitoring and public participation and P<.01 for external consultation). Exceptions were the during the PPP preparation stage (P<.05 for programme-SEA and plan-SEA) and the SEA report review stage (P<.05 for policy-SEA and plan-SEA). Policy-SEAs had an overall good performance, as an open and extensive process was applied, comparing broad policy options. As these usually had no direct consequences for project implementation, authorities were more willing to fully include public participation and external consultation. This underlines the important role of policy-SEA at the top of the decision making cycle.

Sector-specific comparisons

Figure 5.5 shows the differences between the two sectors. While none of the differences were statistically significant, it is indicated that SEA for spatial/land use PPPs involved the general public to a larger extent than SEA for transport PPPs. This was mainly caused by the transport programme-SEAs, which did not involve any public participation at all for a fear of NIMBYism, caused by project orientation of the associated programme.

Scores for regions, SEA types and sectors on SEA procedure

Figure 5.6 presents the average scores for the coverage of procedural stages in the SEAs for the cross-section of 36 PPPs at all administrative levels. While Noord-Holland SEAs and policy-SEAs scored highest, North West England SEAs and programme-SEAs scored lowest. On average, SEAs stages were covered to the same extent in both sectors. The extent to which procedural stages were covered was clearly connected with the SEA type. Thus, while policy-SEA covered procedural stages to the largest extent, programme-SEA covered SEA stages to the smallest extent (P<.01). The main reasons were the integration of policy-SEA into the associated policy and the non-project oriented character of policy-SEA (NIMBYism is unlikely, see Chapter 1). Only one programme-SEA covered procedural stages well, namely the National Spatial 'Plan' (VINEX) review, which followed a formal process, according to the Dutch EIA Decree of 1994. The range of SEA procedural stages covered in plan-SEA was comparatively wide and ranged from 81 per cent (Landscape Plan, *Landschaftsplan* Ketzin) to only 5 per cent (Environment Matrix, *milieumatrix* Amsterdam).

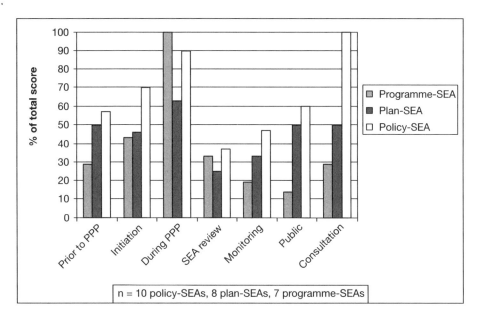

Figure 5.4: *SEA procedural stages considered in the three SEA types*

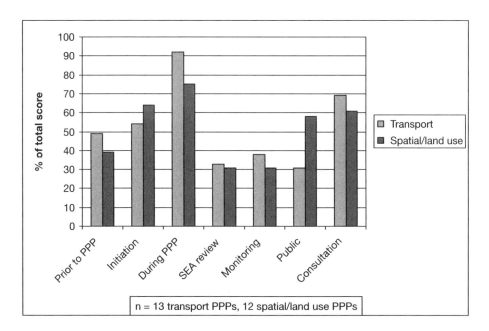

Figure 5.5: *SEA procedural stages considered in the two sectors*

A comparison of the extent to which procedural stages were covered in SEA and in the associated PPP shows that there is scope for improving practice in all SEA types, regions and sectors, if SEAs were more fully integrated into the

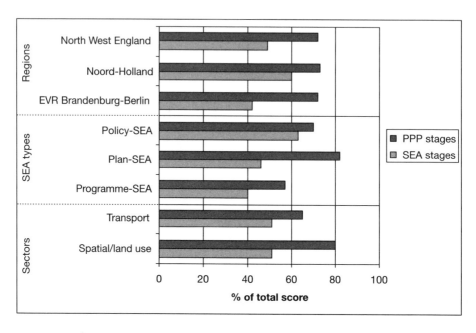

Figure 5.6: *Extent of procedural stages covered in SEA and the associated PPP*

PPP process. The scope for improvement was greater for spatial/land use SEAs with formal procedures than for transport SEAs with informal procedures. The scope for improving SEA through a better integration into existing procedures was greater in plan-SEA and programme-SEA than in policy-SEA. Furthermore, it was greater in North West England and EVR Brandenburg-Berlin than in Noord-Holland. The context variable PPP inter-modality (see Chapter 4) was significantly correlated with the extent to which SEA procedural stages were covered (P<.05). This is mainly explained by the policy-SEA type, covering procedural stages well and considering inter-modal aspects to the largest extent of all SEA types.

IMPACT COVERAGE

Tables 5.4 and 5.5 identify those environmental and socio-economic impacts that were considered in the 25 SEAs for the cross-section of the 36 PPPs at all administrative levels. Five categories were distinguished:

1. Impacts that were directly quantitatively assessed.
2. Impacts that were directly qualitatively assessed.
3. Impacts that were indirectly assessed.
4. Basic requirements, limits or assumptions formulated.
5. No impacts assessed.

Subsequently, the extent of impact coverage is analysed in further detail. Regional, SEA type and sectoral differences are highlighted and explained. The extent to which SEAs combined socio-economic and environmental impacts is also determined.

Table 5.4: *Types of environmental impacts assessed in SEA*

SEA	(1) Fauna	(2) Flora	(3) Soil	(4) Water	(5) Air (+ noise)	(6) Climate	(7) Land-scape & cultural heritage
Environmental Appraisal Lancashire Structure Plan	⇔	⇔	⇔	⇔	⇔	⇔	⇔
Environmental Appraisal Cheshire Structure Plan	⇔	⇔	⇔	⇔	⇔	⇔	⇔
Transport Plan Cheshire TPP	(⇔)	(⇔)	(⇔)	×	⇔	×	(⇔)
Merseyside Package Bid	(⇔)	(⇔)	(⇔)	×	⇔	×	(⇔)
Merseyside Package Bid underlying strategy	×	×	×	×	✓	✓	×
Environmental Appraisal Warrington Local Plan	⇔	⇔	⇔	⇔	⇔	⇔	⇔
Environmental Appraisal Oldham UDP	⇔	⇔	⇔	⇔	⇔	⇔	⇔
Second Transport Structure Plan (SVVII)	×	×	×	×	✓	✓	×
National Spatial Plan (VINEX) review	✓	✓	✓	✓	✓	✓	✓
Vision (*visie*) Noord-Holland	(⇔)	(⇔)	×	(⇔)	(⇔)	×	(⇔)
Transport Plan (RVVP) INVERNO	×	×	×	×	✓	✓	(⇔)
Transport Plan (RVVP) Noord-Holland-Noord	×	×	×	×	✓	✓	×
Transport Plan (RVVP) ROA	×	×	×	×	✓	✓	×
Environment Matrix (*milieumatrix*) Amsterdam	!	!	!	!	!	×	!
Vision (*visie*) Hilversum	(⇔)	(⇔)	×	×	(⇔)	×	(⇔)
Transport Plan (RVVP) Haarlem-IJmond	×	×	×	×	✓	✓	(⇔)
Federal Transport Plan (BVWP) ecological risk	✓	✓	×	✓	(⇔)	×	✓

Table 5.4: *Continued*

SEA	(1) Fauna	(2) Flora	(3) Soil	(4) Water	(5) Air (+ noise)	(6) Climate	(7) Land- scape & cultural heritage
Federal Transport Plan (BVWP)	(⇔)	(⇔)	✗	✗	⇔	(⇔)	(⇔)
Landscape Framework Plan Havelland	!	!	!	!	!	!	!
Road Plan (*Landesstrassenbe- darfsplan*) Brandenb.	(⇔)	(⇔)	✗	⇔	⇔	✗	(⇔)
Integrated Transport Plan (IVP) Brandenburg	⇔	⇔	⇔	⇔	✓	✓	⇔
Land Use Plan (FNP) Berlin, ecological assessment	✓	✓	✓	✓	⇔	(⇔)	✓
Land Use Plan (FNP) Berlin, Landscape Programme	!	!	!	!	!	!	!
Integrated Transport Plan (StEP) Berlin	⇔	⇔	⇔	⇔	✓	✓	⇔
Land Use Plan (FNP) Ketzin, Landscape Plan	✓	✓	✓	✓	⇔	(⇔)	✓

▨ policy-SEA ▢ plan-SEA ▢ programme-SEA
✓   = impacts directly assessed in a quantitative manner
⇔   = impacts directly assessed in a qualitative manner
(⇔) = impacts indirectly assessed
!   = explicitly stated assumptions, impacts not assessed
✗   = no consideration

Table 5.5: *Types of socio-economic impacts assessed in SEA*

SEA	(1) Econo- my	(2) Popula- tion	(3) Housing	(4) Public service	(5) Fiscal	(6) Income	(7) Social impacts
Environmental Appraisal Lancashire Structure Plan	!	!	!	✗	✗	✗	!
Environmental Appraisal Cheshire Structure Plan	!	!	!	!	✗	✗	!
Transport Plan Cheshire TPP	(⇔)	!	✗	(⇔)	✗	✗	(⇔)
Merseyside Package Bid	(⇔)	!	✗	(⇔)	✗	✗	(⇔)

Table 5.5: *Continued*

SEA	(1) Econo-my	(2) Popula-tion	(3) Housing	(4) Public service	(5) Fiscal	(6) Income	(7) Social impacts
Merseyside Package Bid underlying strategy	(⇔)	!	×	✓	✓	×	(⇔)
Environmental Appraisal Warrington Local Plan	!	!	!	!	×	×	!
Environmental Appraisal Oldham UDP	!	!	!	!	×	×	!
Second Transport Structure Plan (SVVII)	(⇔)	!	×	!	✓	×	(⇔)
National Spatial Plan (VINEX) review	✓	!	✓	(⇔)	✓	×	✓
Vision (*visie*) Noord-Holland	⇔	!	×	⇔	×	×	⇔
Transport Plan (RVVP) INVERNO	(⇔)	!	×	✓	✓	×	✓
Transport Plan (RVVP) Noord-Holland-Noord	(⇔)	!	×	✓	✓	×	✓
Transport Plan (RVVP) ROA	(⇔)	!	×	✓	✓	×	(⇔)
Environment Matrix (*milieumatrix*) Amsterdam	!	!	!	!	×	×	!
Vision (*visie*) Hilversum	⇔	⇔	(⇔)	⇔	⇔	⇔	⇔
Transport Plan (RVVP) Haarlem-IJmond	(⇔)	!	×	✓	✓	×	✓
Federal Transport Plan (BVWP) ecological risk	!	!	×	!	×	×	!
Federal Transport Plan (BVWP)	✓	!	×	!	✓	×	⇔
Landscape Framework Plan Havelland	!	!	!	×	×	×	!
Road Plan (*Landesstrassenbe-darfsplan*) Brandenb.	(⇔)	!	×	×	⇔	×	⇔
Integrated Transport Plan (IVP) Brandenburg	(⇔)	!	×	✓	✓	×	✓
Land Use Plan (FNP) Berlin, ecological assessment	!	!	!	!	×	×	!

Table 5.5: *Continued*

SEA	(1) Econo- my	(2) Popula- tion	(3) Housing	(4) Public service	(5) Fiscal	(6) Income	(7) Social impacts
Land Use Plan (FNP) Berlin Landscape Programme	!	!	!	!	✗	✗	!
Integrated Transport Plan (StEP) Berlin	(⇔)	!	✗	✓	✓	✗	✓
Land Use Plan (FNP) Ketzin, Landscape Plan	!	!	!	!	✗	✗	!

[▒▒▒] policy-SEA [   ] plan-SEA [   ] programme-SEA
✓   = impacts directly assessed in a quantitative manner
⇔   = impacts directly assessed in a qualitative manner
(⇔) = impacts indirectly assessed
!   = explicitly stated assumptions, impacts not assessed
✗   = no consideration

General findings

Environmental and socio-economic impacts were assessed in the 25 SEAs to varying extents. Considering all SEAs, environmental impacts were assessed to a greater extent than socio-economic impacts. Three plan-SEAs (including the Environment Matrix, *milieumatrix* Amsterdam, the Landscape Framework Plan, *Landschaftsrahmenplan* Havelland and the Landscape Programme, *Land- schaftsprogramm* Berlin) formulated environmental objectives and provided land suitability maps. Socio-economic impacts were assessed in only 15 SEAs, including all 10 policy-SEAs and 5 of the 7 programme-SEAs. None of the plan-SEAs assessed socio-economic impacts. Figure 5.7 illustrates the overall consideration given to environmental and socio-economic impacts.

While 64 per cent of the environmental impacts were assessed, either directly or indirectly, 25 per cent of the environmental impacts were not assessed at all. Regarding socio-economic impacts, only 31 per cent were assessed, either directly or indirectly and 31 per cent were apparently not assessed at all. Only 11 per cent of the environmental impacts were reflected in assumptions or planning goals. This figure, however, rose to 38 per cent of the socio-economic impacts. The large number of socio-economic impacts reflected in assumptions is mainly explained by the fact that PPPs were usu- ally prepared for meeting economic objectives, particularly those involving plan-SEA application.

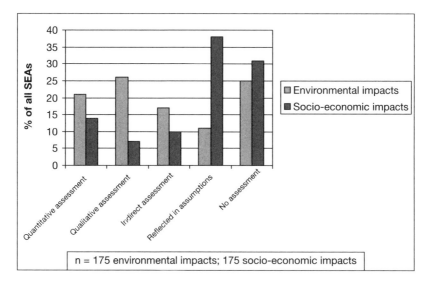

Figure 5.7: *Environmental and socio-economic impacts considered in all SEAs*

Impact types

Environmental impact types

Environmental impact types that were considered in a comparatively large number of SEAs include air (all SEAs, 13 of which were reflected in assumptions) and landscape and cultural heritage (21 SEAs, 3 of which were reflected in assumptions). Soil and water were the two criteria that were considered in the smallest number of SEAs (11 and 10, respectively).

Regional differences were significant for four impact types. Soil was significantly more frequently considered in North West England than in Noord-Holland (P<.05). This was caused by the application of plan-SEAs (environmental appraisals), focusing on location-specific impacts. The more frequent application of policy-SEA in Noord-Holland was responsible for a more non-location-specific approach. Fauna, flora and water were significantly more often considered in EVR Berlin-Brandenburg than in Noord-Holland (P<.05 in all three cases), caused by the application of landscape plans and programmes (*Landschaftspläne und -programme*). These considered a wide range of impacts on the living environment in a systematic manner (according to the Brandenburg Environment Act, *BbgNatSchG*, and the Environment Act Berlin, *NatSchGB*).

Socio-economic impact types

Socio-economic impact types that were considered in a comparatively large number of SEAs include social impacts (all SEAs/associated PPPs, 10 of which were only reflected in assumptions) and public service impacts (21 SEAs/

associated PPPs, 10 of which were only reflected in assumptions). Both in-come and housing were poorly considered.

Transport SEAs considered fiscal (P<.01), social (P<.01), economic (P<.05) and public service (P<.05) impacts significantly more frequently than spatial/land use SEAs, which is mainly explained by the possibility of connecting transport infrastructure development and public funding. While all SEAs/as-sociated PPPs made assumptions on future population development, only the vision (*visie*) Hilversum actually predicted impacts of measures on the future population development (demographic impacts). Not surprisingly, assumptions on housing were made in all spatial/land use SEAs/associated PPPs, but in none of the transport SEAs/associated PPPs (P<.01). Housing impacts were quantitatively assessed only in the National Spatial Plan (VINEX) review and indirectly (through population development) in the Vision (*visie*) Hilversum.

Regional comparisons

Figures 5.8 and 5.9 compare the environmental and socio-economic impacts of SEAs in the three sample regions, including nine SEAs from Noord-Holland, nine SEAs from EVR Brandenburg-Berlin and seven SEAs from North West England.

Only in Noord-Holland were environmental and socio-economic impacts con-sidered to a similar extent. Both North West England and EVR Brandenburg-Berlin considered more environmental than socio-economic impacts. However, a large number of socio-economic impacts were reflected in assumptions of the underly-ing PPP.

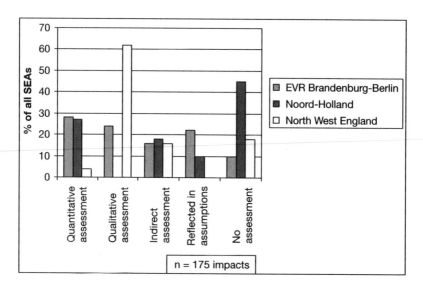

Figure 5.8: *Consideration of environmental impacts in the three sample regions*

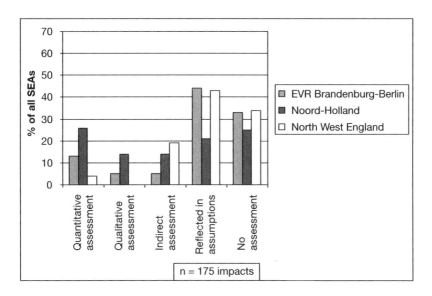

Figure 5.9: *Consideration of socio-economic impacts in the three sample regions*

In EVR Brandenburg-Berlin, on aggregate, significantly more environmental impacts were considered than in Noord-Holland (P<.01). This is explained by the more widespread use of policy-SEA in Noord-Holland, which focused on the assessment of only a few impacts. In EVR Brandenburg-Berlin, on the other hand, the landscape plans and programmes (*Landschaftspläne und -programme*) considered a broad range of purely environmental impacts. Quantitative assessment was more widespread in Noord-Holland and EVR Brandenburg-Berlin than in North West England (P<.05). This was due to the more frequent application of policy-SEA in Noord-Holland and the extensive use of impact maps in EVR Brandenburg-Berlin plan-SEAs. In North West England, environmental impacts were usually assessed only qualitatively, based on the DoE *Good Practice Guide* (1993) for the environmental appraisal of development plans.

Comparisons between SEA types

Figures 5.10 and 5.11 portray the consideration of environmental and socio-economic impacts in the three SEA types, including ten policy-SEAs, eight plan-SEAs and seven programme-SEAs. Policy-SEAs assessed environmental and socio-economic impacts to similar extents; 53 per cent of all possible environmental impacts and 57 per cent of all possible socio-economic impacts were assessed, either directly or indirectly.

While plan-SEA considered significantly more environmental impacts than programme-SEA (P<.01) and policy-SEA (P<.01), it did not assess any socio-economic impacts at all. Socio-economic aspects, however, were frequently reflected in the planning assumptions of the associated plan. Due to environmental

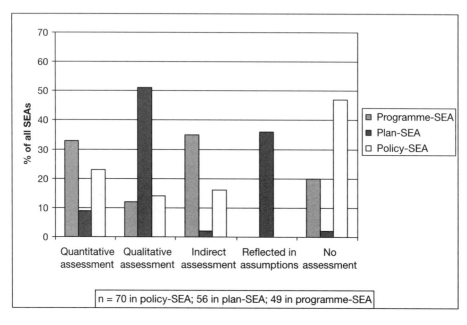

Figure 5.10: *Consideration of environmental impacts in the three SEA types*

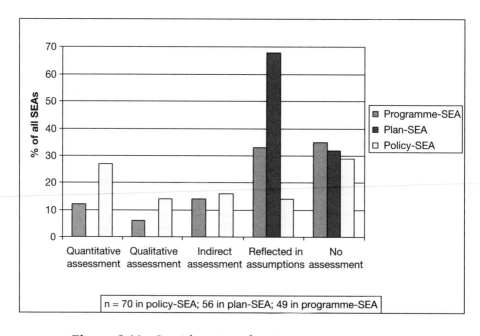

Figure 5.11: *Consideration of socio-economic impacts in the three SEA types*

appraisals in North West England, plan-SEA considered environmental impacts largely in a qualitative way.

Sector-specific comparisons

Figures 5.12 and 5.13 portray the consideration of environmental and socio-economic impacts in transport and spatial/land use SEA, including 12 spatial/land use SEAs and 13 transport SEAs.

Differences between the two sectors were evident for both environmental and socio-economic impacts. While all transport SEAs assessed some socio-economic impacts quantitatively, only one spatial/land use SEA did so, namely the National Spatial Plan (VINEX) review. The Dutch spatial/land use policy-SEAs, the visions (*visies*) Noord-Holland and Hilversum qualitatively assessed socio-economic impacts. All of the other spatial/land use SEAs did not assess any socio-economic impacts at all. This is explained, in particular, by the large extent of plan-SEA application to spatial/land use plans (generally no assessment of socio-economic impacts), and the comparatively widespread use of policy-SEA in transport policies (socio-economic impacts always considered).

Combining socio-economic and environmental impacts

Of all SEA types, only programme-SEA combined socio-economic and environmental impacts, using either cost–benefit analysis (CBA, only in transport-SEAs) or multi-criteria analysis (MCA, in both transport and spatial/land use SEAs). CBA for German transport plans (Federal Transport Infrastructure Plan, BVWP and Land Road Development Plan, *Landesstraßenbedarfsplan* Brandenburg)

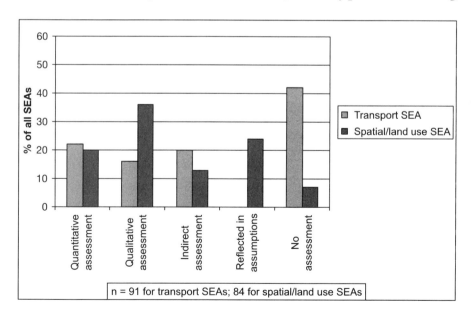

Figure 5.12: *Consideration of environmental impacts in the two sectors*

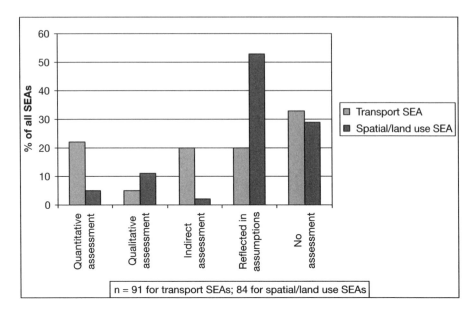

Figure 5.13: *Consideration of socio-economic aspects in the two sectors*

expressed environmental and socio-economic impacts in monetary terms. The MCA for the Cheshire TPP and the Merseyside Package Bid did so in numerical terms.

The German policy-SEAs for the integrated transport policies Brandenburg (IVP) and Berlin (StEP) compared socio-economic and environmental impacts for a wide range of policy measures. Furthermore, the Dutch spatial/land use policy-SEAs, the visions (*visies*), discussed development options in socio-economic terms and provided decision makers with a range of possibilities for development. However, no recommendations were provided, attempting to balance socio-economic and environmental impacts for any of these SEAs. Only the programme-SEA for the National Spatial Plan (VINEX) review (which also involved MCA) selected a number of alternatives and gave clear recommendations to the decision maker, taking environmental and socio-economic impacts into account. All other SEAs (apart from those using MCA and CBA for prioritizing projects in programme-SEA), left the final evaluation to the discretion of the decision maker.

Average scores for the individual SEAs, the regions, SEA types and sectors on impact coverage

This section identifies average scores for the SEA impact coverage, including those impacts that were quantitatively, qualitatively and indirectly assessed. All impacts were weighted equally, as there was no indication at the outset of the research underlying the book whether quantitative, qualitative or indirect assessment would be most effective.[3]

Individual SEAs

Table 5.6 presents the average scores for the individual SEAs. The programme-SEA for the VINEX review obtained the highest score of all SEAs. The second highest score was obtained by three policy-SEAs, namely the vision (*visie*) Hilversum and the integrated transport SEAs/policies (IVP) Brandenburg and (StEP) Berlin, considering both environmental and socio-economic impacts.

Lowest scores were obtained by the three plan-SEAs, not assessing impacts but identifying land suitability, including the Environment Matrix (*milieumatrix*) Amsterdam, the Landscape Framework Plan (*Landschafts-rahmenplan*) Havelland and the Landscape Programme (*Landschaftsprogramm*) Berlin. Low scores were also obtained by the programme-SEA for the Federal Transport Infrastructure Plan (BVWP) and the policy-SEA for the Second Transport Structure Plan (SVVII). While the former did not assess any socio-economic impacts, the latter considered a small number of both environmental and socio-economic impacts.

Table 5.6: *Extent of impacts assessed in SEA*

PPP	Impacts quantitatively assessed: environment/ socio-economic	Impacts qualitatively assessed: environment/ socio-economic	Impacts indirectly assessed: environment/ socio-economic	Overall evaluation
Environmental Appraisal for the Lancashire Structure Plan	0/0	7/0	0/0	⊙
Environmental Appraisal for the Cheshire Structure Plan	0/0	7/0	0/0	⊙
Transport Plan Cheshire TPP	0/0	1/0	4/3	⊙
Merseyside Package Bid	0/0	1/0	4/3	⊙
Merseyside Package Bid underlying strategy	2/0	0/2	0/2	○
Environmental Appraisal for the Warrington Local Plan	0/0	7/0	0/0	⊙
Environmental Appraisal for the Oldham UDP	0/0	7/0	0/0	⊙
Second Transport Structure Plan (SVVII)	2/1	0/0	0/2	○
National Spatial Plan (VINEX) review	7/4	0/0	0/1	●
Vision (*visie*) Noord-Holland	0/0	0/3	5/0	⊙
Transport Plan (RVVP) INVERNO	2/3	0/0	1/1	⊙
Transport Plan (RVVP) Noord-Holland-Noord	2/3	0/0	0/1	○
Transport Plan (RVVP) ROA	2/2	0/0	0/2	○

Table 5.6: *Continued*

PPP	Impacts quantitatively assessed: environment/ socio-economic	Impacts qualitatively assessed: environment/ socio-economic	Impacts indirectly assessed: environment/ socio-economic	Overall evaluation
Environment Matrix (*milieumatrix*) Amsterdam	0/0	0/0	0/0	□
Vision (*visie*) Hilversum	0/0	0/6	4/1	●
Transport Plan (RVVP) Haarlem-IJmond	2/3	0/0	1/1	◉
Federal Transport Plan (BVWP) ecological risk assessment	4/0	0/0	1/0	○
Federal Transport Plan (BVWP)	0/2	1/1	4/0	◉
Landscape Framework Plan Havelland	0/0	0/0	0/0	□
Road Plan (*Landesstraßenbedarfsplan*) Brandenburg	0/0	2/2	3/0	◉
Integrated Transport Plan (IVP) Brandenburg	2/3	5/0	0/1	●
Land Use Plan (FNP) Berlin, ecological assessment	5/0	1/0	1/0	◉
Land Use Plan (FNP) Berlin, Landscape Programme	0/0	0/0	0/0	□
Integrated Transport Plan (StEP) Berlin	2/3	5/0	0/1	●
Land Use Plan (FNP) Ketzin, Landscape Plan	5/0	1/0	1/0	◉

▨ policy-SEA ▭ plan-SEA ▢ programme-SEA

Overall evaluation:
- ■ = 100%
- ● = 75% to under 100%
- ◉ = 50% to under 75%
- ○ = 25% to under 50%
- □ = 0% to under 25%

Regions, SEA types and sectors

Figure 5.14 shows results for the regions, the SEA types and sectors. The lowest average score was achieved by plan-SEA, caused in particular by the failure to assess socio-economic aspects ($P<.01$ with both other SEA types). Highest scores were achieved by policy-SEAs and programme-SEAs. Differences between the regions and the sectors were not statistically significant.

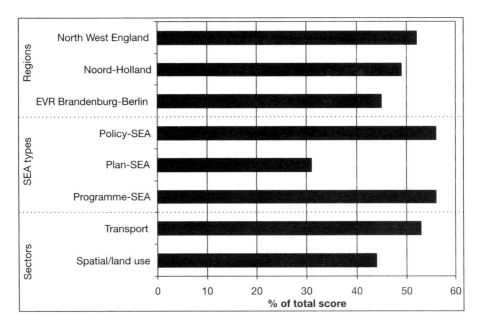

Figure 5.14: *Overall scores for impact coverage for the regions, SEA types and sectors*

The total number of impacts assessed was significantly correlated with the variable PPP relevance (see Chapter 4) in a negative manner (P<.01), that is PPPs with a high relevance assessed only few impacts. This is explained by plan-SEA, which on average had the highest PPP relevance, but did not assess any socio-economic impacts. There was also significant statistical correlation between the extent to which environmental impacts were assessed in a qualitative way and the time needed for SEA preparation (P<.01), in other words those SEAs involving quantitative assessment took significantly longer to be prepared. In addition, the extent to which impacts were quantitatively assessed was correlated with the extent to which SEA procedural stages were covered (P<.05). This is mainly explained by the extensive procedural coverage in policy-SEA, which quantitatively assessed both environmental and socio-economic impacts.

OTHER METHODOLOGICAL ASPECTS

This section explains other methodological aspects of SEA application, including the use of methods and techniques employed in (or for) SEA reports. Observations are presented by region, SEA type and sector.

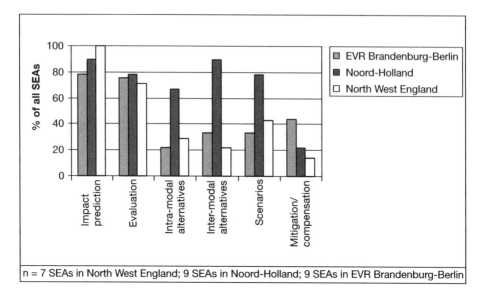

Figure 5.15: *Methods used in SEA documentation*

Methods

Regions

Figure 5.15 shows the extent to which the six methods introduced in Chapter 2 were used in SEA reports in the three sample regions. Impact prediction and impact evaluation were the methods that were on average most frequently used. Only three plan-SEAs, namely the Environment Matrix (*milieumatrix*) Amsterdam, the Landscape Framework Plan (*Landschaftsrahmenplan*) Havelland and the Landscape Programme (*Landschaftsprogramm*) Berlin did not assess impacts, but identified land suitability. Mainly caused by the large extent of policy-SEA application, Noord-Holland SEAs considered scenarios, intra-modal and inter-modal alternatives (P<.01) to a larger extent than North West England and EVR Brandenburg-Berlin SEAs.

SEA types

Table 5.7 identifies the extent to which methods were used in the three SEA types. As expected, policy-SEA considered scenarios and inter-modal alternatives particularly well (difference with programme-SEA at P<.01) and plan-SEA evaluated impacts to a significantly larger extent than programme-SEA (P<.05). All programme-SEAs compared impact magnitudes for different projects, but none considered scenarios and inter-modal alternatives.

Differences in the application of methods within a certain SEA type were most evident for plan-SEA. While German landscape plans and programmes (*Landschaftspläne und -programme*) and the Environment Matrix (*milieumatrix*) Amsterdam focused on setting environmental objectives and identifying land suitability (as instruments of the precautionary principle), English environmental appraisals focused on the qualitative prediction of environmental impacts, mainly using impact matrices.

Table 5.7: *Methods in documentation for the three SEA types*

Methods	Policy-SEA	Plan-SEA	Programme-SEA
Mitigation/compensation	✗		
Scenarios	✓		✗
Inter-modal alternatives	✓	✗	✗
Intra-modal alternatives			
Evaluation/objective setting		✓	
Impact prediction	✓		✓

✓   method applied in all SEAs
▭   method applied in some of the SEAs
✗   method applied in none or only one of the SEAs

Sectors

Figure 5.16 shows the use of methods in transport and spatial/land use SEAs. Mitigation/compensation measures were only considered in spatial/land use SEAs. Considering the direct link between some transport PPPs (in particular those involving programme-SEA) and public funding, it is surprising that no transport SEAs considered mitigation, as the mitigation of impacts involves costs that can differ considerably for different alternatives. While spatial/land

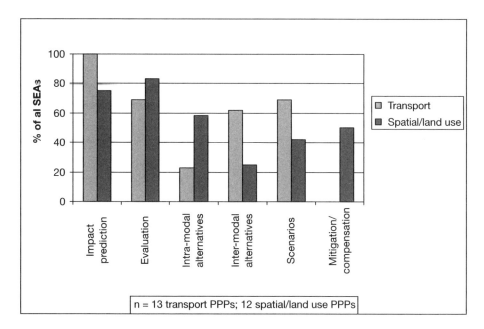

Figure 5.16: *Methods used in SEA documentation for the two sectors*

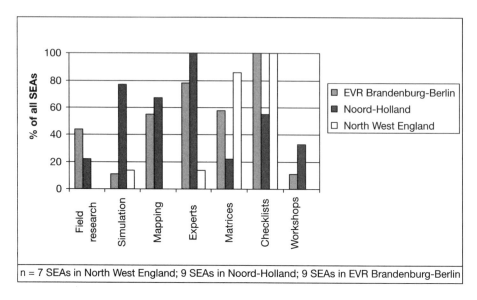

n = 7 SEAs in North West England; 9 SEAs in Noord-Holland; 9 SEAs in EVR Brandenburg-Berlin

Figure 5.17: *Techniques used in SEA documentation*

use SEAs focused on site (intra-modal) alternatives, transport SEAs focused on inter-modal alternatives (difference between the sectors in both cases at P<.01).

Techniques

Regions

Figure 5.17 shows the techniques used in SEA reports. On average, checklists were most frequently used in the three sample regions. While the range of techniques used in Noord-Holland and EVR Brandenburg-Berlin SEAs was comparatively extensive, in North West England, mainly matrices and checklists were used (following the *Good Practice Guide*, DoE, 1993). Furthermore, SEA preparation times in North West England were considerably shorter than in the other two regions.

Mapping and expert consultation were used significantly less in North West England than in Noord-Holland (P<.01) as well as in EVR Brandenburg-Berlin (P<.05). Furthermore, simulation techniques were used to a significantly larger extent in Noord-Holland than in both of the other regions (P<.01). This is explained by the more frequent use of policy-SEAs, which all apply simulation techniques. Caused by the landscape plans and programmes, field research was most frequently used in EVR Brandenburg-Berlin (P<.01).

SEA types

Table 5.8 identifies those techniques that were used or not used. While all policy-SEAs used simulation and expert consultation, none used matrices. While all German and Dutch plan-SEAs included expert consultation and mapping, none of the North West England environmental appraisals used these techniques. Field research was consistently applied in German plan-SEAs (landscape plans and programmes). The lack of workshops in programme-SEA preparation is explained by a reluctance on the part of decision makers to accept any external inputs for prioritizing transport projects, reflecting the strong status of transport departments within authorities.

Table 5.8: *Techniques in documentation for the three SEA types*

Technique	Policy-SEA	Plan-SEA	Programme-SEA
Field research	✗		
Simulation	✓	✗	✗
Mapping		(✓)	
Expert consultation	✓	(✓)	
Matrices		✓	
Checklists		✓	✓
Workshops			✗

✓	= technique applied in all SEAs
(✓)	= technique applied in all SEAs, except those in North West England
☐	= technique used in some of the cases
✗	= technique applied in none or only one of the SEAs

Sectors

Figure 5.18 shows the techniques used in transport and spatial/land use SEAs. Mapping, field research and workshops were applied to a significantly larger

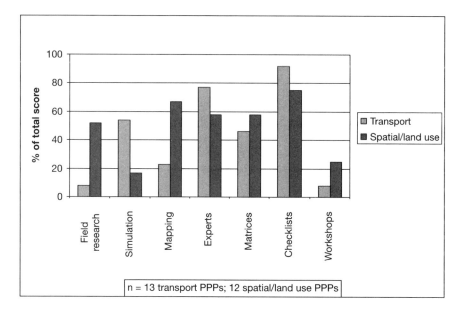

Figure 5.18: *Techniques used in SEA documentation for the two sectors*

extent in spatial/land use SEA than in transport SEA (P<.01). Simulation techniques were applied to a significantly larger extent in transport PPPs (P<.01). The differences are explained by the comparatively large number of policy-SEAs in the transport sector. Furthermore, mapping was applied in all Dutch and German plan-SEAs for spatial/land use plans.

Average scores for the individual SEAs, the regions, SEA types and sectors on the other methodological aspects

Individual SEAs

Table 5.9 identifies the overall scores for each of the individual SEAs. The maximum numbers of methods that could possibly have been considered in the three SEA types are five in policy-SEA and plan-SEA and four in programme-SEA (following Table 5.7). The maximum number of techniques that could have been considered is six in policy-SEA and plan-SEA and five in programme-SEA (following Table 5.8).

The programme-SEA for the National Spatial Plan (VINEX) review obtained the highest score (100 per cent). Furthermore, high scores of over 75 per cent were obtained by the plan-SEAs, Environment Matrix (*milieumatrix*) Amsterdam and Landscape Programme (*Landschaftsprogramm*) Berlin, and the policy-SEAs for the Regional Transport Plan (RVVP) Haarlem-IJmond and the Integrated Transport Plan (StEP) Berlin.

Table 5.9: *Overall evaluation of the use of methods and techniques for all SEAs*

PPP	Number of methods used*	Number of techniques used*	Overall evaluation
Environmental Appraisal for the Lancashire Structure Plan	3 (5)	2 (6)	○
Environmental Appraisal for the Cheshire Structure Plan	5 (5)	2 (6)	◉
Transport Plan Cheshire TPP	1 (4)	2 (5)	○
Merseyside Package Bid	1 (4)	2 (5)	○
Merseyside Package Bid underlying strategy	5 (5)	3 (6)	◉
Environmental Appraisal for the Warrington Local Plan	3 (5)	2 (6)	○
Environmental Appraisal for the Oldham UDP	4 (5)	2 (6)	◉
Second Transport Structure Plan (SVVII)	5 (5)	2 (6)	◉
National Spatial Plan (VINEX) review	4 (4)	5 (5)	■
Vision (*visie*) Noord-Holland	4 (5)	4 (6)	◻
Transport Plan (RVVP) INVERNO	4 (5)	3 (6)	◉
Transport Plan (RVVP) Noord-Holland-Noord	4 (5)	3 (6)	◉

Table 5.9: *Continued*

PPP	Number of methods used*	Number of techniques used*	Overall evaluation
Transport Plan (RVVP) ROA	4 (5)	4 (6)	⊙
Environment Matrix (*milieumatrix*) Amsterdam	2 (4)	6 (6)	●
Vision (*visie*) Hilversum	4 (5)	4 (6)	⊙
Transport Plan (RVVP) Haarlem-IJmond	5 (5)	4 (6)	●
Federal Transport Plan (BVWP) ecological risk assessment	2 (4)	4 (5)	⊙
Federal Transport Plan (BVWP)	2 (4)	3 (5)	⊙
Landscape Framework Plan Havelland	2 (5)	5 (6)	⊙
Road Plan (*Landesstraßenbedarfsplan*) Brandenburg	1 (4)	3 (5)	O
Integrated Transport Plan (IVP) Brandenburg	3 (5)	4 (6)	⊙
Land Use Plan (FNP) Berlin, ecological assessment	4 (4)	2 (5)	⊙
Land Use Plan (FNP) Berlin, Landscape Programme	2 (5)	5 (6)	⊙
Integrated Transport Plan (StEP) Berlin	4 (5)	5 (6)	●
Land Use Plan (FNP) Ketzin, Landscape Plan	4 (5)	5 (6)	●

Note: * possible numbers in brackets, see Tables 5.7 and 5.8

▨ policy-SEA ▢ plan-SEA ▢ programme-SEA

Overall evaluation:
■ = 100%
● = 75% to under 100%
⊙ = 50% to under 75%
O = 25% to under 50%
▫ = 0% to under 25%

Regions, SEA types and sectors

Figure 5.19 shows the overall scores for the regions, SEA types and sectors. North West England SEAs obtained significantly lower scores than Noord-Holland SEAs (P<.01) and EVR Brandenburg-Berlin SEAs (P<.05). This was mainly due to the use of fewer techniques in North West England. There were no significant differences between the SEA types or between the sectors.

The extent to which methods and techniques were applied was correlated with the extent to which SEA procedural stages were covered (P<.01), thus underlining the importance of a full coverage of SEA procedural stages. While

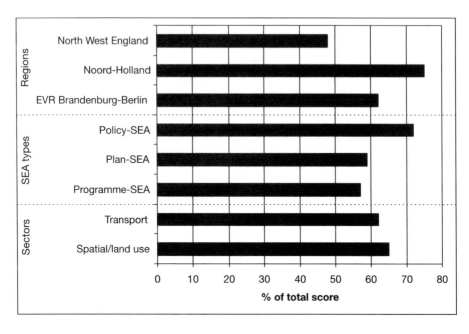

Figure 5.19: *Overall scores for the regions, SEA types and sectors*

there was no correlation with the average impact range, there was significant correlation of the use of methods and techniques and the extent to which impacts were quantitatively assessed (P<.01).

SEA PREPARATION TIMES

Figure 5.20 shows the SEA preparation times in the three sample regions (preparation times for the individual SEAs are provided in Table 5.10). While all SEAs in North West England took less than a person-year to undertake, most of Noord-Holland and EVR Brandenburg-Berlin SEAs took more than a person-year to undertake. The number of authorities that were not able to provide an answer to SEA preparation times was particularly high in Noord-Holland. This was mainly caused by the greater number of policy-SEAs in this region, as authorities were often unable to answer the question as to whether there was separate SEA documentation. For three of the nine SEAs in EVR Brandenburg-Berlin, preparation times were said to have been more than three person-years, namely the plan-SEAs, the Landscape Framework Plan (*Landschaftsrahmenplan*) Havelland, the Landscape Programme (*Landschaftsprogramm*) Berlin (both of which following formal procedures) and the programme-SEA, the Ecological Conflict Assessment (*ökologische Konfliktanalyse*) for the Land Use Plan (FNP) Berlin. For three of the nine PPPs that involved SEA preparation in Noord-Holland, authorities said that preparation times were between two and three person-years, namely for the

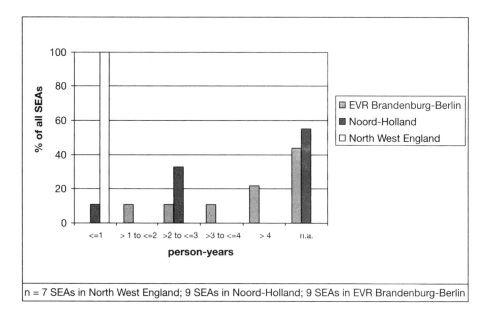

n = 7 SEAs in North West England; 9 SEAs in Noord-Holland; 9 SEAs in EVR Brandenburg-Berlin

Figure 5.20: *SEA preparation times for the three sample regions*

integrated transport plans (RVVPs) Haarlem-IJmond and ROA and the SEA of the National Spatial Plan (VINEX) review.

Postal questionnaire results from local authorities on local plan-SEAs in North West England and EVR Brandenburg-Berlin confirmed the above findings. While all of the authorities in North West England said that environmental appraisals took less than a person-year to prepare, 88 per cent of EVR Brandenburg-Berlin authorities said that it took longer than a person-year to prepare the landscape plans (*Landschaftspläne*).

SUMMARY

A minimum number of 80 SEAs (broadly defined) were identified in the three sample regions that are classified into three SEA types. For convenience and in order to avoid any further confusion, existing terminology is used and the SEA types are called policy-SEA, plan-SEA and programme-SEA. Policy-SEA was applied to a comparatively large extent in Noord-Holland, having an open participation process with widespread consultation and participation. In EVR Brandenburg-Berlin and North West England, plan-SEAs were mostly under-taken with no public participation at higher levels of decision making. Programme-SEA was generally applied to a lesser extent than the other two SEA types. The extent to which the different SEA types were applied in the three regions reflected the different planning approaches taken. While the consensus-led, quasi-top-down planning approach in The Netherlands involved public participation at all administrative levels, the centrally guided, local plan making approach in North West England and the public administration consensus-led counter-current approach in EVR Brandenburg-Berlin involved the general public only at lower tiers. Individual scores for SEA procedures, impact coverage and the use of methods and techniques (other methodological aspects) and SEA preparation times are summarized in Table 5.10.

The programme-SEA for the National Spatial Plan (VINEX) review obtained the highest average score of all of the assessments for SEA procedure, impact coverage and the other methodological aspects. Other SEAs that scored comparatively highly include mostly policy-SEAs and the Landscape Plan (*Landschaftsplan*) Ketzin. SEAs that obtained the lowest scores include the transport programme-SEAs, in particular.

Three plan-SEAs included land suitability maps and defined environmental objectives for the associated plan, and therefore obtained only low scores on the impact range. These include the Environment Matrix (*milieumatrix*) Amsterdam, the Landscape Framework Plan (*Landschaftsrahmenplan*) Havelland and the Landscape Programme (*Landschaftsprogramm*) Berlin.

Table 5.10: *SEA variables scores*

PPP	SEA process	Impact coverage	Other methodological aspects	Preparation times in years
Environmental Appraisal Lancashire Structure Plan	○	◉	○	<1
Environmental Appraisal Cheshire Structure Plan	○	◉	◉	<1
Transport Plan Cheshire TPP	○	◉	○	<1
Merseyside Package Bid	○	◉	○	<1
Merseyside Package Bid underlying strategy	◉	○	◉	n/a
Environmental Appraisal Warrington Local Plan	○	◉	○	<1
Environmental Appraisal Oldham UDP	○	◉	◉	<1
Second Transport Structure Plan (SVVII)	●	○	◉	n/a
National Spatial Plan (VINEX) review	●	●	■	2–3
Vision (*visie*) Noord-Holland	◉	◉	◉	n/a
Transport Plan (RVVP) INVERNO	◉	◉	◉	n/a
Transport Plan (RVVP) Noord-Holland-Noord	◉	○	◉	<1
Transport Plan (RVVP) ROA	◉	○	◉	3-4
Environment Matrix (*milieumatrix*) Amsterdam	□	□	●	n/a
Vision (*visie*) Hilversum	◉	●	◉	n/a

Table 5.10: *Continued*

PPP	SEA process	Impact coverage	Other methodological aspects	Preparation times in years
Transport Plan (RVVP) Haarlem-IJmond	◉	◉	●	3–4
Federal Transport Plan (BVWP) ecological risk	□	○	◉	2–3
Federal Transport Plan (BVWP)	◉	◉	◉	n/a
Landscape Framework Plan Havelland	◉	□	◉	4–5
Road Plan (*Landesstrassenbedarfsplan*) Brandenburg	□	◉	○	n/a
Integrated Transport Plan (IVP) Brandenburg	◉	●	◉	n/a
Land Use Plan (FNP) Berlin, ecological assessment	○	◉	◉	3–4
Land Use Plan (FNP) Berlin, Landscape Programme	◉	□	◉	4–5
Integrated Transport Plan (StEP) Berlin	◉	●	●	n/a
Land Use Plan (FNP) Ketzin, Landscape Plan	●	◉	●	1–2

☐ policy-SEA ☐ plan-SEA ☐ programme-SEA

Overall evaluation:

■ = 100%
● = 75% to under 100%
◉ = 50% to under 75%
○ = 25% to under 50%
□ = 0% to under 25%

Chapter 6

Opinions and attitudes of authorities

Chapter 6 refers to objective 3 of the book and identifies the opinions of authorities about current SEA practice and their attitudes towards an application of formalized SEA. Results are based on interviews on 36 PPPs at all administrative levels and on postal questionnaires at the local level.

OVERALL PICTURE

Figure 6.1 shows the average scores for authorities opinions on the quality and the influence of current assessments, and attitudes towards the application of formalized SEA, representing a cross-section of PPPs (interview results). Figure 6.1 is based on an evaluation, ranking from 0 (most negative) to 3 (most positive).

On the whole, opinions on the influence of current assessments in the PPP process were less positive than the opinions on the quality of the assessments. Most authorities thought that an integration of formalized SEA into the existing process was possible, but also feared that formalized SEA would delay its preparation. A majority of authorities thought that formalized SEA could lead to project acceleration and to a better consideration of the environment in PPP preparation. Figure 6.2 shows the average scores of the opinions and attitudes of authorities for the three sample regions. Opinions on the influence of SEA in PPP formulation were significantly less positive in North West England than in both EVR Brandenburg-Berlin (P<.01) and Noord-Holland (P<.01). Regarding attitudes in the three regions, significantly fewer authorities in EVR Brandenburg-Berlin than in the other two regions thought that an integration of formal SEA into the PPP process was possible (P<.01). Significantly fewer authorities in EVR Brandenburg-Berlin than in Noord-Holland thought that formal SEA would accelerate project preparation (P<.05), but rather that it could lead to a delay of the formulation process (P<.05). Finally, significantly more authorities in North West England than in EVR Brandenburg-Berlin thought that SEA would lead to a better consideration of the environment (P<.01).

The opinions and attitudes of local authorities did not differ as much between the three regions as was observed for the cross-section of PPPs.[1] While opinions on the quality of current assessments were similar in North West England and EVR Brandenburg-Berlin, attitudes towards formalized SEA were slightly better in EVR Brandenburg than in North West England. Differences between the regions, however, were not statistically significant. Local authorities

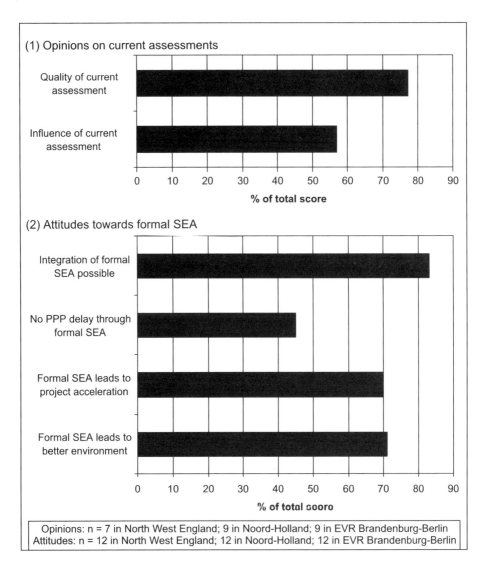

Figure 6.1: *Opinions and attitudes on current SEA and formalized SEA*

in EVR Brandenburg-Berlin had comparatively positive attitudes towards formalized SEA. This was unexpected, as past studies had suggested that attitudes in Germany were generally rather negative (see Chapter 1). As will be shown later, this is particularly explained by the use of statutory and mandatory landscape plans (*Landschaftspläne*) to local land use plans (FNPs) in the *Land* Brandenburg.

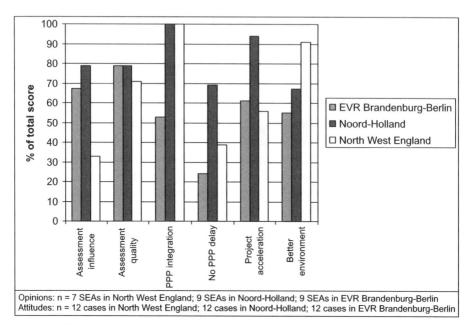

Figure 6.2: *Opinions of authorities on current SEA and attitudes towards formalized SEA representing the cross-section of 36 PPPs by region*

OPINIONS ON CURRENT SEA

This section considers the opinions of authorities on current assessments, including their influence on PPP preparation and their overall quality. Results are presented for three presentation aspects: the regions; SEA types; and sectors.

Influence of SEA in PPP preparation

Cross-section of 36 PPPs

Figure 6.3 shows the responses of interviewed authorities to the question 'how influential do you think the assessment was in PPPs preparation?' Views in North West England were significantly more negative than in both Noord-Holland (P<.05) and EVR Brandenburg-Berlin (P<.01).

While all authorities in North West England said that assessments were only marginally influential, most authorities in Noord-Holland (61 per cent) said that assessments were very influential. All of the authorities in EVR Brandenburg-Berlin that were able to reply to the question (55 per cent) said that assessments were reasonably influential. One SEA in Noord-Holland was conducted after PPP preparation and was therefore said not to have been influential at all. Most of the authorities that were unable to answer the question undertook policy-SEAs. This is not surprising, as policy-SEA is always fully integrated into the associated policy. Most of the authorities responsible for the preparation of policy-SEA that were able to answer the question said that SEA was very influential.

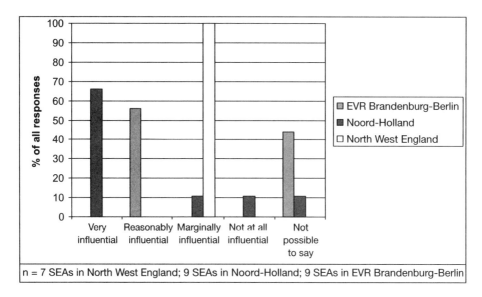

Figure 6.3: *Views about the influence of current SEA in PPP formulation by region*

Figure 6.4 shows the replies of the authorities in terms of the three SEA types (including ten policy-SEAs, eight plan-SEAs and seven programme-SEAs). While

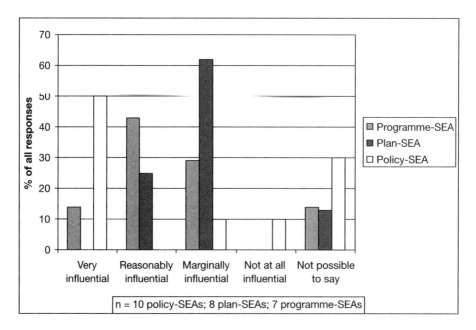

Figure 6.4: *Views about the influence of current SEA in PPP formulation by SEA type*

policy-SEA and plan-SEA appeared to have been the most influential, differences were not statistically significant.

While almost twice as many authorities preparing transport SEAs than authorities preparing spatial/land use SEAs thought that assessments were either very influential (policy-SEA) or reasonably influential (programme-SEA), differences were not statistically significant.

It was apparent that the status of the SEA was of some importance to the differences found. Thus, all non-statutory plan-SEAs were said to have been only marginally influential (including the environmental appraisals in North West England and the Environment Matrix, *milieumatrix* Amsterdam). All statutory plan-SEAs, on the other hand, were said to have been reasonably influential (landscape plans and programmes, *Landschaftspläne und -programme* in EVR Brandenburg-Berlin). The programme-SEA for the National Spatial Plan (VINEX) review followed a formal process, as laid out in the national EIA Decree and was also said to have been very influential in PPP preparation.

Local land use PPPs

Figure 6.5 shows the views of local authorities about the influence of SEA for local land use PPPs (postal questionnaire results). Noord-Holland is not included, as information was obtained for only one SEA at the local level. While opinions in EVR Brandenburg-Berlin were more positive than opinions in North West England, the difference between the two regions were not statistically significant. Observed differences are most likely explained by SEA preparation times and the status of the SEA. While landscape plans (*Landschaftspläne*) in

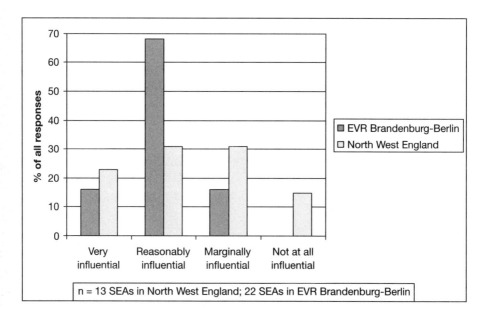

Figure 6.5: *Views of local authorities in North West England and EVR Brandenburg-Berlin on the influence of current SEA*

EVR Brandenburg-Berlin were statutory, applied a formalized procedure and, on average, took more than a person-year to prepare, environmental appraisals in North West England were non-statutory, did not follow a formal procedure and, on average, took less than a person-year to prepare.

Quality of SEA

Cross-section of PPPs

Figure 6.6 shows the responses of authorities, representing the cross-section of 36 PPPs at all administrative levels to the question 'in your opinion, what is the quality of the assessment?'. All of the authorities who replied to the question said that quality was either fair, reasonable or very good. None said that SEA quality was poor. Differences between the regions, however, were not statistically significant.

Figure 6.7 shows the replies of the authorities in terms of the three SEA types. While authorities preparing plan-SEAs judged the quality to be somewhat better than authorities preparing policy-SEAs and programme-SEAs, differences failed to be statistically significant. 20 per cent of the authorities preparing policy-SEAs were not able to answer the question as they thought it was impossible to distinguish between the SEA and the associated policy.

Figure 6.8 presents views about the quality of transport SEAs and spatial/land use SEAs. In contrast to regional and SEA-type differences, sectoral differences were found to be statistically significant ($P<.05$). While 59 per cent of the authorities responsible for the preparation of spatial/land use SEAs said that they were of very good quality, this figure fell to 23 per cent for transport SEAs. All SEAs that were said to have been of fair quality were transport

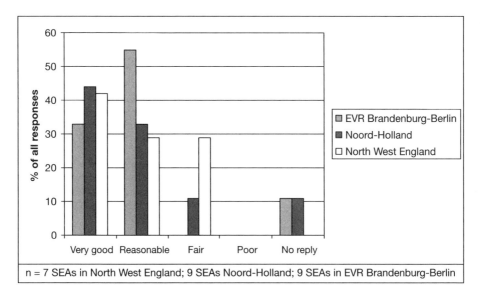

n = 7 SEAs in North West England; 9 SEAs Noord-Holland; 9 SEAs in EVR Brandenburg-Berlin

Figure 6.6: *Views on the quality of current SEA by region*

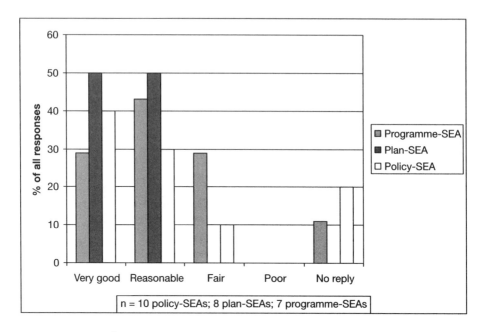

Figure 6.7: *Views on the quality of current SEAs by SEA type*

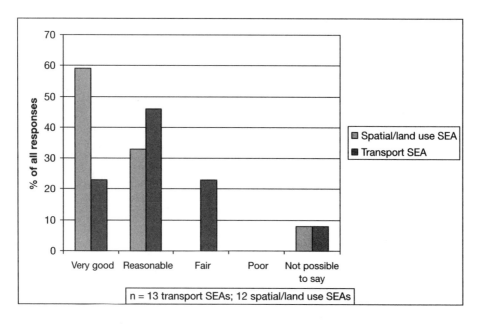

Figure 6.8: *Views on the quality of current SEA by sector*

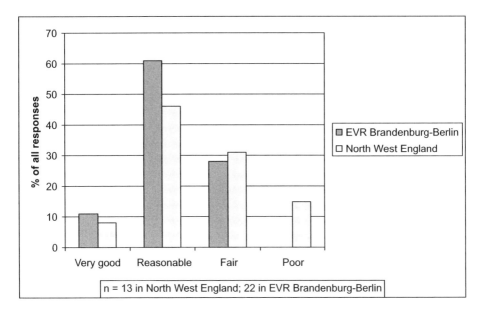

Figure 6.9: *Views of local authorities on the quality of current SEA in EVR Brandenburg-Berlin and North West England*

SEAs. Two procedural stages were of particular importance for the perception of good quality SEAs. These include the initiation stage (scoping) (P<.01) and the public participation stage (P<.05). While the average preparation times of all PPPs were 1.5 to 2.5 years, this figure rose to 2.3 to 3.3 years for those SEAs that were said to have been of good quality.

Local land use policies, plans and programmes

Figure 6.9 shows the responses of authorities responsible for the preparation of local land use policies, plans and programmes (postal questionnaire results). Only North West England and EVR Brandenburg-Berlin were considered, as information on only one local-level SEA was obtained in Noord-Holland. Most authorities thought that their assessments were of either reasonable or fair quality. Only a few authorities in North West England said that their assessments were of poor quality. While EVR Brandenburg-Berlin authorities gave their assessments slightly higher quality scores, differences failed to be statistically significant.

Overall evaluation of the opinions of authorities

Individual SEAs

Table 6.1 shows the opinions of authorities on the quality and the influence of SEA for each individual assessment. An average opinion score is calculated and used in statistical analysis with the context variables (Chapter 4), SEA variables (Chapter 5) and the other examined SEA aspects (see Chapters 7 to 8).

Table 6.1: *Overall evaluation of opinions on current SEA*

PPP	Influence in PPP making	Quality of SEA	Overall evaluation
Environmental Appraisal Lancashire Structure Plan	(⇔)	✓	◉
Environmental Appraisal Cheshire Structure Plan	(⇔)	⇔	◉
Transport Plan Cheshire TPP	(⇔)	(⇔)	○
Merseyside Package Bid	(⇔)	(⇔)	○
Merseyside Package Bid underlying strategy	(⇔)	✓	◉
Environmental Appraisal Warrington Local Plan	(⇔)	✓	◉
Environmental Appraisal UDP Oldham	(⇔)	⇔	◉
Second Transport Structure Plan (SVVII)	✓	✓	■
National Spatial Plan (VINEX) review	✓	✓	■
Vision (*visie*) Noord-Holland	n/a	n/a	n/a
Transport Plan (RVVP) INVERNO	✓	(⇔)	¤
Transport Plan (RVVP) Noord-Holland-Noord	✗	⇔	○
Transport Plan (RVVP) ROA	✓	⇔	●
Environment Matrix (*milieumatrix*) Amsterdam	(⇔)	⇔	◉
Vision (*visie*) Hilversum	✓	✓	■
Transport Plan (RVVP) Haarlem-IJmond	✓	✓	■
Federal Transport Plan (BVWP) ecological risk	⇔	⇔	◉
Federal Transport Plan (BVWP)	⇔	⇔	◉
Landscape Framework Plan Havelland	⇔	✓	●
Road Plan (*Landesstraßenbedarfsplan*) Brandenburg	⇔	⇔	◉
Integrated Transport Plan (IVP) Brandenburg	n/a	⇔	n/a
Land Use Plan (FNP) Berlin, ecological assessment	n/a	✓	n/a
Land Use Plan (FNP) Berlin, Landscape Programme	n/a	✓	n/a

Table 6.1: *Continued*

PPP	Influence in PPP making	Quality of SEA	Overall evaluation
Integrated Transport Plan (StEP) Berlin	n/a	n/a	n/a
Land Use Plan (FNP) Ketzin, Landscape Plan	⇔	⇔	⊙

☐ policy-SEA   ☐ plan-SEA   ☐ programme-SEA

Evaluation of criteria:
✓ = very influential/very good quality (scores 3)
⇔ = reasonably influential/reasonable quality (scores 2)
(⇔) = marginally influential/fair quality (scores 1)
✗ = not at all influential/poor quality (scores 0)
n.a. = no answer

Overall evaluation (on the basis of criteria scores):
■ = met to 100%
● = met from 75% to under 100%
⊙ = met from 50% to under 75%
○ = met from 25% to under 50%
◻ = met from 0% to under 25%

Highest scores for the influence and quality of SEA were achieved by four SEAs which were all from Noord-Holland. Three of the SEAs that obtained the highest overall scores were policy-SEAs and one was a programme-SEA, namely the National Spatial Plan (VINEX) review, which followed a formalized project-EIA procedure, as laid out in the Dutch EIA Decree.

Most SEAs obtained moderate scores of 50 per cent to 75 per cent. The only three SEAs that obtained low scores of under 50 per cent included two transport programme-SEAs from North West England that relied entirely on multi-criteria analysis. Furthermore, it included a policy-SEA in Noord-Holland of which the responsible authority said that SEA was only conducted after the underlying policy was decided on. In conclusion, high scores were achieved either in policy-SEAs or in assessments that followed formalized procedures.

Regions, SEA types and sectors

Figure 6.10 shows the overall evaluation of the opinions of authorities, representing a cross-section of 36 PPPs at all administrative levels, referring to the regions, SEA types and sectors. Noord-Holland SEAs, policy-SEAs and spatial/land use SEAs obtained the highest overall scores. Of all presentation aspects, only regional differences were significant between Noord-Holland and North West England (P<.05) and between EVR Brandenburg-Berlin and North West England (P<.01).

The overall score of PPP makers' opinions was significantly correlated with the time needed to undertake the SEA (P<.01), in other words the more time and therefore funding that was available to undertake an SEA, the higher the

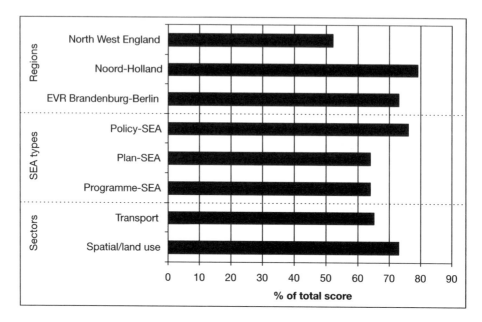

Figure 6.10: *Opinions on current SEAs by region, SEA type and sector*

overall SEA opinion score. There was also significant correlation between authorities' opinions and the extent to which methods and techniques were used (P<.01) and the extent to which the SEA procedural stages were covered (P<.01). This is explained, in particular, by the high opinions of the authorities preparing policy-SEA, covering stages comparatively extensively and using a wide variety of methods and techniques. Stages that proved to have been of particular importance for the high opinions of authorities included scoping (P<.01) and consultation (P<.05). There was also a correlation between the opinions of authorities and the extent to which mitigation was conducted (P<.05), impact mapping was used (P<.01) and environmental impacts were assessed in a quantitative manner (P<.05).

ATTITUDES OF AUTHORITIES TOWARDS FORMALIZED SEA

This section considers the attitudes of authorities towards formalized SEA. Four aspects are examined, including the consideration of the integration of formalized SEA into the existing PPP process, a possible delay through SEA preparation, an acceleration of project preparation and a better consideration of environmental impacts in the process. While the previous section compared an unequal number of cases in the three regions (seven SEAs in North West England, nine SEAs in Noord-Holland and nine SEAs in EVR Brandenburg-Berlin), this section presents the results for an equal number of 12 authorities in each region (representing 12 PPPs in each region).

Integration of SEA into the PPP process

Cross-section of PPPs

Figure 6.11 shows the responses of the authorities, representing the cross-section of 36 PPPs at all administrative levels to the question 'do you think the integration of formal SEA into the PPP process is possible?'. It was found that attitudes in EVR Brandenburg-Berlin were significantly more negative than those in North West England (P<.05) and Noord-Holland (P<.01). This is not unexpected, considering the findings of other studies regarding attitudinal problems towards SEA in Germany (a different picture, however, arises if only the local level is considered – see further below). While all of the authorities in Noord-Holland considered integration possible, ten authorities in North West England and three authorities in EVR Brandenburg-Berlin felt that this was possible. There were no significant differences between the results for the SEA types and the sectors.

The only two authorities that did not consider an integration of SEA into the PPP process possible were from EVR Brandenburg-Berlin. Two reasons were provided. Firstly, in one case, it was said that only a general development outline was prepared and that SEA could therefore not be applied.[2] Secondly, it was claimed that environmental impacts were already well considered and that formalized SEA was therefore not needed. The introduction of SEA was thought to be rather counterproductive and it was concluded that formal SEA would not improve existing practice.

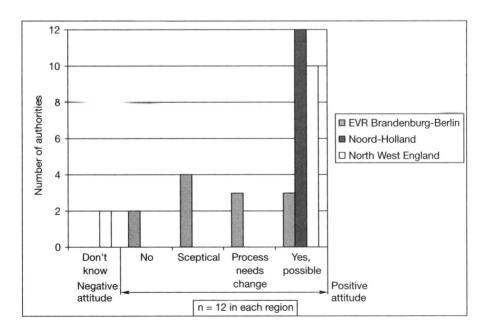

Figure 6.11: *Views on the possibility of integrating formalized SEA into the PPP process*

Some authorities in Noord-Holland responsible for the preparation of regional transport plans considered formalized SEA to be able to simplify current practice as only one assessment would need to be undertaken. For the regional plans in Noord-Holland (*streekplannen*), it was claimed that existing assessments started too late and that formalized SEA provisions were therefore needed.

Regarding the reasons for not having conducted SEA, one authority responsible for the preparation of a statutory land use plan in Noord-Holland said that it attempted to do so, but failed, as environmental objectives and targets were unclear. Furthermore, four authorities in EVR Brandenburg-Berlin were very sceptical as to whether an integration of SEA into the PPP process was possible at all. Two of them said that the preparation process would need to change in order to facilitate SEA application.

There was significant correlation of the view about a possible integration of formalized SEA into the PPP process with SEA preparation times (P<.05). The correlation coefficient was negative, that is longer preparation times were the reason for local authorities to have more negative attitudes towards the possibility of the integration of formalized SEA into the PPP process.

Local land use policies, plans and programmes

All authorities responsible for the preparation of local land use policies, plans and programmes in the three regions thought that, in principle, formalized SEA could be integrated into the existing preparation process. In order to make a final decision, however, the form of SEA would need to be clarified. In North West England and EVR Brandenburg-Berlin, the authorities thought that formalized SEA should be built into the existing assessment instruments of environmental appraisal and landscape plans (*Landschaftspläne*). In Noord-Holland, most of the authorities were convinced that actions proposed in local land use plans would only very rarely have significant impacts to such an extent that SEA would be needed. Consequently, they usually thought that SEA should rather be applied at the level of regional plans (*streekplannen*).

Delay of PPP formulation

Cross-section of PPPs

Figure 6.12 shows the responses of the authorities representing the cross-section of 36 PPPs at all administrative levels to the question 'do you think formal SEA could delay policy, plan or programme preparation?'. Not unexpectedly, perceptions in EVR Brandenburg-Berlin were the most negative (significantly less positive than perceptions in Noord-Holland; P<.05). While six authorities in EVR Brandenburg-Berlin thought that formalized SEA would lead to a delay of PPP preparation, four authorities in North West England and only three authorities in Noord-Holland thought that this was possible.

All of the EVR Brandenburg-Berlin authorities thought that past experience had proven that the introduction of new planning instruments would delay PPP preparation. Two Dutch authorities argued that the planning system

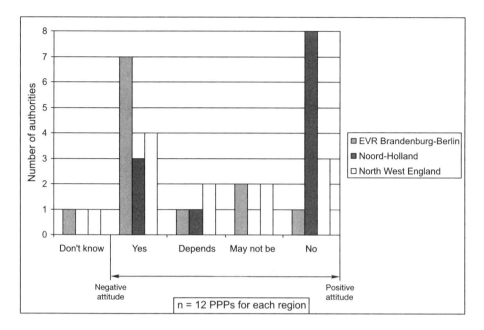

Figure 6.12: *Views on a possible delay of PPP preparation through formalized SEA*

in general was too slow and were sceptical about the introduction of formalized SEA. Some authorities in North West England, on the other hand, argued that the benefits might outweigh the problems connected with formalized SEA application, and that a slight delay would not necessarily be a problem if plan quality were to be improved.

There were no significant differences between the views on possible PPP preparation delays of transport authorities and of spatial/land use authorities. There were, however, significant differences between the attitudes of authorities preparing different SEA types. Those authorities undertaking policy-SEAs had significantly better attitudes than those preparing plan-SEAs (P<.01) and programme-SEAs (P<.01). This is not unexpected, as delays due to NIMBYism (see Chapter 1) is only likely in project-oriented SEA. The expectation that SEA would delay PPP preparation was correlated with the context variable PPP relevance. This could be expected, as PPP with a high relevance included specific projects. The possibility of public opposition was therefore increased. The extent to which current assessments covered SEA procedural stages had a positive impact on the attitudes of authorities, as there was an expectation that existing SEA procedures would need only few changes (P<.05). In particular, those authorities involving the procedural stages of external consultation (P<.01) and SEA report review (P<.05) did not think that formalized SEA would be likely to delay PPP preparation.

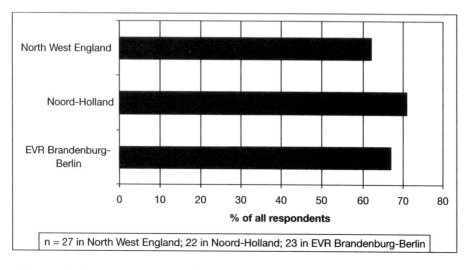

Figure 6.13: *Expectations of local authorities for formalized SEA to delay PPP preparation*

Local land use policies, plans and programmes

Attitudes expressed by authorities responsible for the preparation of local land use PPPs differed from those of the cross-section of 36 PPPs at all administrative levels. Attitudes were most positive in EVR Brandenburg-Berlin and most negative in Noord-Holland (see Figure 6.13). Two main reasons are provided for these differences. Firstly, in EVR Brandenburg-Berlin, there appeared to be a perception that formalized SEA would not change existing practice (the preparation of landscape plans, *Landschaftspläne*) to any great extent. To some extent, this perception is confirmed in Chapter 8, which shows that the SEA (landscape plan, *Landschaftsplan*) for the local Land Use Plan (FNP) Ketzin, meets the requirements of the EC SEA Directive proposal to the largest extent of any of the examined SEAs. The more negative attitudes of local authorities in Noord-Holland appear to have been related to:

- the small size of the geographical areas administered by the local authority; and
- the planning approach (society consensus-led, quasi-top-down).

Local authorities in Noord-Holland usually believed that decisions with significant impacts were all made at higher tiers and that the environmental implications should be dealt with there. SEA application at the local level was therefore not perceived to be useful.[3]

Project acceleration

Cross-section of PPPs

Figure 6.14 shows the responses of interviewed authorities to the question 'do you think formalized SEA would be able to accelerate project preparation?'. Attitudes in Noord-Holland were significantly more positive than in EVR Brandenburg-Berlin (P<.05). While nine authorities in Noord-Holland thought that project acceleration was possible, this opinion was shared by only four authorities in North West England and only three authorities in EVR Brandenburg-Berlin. The only three authorities that explicitly said that SEA would lead to a delay in project preparation were from North West England. All three authorities argued that the same people were responsible for PPP and project preparation and that the introduction of an additional planning instrument would increase the work load of local authorities and therefore delay project preparation. One authority responsible for the preparation of a transport SEA said that depending on the transport mode, projects might be delayed or accelerated.[4] The more positive views in Noord-Holland were probably caused by current experiences in The Netherlands with the application of big-project SEA/EIA to the regional plans (*streekplannen*), which substitute for project-EIA and can therefore indeed lead to project acceleration.

There were no significant differences for transport and spatial/land use SEAs. Furthermore, differences between authorities preparing SEA and authorities not preparing SEA were not significant. While the views of the authorities

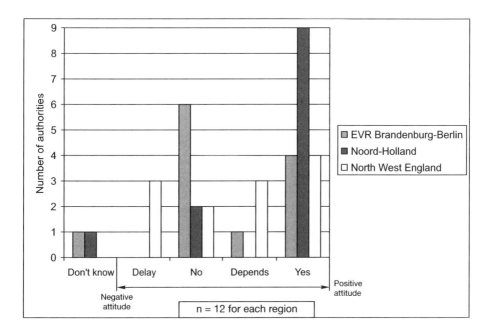

Figure 6.14: *Views on the possibility of accelerating project preparation through formalized SEA*

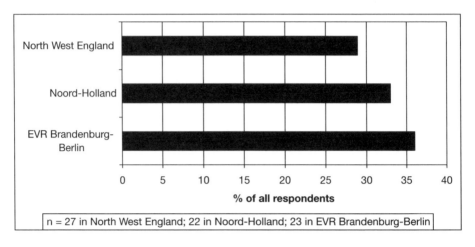

Figure 6.15: *Views of local authorities on the possibility of accelerating project preparation through formalized SEA*

preparing policy-SEAs were more positive than those preparing plan-SEAs and programme-SEAs, the differences failed to be statistically significant.

Local land use PPPs

Local authorities in the three sample regions had similar perceptions on possible project acceleration through the use of SEA (Figure 6.15), with only between 29 per cent and 36 per cent of the local authorities thinking that SEA might be able to lead to project acceleration. While attitudes were slightly better in EVR Brandenburg-Berlin than in the other two regions, such differences were not statistically significant.

Better consideration of environmental impacts

Cross-section of PPPs

Figure 6.16 shows the responses of interviewed authorities to the question 'do you think formalized SEA would lead to a better consideration of environmental impacts?'. Perceptions were most positive in North West England and most negative in EVR Brandenburg-Berlin (P<.05). Three authorities in EVR Brandenburg-Berlin believed that environmental objectives were sufficiently considered and thought that SEA would not have any additional benefits. One authority in Noord-Holland thought that the city regional administrative level was not suitable for SEA application and suggested that suitable levels were national and *Provincie* levels. Another authority preparing a spatial/land use policy-SEA said that current assessments considered environmental aspects sufficiently. One authority responsible for the preparation of an inter-provincial plan said that the consideration of the environment in the National Spatial Plan (VINEX) review was sufficient and that SEA was therefore not required at the inter-provincial level. One authority in the UK believed that the setting of

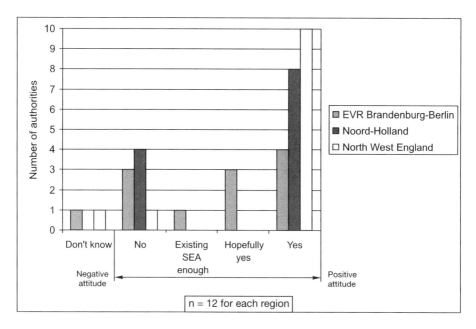

Figure 6.16: *Views on the possibility of formalized SEA leading to a better consideration of environmental concerns*

clear objectives and standards at the regional level would be more important than the application of SEA.

There were no significant differences between the attitudes of authorities of spatial/land use and transport SEAs. While authorities preparing policy-SEAs and plan-SEAs had more positive attitudes than those preparing programme-SEAs, the differences between the SEA types failed to be statistically significant. There were also no significant differences between the attitudes of authorities preparing SEA and those not preparing SEA.

SEA preparation times were significantly correlated with the attitudes of authorities in a negative manner, that is longer preparation times meant that attitudes were more negative (P<.05). This was explained, in particular, by the observed patterns in EVR Brandenburg-Berlin. Furthermore, there was a significant statistical correlation with the context variable PPP relevance (P<.01). Attitudes towards formalized SEA were therefore most positive among decision makers that prepared PPPs with a high relevance. These included, in particular, those North West England authorities preparing development plans.

Local land use PPPs

Figure 6.17 shows the views of the local authorities in the three sample regions about whether formalized SEA would lead to a better consideration of environmental concerns. Local authorities in EVR Brandenburg-Berlin had significantly more positive attitudes than the authorities in North West England (P<.01) and Noord-Holland (P<.01). This most likely reflects the experience

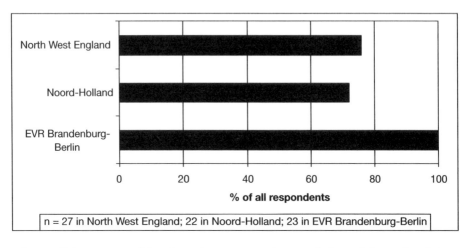

North West England

Noord-Holland

EVR Brandenburg-Berlin

% of all respondents

n = 27 in North West England; 22 in Noord-Holland; 23 in EVR Brandenburg-Berlin

Figure 6.17: *Views of local authorities on the possibility of formalized SEA leading to a better consideration of environmental concerns*

with current SEA practice (landscape plans, *Landschaftspläne*), which is generally perceived to be rather positive.

Overall evaluation of the attitudes of authorities

Individual PPPs

Table 6.2 shows the results of the attitudes of authorities towards formalized SEA for each individual PPP. No overall score is calculated for the Merseyside Package Bid and the Federal Spatial Orientation Framework (ROPOrient), as only one of the four questions was answered.

The highest attitude scores were obtained for six PPPs in Noord-Holland and one in North West England. Low scores of under 50 per cent were obtained for five PPPs in EVR Brandenburg-Berlin and one in Noord-Holland. The highest scores were either obtained by PPPs involving the preparation of policy-SEA or by those that did not involve any SEA at all. Further explanations for the observed patterns are provided below.

Table 6.2: *Overall evaluation of attitudes towards the application of formalized SEA*

Variable PPPs	Integration	No PPP preparation delay	Project acceleration	Better environment	Overall evaluation
Trunk Roads Programme	na	(⇔)	⇔	✓	⊙
North West Transport Strategy	✓	(⇔)	⇔	✗	⊙
Regional Planning Guidance RPG 13	✓	✓	✓	✓	■
Lancashire Structure Plan	✓	✓	✗	✓	●
Cheshire Structure Plan	✓	✗	✓	✓	●

Table 6.2: *Continued*

Variable PPPs	Integration	No PPP preparation delay	Project acceleration	Better environment	Overall evaluation
Trunk Roads Programme	na	(⇔)	⇔	✓	⊙
North West Transport Strategy	✓	(⇔)	⇔	✗	⊙
Regional Planning Guidance RPG 13	✓	✓	✓	✓	■
Lancashire Structure Plan	✓	✓	✗	✓	●
Cheshire Structure Plan	✓	✗	✓	✓	●
Lancashire TPP	✓	✗	✗	✓	⊙
Cheshire TPP	✓	✗	(⇔)	✓	⊙
Merseyside Package Bid	na	na	✓	na	na
Greater Manchester Package Bid	✓	✓	✗	✓	●
Warrington Local Plan	✓	✗	✓	✓	●
Oldham Unitary Development Plan	✓	✗	(⇔)	✓	⊙
Salford Unitary Development Plan	✓	⇔	⇔	✓	●
Second Transport Structure Plan (SVVII)	✓	✓	✓	✓	■
National Spatial Plan (VINEX) review	✓	(⇔)	✓	✓	●
Inter-provincial Urbanization Vision (IPVR)	✓	✗	✓	✗	⊙
Development Vision (*Ontwikkelingsvisie*) Noord-Holland	✓	✓	na	✗	⊙
Regional Plans (*Streekplannen*)	✓	✓	✓	✓	■
Integrated Transport Vision Randstad North (INVERNO)	✓	✓	✓	✓	■
Transport Plan (RVVP) Noord-Holland-Nord	✓	✓	✓	✓	■
Structure Plan (*Structuurplan*) ROA	✓	✓	✓	✓	■
Transport Plan (RVVP) ROA	✓	✗	⇔	✗	○
Structure Plan (*Structuurplan*) Amsterdam	✓	✗	⇔	✓	⊙
Future Vision (*Toekomstvisie*) Hilversum	✓	✓	✓	✗	●
Transport Plan (RVVP) Haarlem-IJmond	✓	✓	✓	✓	■

Table 6.2: *Continued*

Variable PPPs	Integration	No PPP preparation delay	Project acceleration	Better environment	Overall evaluation
Federal Transport Infrastructure Plan (BVWP)	(⇔)	×	(⇔)	⇔	○
Spatial Orientation Framework (RopOrient)	×	na	na	na	na
Land Development Programme (LEPro)	⇔	⇔	(⇔)	×	○
Land Development Plan EVR Brb (LEPeV)	⇔	×	⇔	⇔	◉
Regional Plan (*Regionalplan*) Havelland-Flaming	(⇔)	×	✓	✓	◉
Development Concept (*Kreisentwicklungskonzept*) Hav.	(⇔)	(⇔)	✓	⇔	◉
Road Development Plan (*Landesstraßenplan*) Brb.	✓	×	✓	⇔	◉
Integrated Transport Plan (IVP) Brandenburg	✓	⇔	✓	✓	●
Local Land Use Plan (FNP) Berlin	×	×	(⇔)	(⇔)	□
City Development Plan (StEP) Transport Berlin	(⇔)	✓	(⇔)	×	○
District Development Plan (*Bereichsplan*) Charlot'burg	⇔	×	(⇔)	×	○
Local Land Use Plan (FNP) Ketzin	✓	×	(⇔)	✓	◉

☐ policy-SEA   ☐ plan-SEA   ☐ programme-SEA   ▨ no SEA

Criteria scores:
✓   = positive (scores 3)
⇔   = hopeful that effect is positive (scores 2)
(⇔)   = not sure/maybe (scores 1)
×   = negative (scores 0)

Overall evaluation (on the basis of criteria scores):
■   = 100%
●   = 75% to under 100%
◉   = 50% to under 75%
○   = 25% to under 50%
□   = 0% to under 25%

Regions, SEA types, sectors and general SEA application

Figure 6.18 shows the overall scores for the regions, SEA types, sectors and general SEA application. EVR Brandenburg-Berlin authorities had significantly

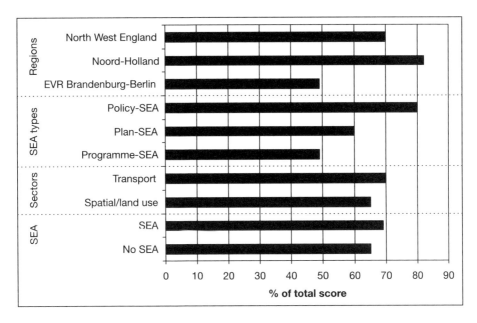

Figure 6.18: *Overall scores for attitudes towards formalized SEA by region, SEA type, sector, and PPPs with and without SEA*

more negative attitudes than the authorities in Noord-Holland (P<.01) and North West England (P<.05). The attitudes of the Noord-Holland authorities were the most positive. There were no significant differences between the attitudes of authorities preparing SEA and those not preparing SEA. The attitudes of authorities preparing policy-SEAs, however, were significantly more positive than those preparing plan-SEAs (P<.05) and programme-SEAs (P<.05). Differences were particularly evident for a possible delay of PPP preparation, caused by the application of formalized SEA. While authorities with policy-SEAs thought that formalized SEA would not delay PPP making, authorities with programme SEAs had comparatively negative attitudes.

The observed patterns are most likely explained by a more positive experience with SEA in The Netherlands, where big-project SEA/EIA is currently applied to regional plans (*streekplannen*), substituting for project-EIA. Furthermore, the attitudes of authorities responsible for the preparation of policy-SEAs were more positive than those of the other SEA types. They are furthest away from project implementation and opposition appears to be less likely, in other words the likelihood of NIMBYism is reduced (see Chapter 1).

Local authorities

Postal questionnaire results suggest that attitudes at the local level were the most positive in EVR Brandenburg-Berlin and the most negative in Noord-Holland (P<.01). This is most likely explained by the application of current SEA in the form of landscape plans (*Landschaftspläne*) at the local level in EVR Brandenburg-Berlin, which are potentially fulfilling requirements of the

EC SEA Directive to a large extent (see also Chapter 8). Expectations are that current practice will not result in too many changes. Negative attitudes at the local level in Noord-Holland are most likely explained by a perception within authorities that SEA should not be applied at the local level but at higher tiers, where the 'real' impacts occur.

SUMMARY

Opinions on the influence of existing SEA in PPP making were significantly more negative in North West England than in Noord-Holland and in EVR Brandenburg-Berlin. This was explained by SEA preparation times, which were usually less than a person-year in North West England and more than a person-year in the other two regions. Furthermore, the status of the SEA appears to have had an impact, as statutory SEAs were said to have been of greater influence than non-statutory SEAs. Regarding the opinions on the quality of current SEA, while there were no significant differences between the three regions, the quality of current transport SEAs was said to have been significantly better than those of spatial/land use SEAs. Local authorities had similar opinions on the quality and influence of SEAs in North West England and EVR Brandenburg-Berlin. As only one SEA was undertaken at the local level in Noord-Holland, this region could not be considered.

Opinions were significantly correlated with the extent to which methods and techniques were used, SEA procedural stages were covered and impacts were assessed in a quantitative manner. Furthermore, longer SEA preparation times meant that the opinions on current SEA were more positive.

Regarding the attitudes towards formalized SEA, it was found that while a majority of authorities considered an integration of formalized SEA possible, there was widespread fear that it would also lead to a delay of policy, plan and programme preparation. The attitudes of authorities for the cross-section of 36 PPPs at all administrative levels were, on average, the most negative in EVR Brandenburg-Berlin and the most positive in Noord-Holland. The attitudes of local authorities tended to be different from those of authorities representing a cross-section of PPPs at all administrative levels. The authorities in EVR Brandenburg-Berlin were the most positive, while they were the most negative in Noord-Holland. This is most likely explained by the experience with local-level SEA which is most extensive in EVR Brandenburg-Berlin (in the form of landscape plans, *Landschaftspläne*) and least extensive in Noord-Holland.

While there was no significant correlation between current SEA practice and attitudes towards formalized SEA, attitudes were to some extent correlated with SEA preparation times. Thus, longer preparation times were usually accompanied by more negative attitudes. Authorities undertaking policy-SEAs and authorities undertaking SEA with an extensive coverage of procedural stages tended to have more positive attitudes towards formalized SEA than authorities that did not. This is explained by a perception that the introduction of formalized SEA will not change current practice to any large extent.

Chapter 7

The Consideration of Sustainability Aspects

Chapter 7 refers to objective 4 of the book and identifies whether SEA application leads to a better consideration of sustainability objectives, targets and measures. In this context, the framework provided in Chapter 2 is used and reference is made to the Fifth Environmental Action Programme of the EC (1993a). Interview results are presented for the cross-section of 36 PPPs at all administrative levels, and postal questionnaire results are presented for local land use PPPs. This chapter is divided into six sections. The first provides an overall picture of the extent to which sustainability aspects were considered in the PPPs and the influence of SEA in this context. The next three describe and analyse the consideration of sustainability objectives, targets and measures in further detail. The results are evaluated in and the fourth section, and overall sustainability scores identified. Finally, the results of the chapter are summarized.

OVERALL PICTURE

This section provides an overall picture of the consideration of sustainability aspects and the influence of SEA. The results for all of the PPPs are presented and regional characteristics are portrayed.

All PPPs

Figure 7.1 shows the consideration of sustainability objectives[1], targets[2] and measures[3] for the cross-section of 36 PPPs at all administrative levels in the three sample regions with and without SEA application. While SEA was not able to lead to a better consideration of objectives and targets, the consideration of sustainability measures was significantly better in PPPs with SEA ($P<.05$). Objectives were acknowledged to a comparatively large extent (80 per cent), either explicitly or implicitly.[4] Targets and measures were considered considerably less (under 50 per cent). Explicit targets were only considered to a small extent.

The results for local land use PPPs in the three regions differed from the results for the cross-section of 36 PPPs at all administrative levels (Figure 7.2). SEA preparation led to a significantly better consideration of sustainability objectives[5], targets[6] and measures[7] ($P<.01$). Objectives, targets and measures were, however, not considered to the same extent. While objectives were considered

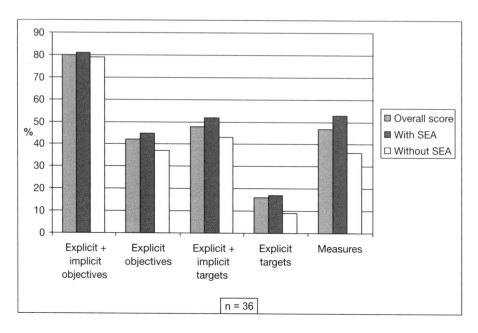

Figure 7.1: *Sustainability aspects in the cross-section of PPPs*

to the largest extent, measures were considered to the least extent. In order to meet the principles of sustainable development, PPP formulation processes

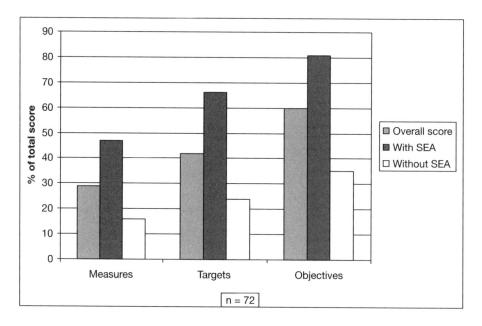

Figure 7.2: *Sustainability aspects in local land use PPPs with and without SEA*

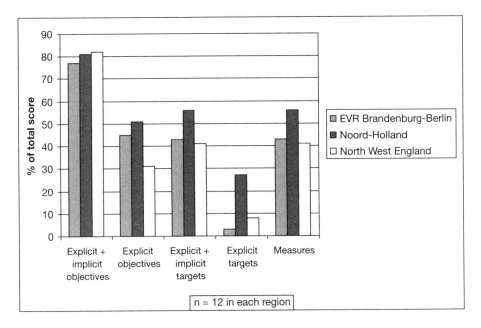

Figure 7.3: *Explicit objectives, explicit targets and measures by region*

should, however, have considered sustainability objectives, targets and measures equally (see Figure 1.1).

Regional patterns

Figure 7.3 shows the extent to which sustainability objectives, targets and measures were explicitly considered within the cross-section of 36 PPPs at all administrative levels in the three sample regions (following interview results). In Noord-Holland, PPPs obtained the highest regional scores for all three sustainability aspects. Explicit targets were considered to a significantly larger extent in Noord-Holland than in EVR Brandenburg-Berlin (P<.05).

Figure 7.4 shows the extent to which objectives, targets and measures were considered in local land use PPPs. In contrast to the cross-section of 36 PPPs at all administrative levels, the largest numbers of objectives, targets and measures were proposed in EVR Brandenburg-Berlin and the smallest numbers in Noord-Holland. In EVR Brandenburg-Berlin, PPPs considered all three sustainability aspects to a significantly larger extent than those in Noord-Holland (P<.01), and targets were considered to a significantly larger extent than those in North West England (P<.01). North West England PPPs considered explicit objectives and measures to a significantly larger extent than those in Noord-Holland (P<.01).

Subsequent sections discuss the consideration of sustainability objectives, targets and measures in further detail. The results are presented in general terms and for PPPs with and without SEA. Furthermore, the results for three presentation aspects are portrayed: the regions, SEA types and sectors.

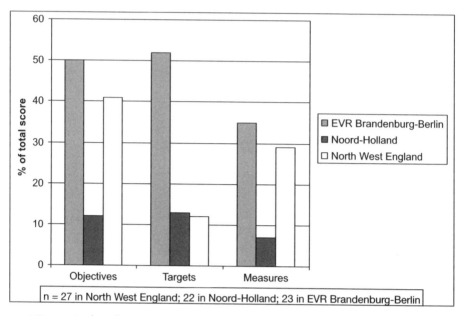

Figure 7.4: *Objectives, targets and measures in local land use PPPs*

SUSTAINABILITY OBJECTIVES

This section describes, analyses and discusses the consideration of sustainability objectives in PPPs and the role of SEA in the three sample regions. It firstly deals with the cross-section of 36 PPPs at all administrative levels (interview results). Secondly, the results for local land use PPPs are presented (postal questionnaire results).

Cross-section of PPPs

Figure 7.5 shows the total number of objectives considered in each PPP. Sixteen of them considered all of the objectives, either explicitly or implicitly, and only the National Spatial Plan (VINEX) review considered all seven objectives explicitly.

Explicit objectives were considered to the largest extent in Noord-Holland (3.6 per case) and to a large extent in EVR Brandenburg-Berlin (3.2 per case). They were considered to the smallest extent in North West England (2.2 per case). Three cases did not consider any explicit objectives at all, namely the North West Transport Strategy, the Cheshire TPP and the Structure Plan (*Structuurplan*) ROA. Of these three, only the Cheshire TPP involved SEA preparation. The extent to which objectives were explicitly considered in PPPs was significantly correlated with two of the SEA variables, the extent to which procedural stages were covered in SEA (P<.05) and the extent to which impacts were assessed in a quantitative manner (P<.05).

Figure 7.6 shows the extent to which individual sustainability objectives were either explicitly considered, or not considered at all, in the three sample

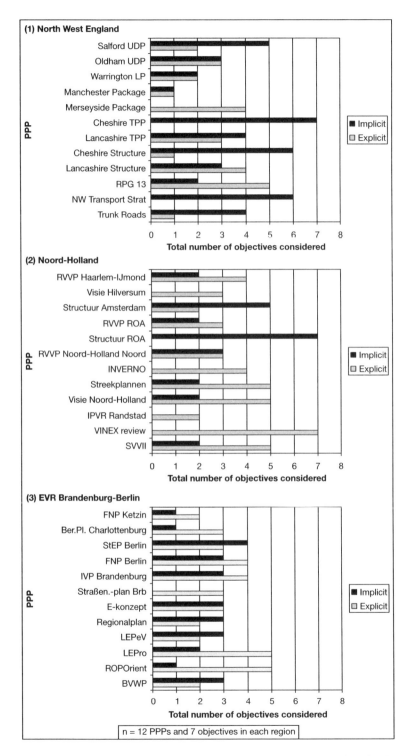

Figure 7.5: *Sustainability objectives considered in the individual PPP*

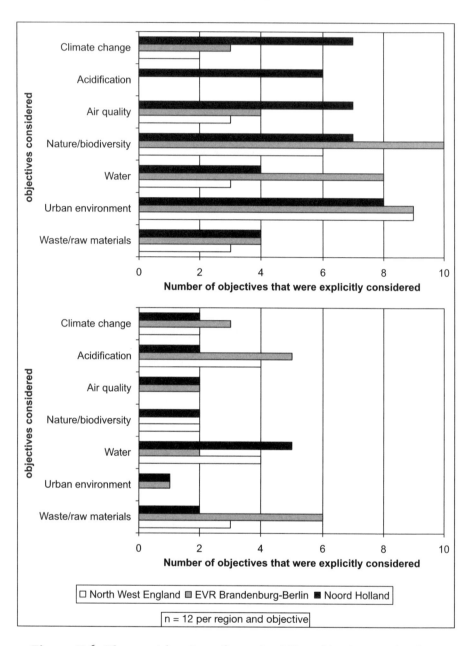

Figure 7.6: *The consideration of sustainability objectives in the three sample regions*

regions. For those PPPs that were not included in either category, authorities said that objectives were implicitly considered. Nature/biodiversity and the urban environment were those objectives that were considered to the largest extent in the three regions and waste/raw material consumption was comparatively poorly considered. In Noord-Holland, PPPs considered climate change

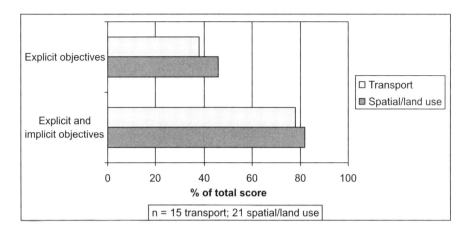

Figure 7.7: *Sustainability objectives considered in the two sectors*

(P<.05) and acidification (P<.01) to a significantly larger extent than those in North West England. Acidification was also considered to a considerably larger extent in Noord-Holland than in EVR Brandenburg-Berlin (P<.01). The extensive consideration of these two objectives in Noord-Holland is explained by the comparatively large number of transport policy-SEAs, taking a more global perspective on impacts. Water was considered to a significantly larger extent in EVR Brandenburg-Berlin than in North West England (P<.05). This was caused by the obligatory consideration of water in EVR Brandenburg-Berlin landscape plans (*Landschaftspläne*).

Figure 7.7 shows that the objectives were considered to a slightly larger extent in the spatial/land use sector than in the transport sector. Differences were, however, not statistically significant. The average numbers of all objectives (explicit and implicit) considered in transport and spatial/land use PPPs varied between 5.4 and 5.7 in Noord-Holland and EVR Brandenburg-Berlin. In North West England, PPPs in the spatial/land use sector considered objectives to a larger extent than those in the transport sector. On average, 6.5 objectives were considered in the spatial/land use sector and 5.1 objectives were considered in the transport sector.

Individual objectives were considered to varying extents in transport and spatial/land use PPPs. Only the objective, urban environment was considered to a similar extent in both sectors. Three explicit objectives were predominantly considered in transport PPPs, namely, climate change (P<.01), acidification (P<.05) and air quality (P<.05). This is mainly explained by the comparatively large number of transport policy-SEAs. While 8 of the 13 transport SEAs were policy-SEAs, only 2 of 12 spatial/land use SEAs were policy-SEAs. Those objectives that were significantly more frequently considered in the spatial/land use sector than in the transport sector include, nature and biodiversity (P<.01) and water (P<.01).

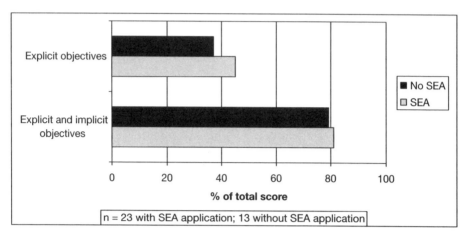

Figure 7.8: *Sustainability objectives and SEA application*

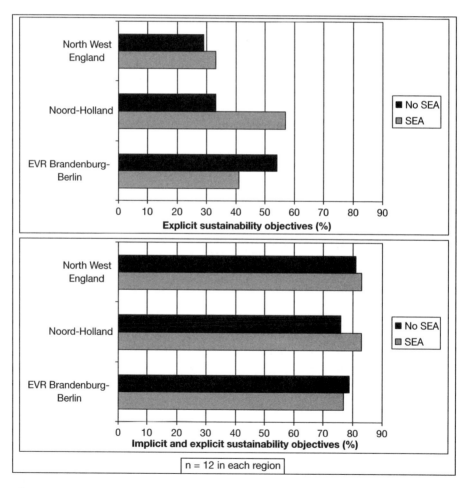

Figure 7.9: *Sustainability objectives and SEA application per sample region*

SEA application

Figure 7.8 shows the extent to which sustainability objectives were considered in PPPs with and without SEA. While SEA led to the consideration of slightly more objectives, differences were not statistically significant. For one individual objective, PPPs with SEA obtained a significantly higher score, namely, for acidification ($P<.05$). This is mainly due to the frequent consideration of this objective in policy-SEA.

Figure 7.9 shows the regional differences of PPPs with and without SEA. While in North West England and Noord-Holland, SEA application led to a slightly better consideration of sustainability objectives, in EVR Brandenburg-Berlin, PPPs that did not involve SEA considered more sustainability objectives than those with SEA. Differences were, however, not statistically significant. Two cases without SEA are mainly responsible for the rather unexpected finding in EVR Brandenburg-Berlin, namely the National Spatial Orientation Framework (*Raumordnungspolitischer Orientierungsrahmen,* ROPOrient) and the Land Development Programme (LEPro) Brandenburg. These two cases considered the largest numbers of explicit objectives of any case in EVR Brandenburg-Berlin. Both cases were policy statements at the *Land* level,

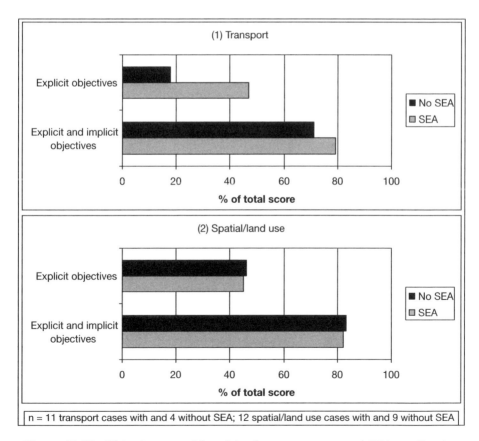

Figure 7.10: *Objectives considered in the two sectors and SEA application*

providing lower tiers with development objectives, including environmental/ sustainability objectives.

If a distinction is made between the two sectors (Figure 7.10), it can be seen that SEA application in the transport sector led to a significantly better consideration of explicit objectives (P<.05). Spatial/land use PPPs with SEA scored slightly lower than those without SEA. This is mainly explained by the two EVR Brandenburg-Berlin cases that did not involve SEA, but that scored highly on the consideration of explicit objectives (see also previous section). Differences, however, failed to be statistically significant.

SEA types

Figure 7.11 compares the consideration of sustainability objectives in PPPs involving the three SEA types and those not involving SEA at all. Policy-SEA clearly led to higher scores on explicit objectives and differences were statistically significant between policy-SEAs and plan-SEAs (P<.01). Policy-SEAs scored significantly better than plan-SEAs on three objectives, namely, climate change (P<.01), acidification (P<.01) and air quality (P<.05). For nature and biodiversity, plan-SEAs scored significantly better than policy-SEAs (P<.05). Policy-SEAs scored significantly better than PPPs without SEA on climate (P<.01) and acidification (P<.01). The comparatively high effectiveness of policy-SEA for leading to a better consideration of explicit objectives is explained by its early application in the planning cycle. This allows for the consideration of a wide range of alternatives and a large number of objectives. As projects usually cannot be clearly located, authorities do not need to fear public opposition due to NIMBYism (see Chapter 1).

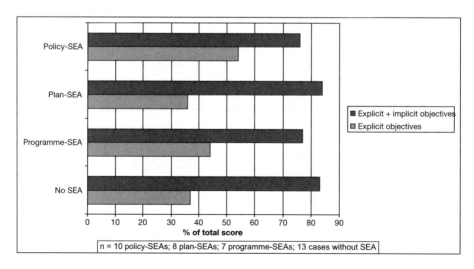

Figure 7.11: *SEA types and the consideration of sustainability objectives*

Local land use PPPs

General remarks

Figure 7.12 shows the extent to which sustainability objectives were considered in local land use PPPs in the three sample regions (postal questionnaire results). General and transport-specific objectives were distinguished in order to illustrate the importance of considering land use PPPs when dealing with transport infrastructure planning.

In contrast to the findings for the cross-section of 36 PPPs at all administrative levels, on average, more sustainability objectives were considered in EVR Brandenburg-Berlin and North West England than in Noord-Holland. There are two main reasons for the differences between the two sets, namely a different extent of SEA application in the three regions and different planning approaches. While only 1 SEA was undertaken for 22 cases at the local level in Noord-Holland, 13 of the 27 cases in North West England and 21 of the 23 cases in EVR Brandenburg-Berlin involved SEA preparation (environmental appraisals and landscape plans, *Landschaftspläne*; see subsequent paragraph on SEA application). In The Netherlands, policy objectives were identified at higher tiers[8], and were to be considered at all other decision making levels. Local land use PPPs therefore considered environmental objectives only indirectly through national, provincial and regional policy.

In contrast to the other two regions in Noord-Holland, new development areas with significant impacts on the environment were mostly proposed and assessed either at national or at regional levels of decision making. Local authorities in North West England and EVR Brandenburg-Berlin on average identified and considered objectives more actively and explicitly than local authorities in Noord-Holland, and SEA application led to a better consideration of sustainability objectives.

Nature and biodiversity, and the urban environment were the two objectives that were most frequently considered in local land use PPPs. As a general objective, nature and biodiversity was considered in all local land use PPPs in EVR Brandenburg-Berlin (mainly through the landscape plans, *Landschaftspläne*). The urban environment was the most frequently mentioned transport-specific objective. All general objectives were considered to a significantly larger extent in EVR Brandenburg-Berlin and in North West England than in Noord-Holland (P<.01). Regarding transport-specific objectives, the objectives of nature and biodiversity (P<.01) and air quality (P<.05) were significantly more frequently considered in EVR Brandenburg-Berlin than in Noord-Holland, which is explained by the consistent use of landscape plans and programmes (*Landschaftspläne und -programme*).

SEA application

SEA application had a positive effect on the extent to which sustainability objectives were considered in local land use PPPs (Figure 7.13). All four objectives were considered to a significantly larger extents in cases with SEA than in cases without SEA (P<.01). The only region that allowed the differences to

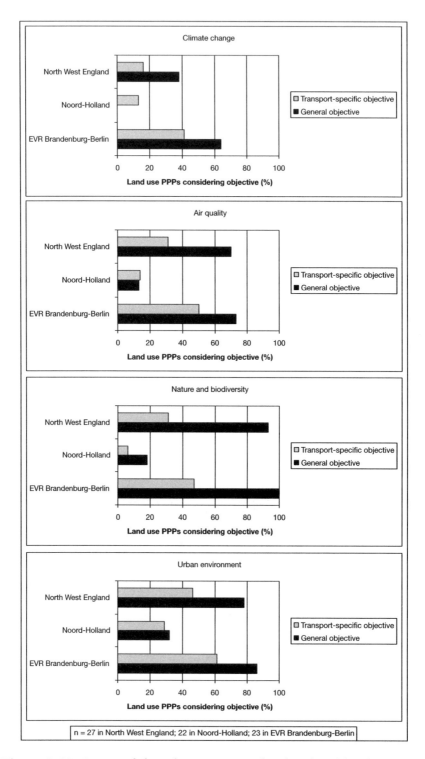

Figure 7.12: *Sustainability objectives considered in local land use PPPs*

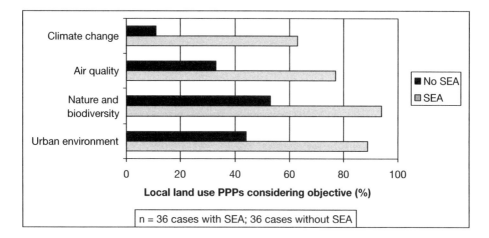

Figure 7.13: *SEA application and the consideration of sustainability objectives in local land use PPPs*

be compared was North West England, as 13 of 27 cases involved SEA preparation (as opposed to 21 of 23 in EVR Brandenburg-Berlin and 1 of 22 in Noord-Holland). It was found that SEA application led to a significantly better consideration of sustainability objectives in local land use PPPs in North West England (P<.01).

SUSTAINABILITY TARGETS

This section describes and analyses the consideration of sustainability targets in the three sample regions. Similarly to the previous section on sustainability objectives, it deals separately with the cross-section of 36 PPPs at all administrative levels (interview results) and with local land use PPPs (postal questionnaire results).

Cross-section of PPPs

General remarks

Figure 7.14 shows the total number of targets considered in each PPP in the three sample regions. The maximum possible number to be considered were five targets. Sixteen (70 per cent) of the total number of 23 explicit targets that were considered in all PPPs were from Noord-Holland. While 1.3 targets were on average explicitly considered in each PPP in Noord-Holland, this figure fell to 0.4 targets in North West England and to 0.2 targets in EVR Brandenburg-Berlin. Regional differences were significant for explicit targets between Noord-Holland and EVR Brandenburg-Berlin (P<.05).

As well as the five targets proposed in the Fifth Environmental Action Programme, a number of other targets were also considered in the three sample regions. The most frequently mentioned targets included:

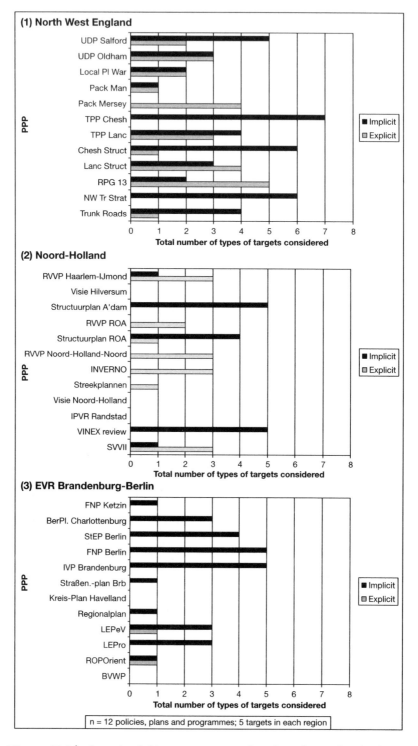

Figure 7.14: *Sustainability targets considered in the individual PPP*

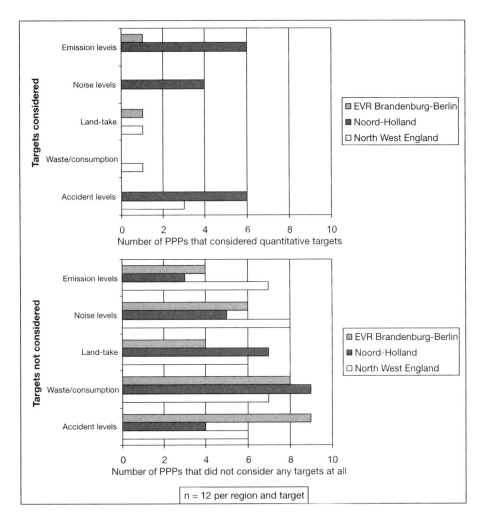

Figure 7.15: *The consideration of sustainability targets by region*

- Reducing mobility and road traffic growth.
- 'Improving' ratios of public and private transport (changing the modal split).
- Better safety standards.
- Greater punctuality of trains and faster trains.
- Higher car occupancies.
- Reduction of congestion.
- Public transport growth.

Figure 7.15 presents PPPs in each sample region that either considered targets explicitly or not at all. Those that were not included in either category said that targets were implicitly considered. In Noord-Holland, PPPs considered emissions and noise targets to a significant larger extent than those in North

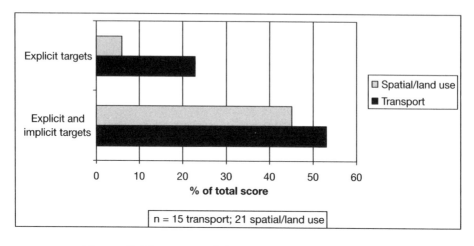

Figure 7.16: *Sustainability targets in the two sectors*

West England (P<.01 and P<.05, respectively) and in EVR Brandenburg-Berlin (P<.05 in both cases). Furthermore, accident levels were considered to a significantly larger extent in Noord-Holland than in EVR Brandenburg-Berlin (P<.01).

Differences are mainly explained by the larger extent to which policy-SEA was applied in Noord-Holland, allowing the consideration of a wider range of issues (see also Chapter 8). In Noord-Holland, in contrast to the other regions, clear targets were defined in the environmental policy plans (*milieubeleidsplannen*) that were prepared at all administrative levels. Figure 7.16 shows the overall extent to which targets were considered in both sectors. While the extent to which all targets (explicit and implicit) were considered was similar for both sectors, explicit targets were considered to a significantly larger extent in the transport sector (P<.05). This is particularly explained by

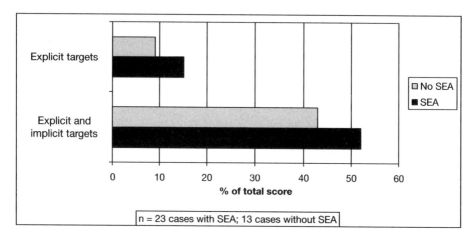

Figure 7.17: *Sustainability targets and SEA application*

the large extent to which accident and noise targets were considered in the transport sector.

SEA application

Figure 7.17 shows the extent to which targets were considered in PPPs with and without SEA. While SEA led to the consideration of more objectives on both occasions, differences failed to be statistically significant.

Figure 7.18 shows the influence SEA had on the consideration of sustainability targets in the three sample regions. While in North West England and in Noord-Holland, SEA application led to a better consideration of sustainability targets, in EVR Brandenburg-Berlin, policies, plans and programmes without SEA obtained higher scores than those with SEA. This is mainly due to a good performance of two cases that did not involve SEA preparation, namely the Land Development Programme (LEPro) Brandenburg and the Land Devel-

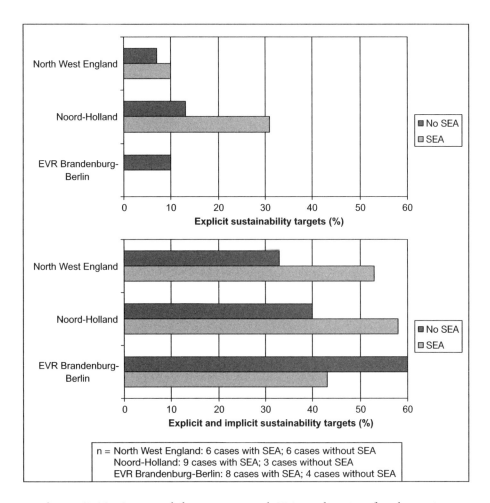

Figure 7.18: *Sustainability targets and SEA application for the regions*

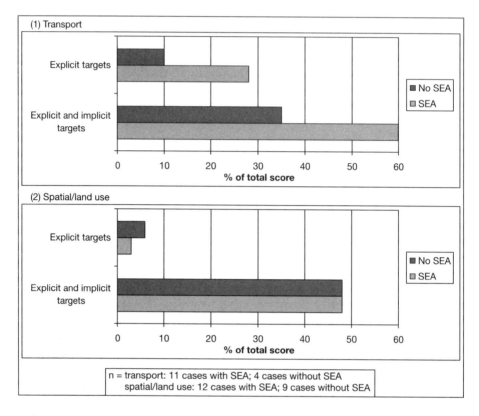

Figure 7.19: *Sustainability targets in the two sectors and SEA application*

opment Plan (*Landesentwicklungsplan*) EVR Brandenburg-Berlin. Differences, however, failed to be statistically significant.

Figure 7.19 shows the extent to which sustainability targets were considered in spatial/land use and transport PPPs with and without SEA. While SEA in the transport sector had a positive effect on the consideration of sustainability targets, those spatial/land use PPPs that did not involve SEA preparation scored slightly higher than those with SEA. Differences were, however, not statistically significant. The observed patterns are explained firstly by the more extensive use of policy-SEA in the transport sector, particularly in The Netherlands (due to the requirements formulated in the Second Transport Structure Plan). Secondly, spatial/land use PPPs without SEA in EVR Brandenburg-Berlin scored comparatively highly. This is caused by two cases, namely the Land Development Programme (*Landesentwicklungsprogramm,* LEPro) and the Land Development Plan (*Landesentwicklungsplan,* LEP) EVR Brandenburg-Berlin, both of which identify policies and provide different possibilities for development.

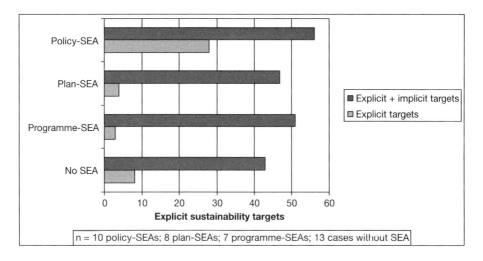

Figure 7.20: *Sustainability targets and SEA types*

SEA types

There was no significant correlation between any of the five individual targets and the general application of SEA. Regarding SEA types (Figure 7.20), policy-SEAs considered explicit targets to a significantly larger extent than programme-SEAs (P<.05). Furthermore, policy-SEAs considered a number of individual targets to a larger extent than plan-SEAs, namely emissions (P<.01), noise (P<.05) and accidents (P<.05). Policy-SEAs also considered a significantly larger number of noise targets than PPPs without SEA (P<.01).

Fifth Environmental Action Programme reduction targets

Table 7.1 shows the PPPs that considered sustainability targets in a quantitative manner that were at least as strict as those introduced in the Fifth Environmental Action Programme.

With the exception of two cases, namely the Federal Spatial Orientation Framework (*Raumordnungspolitischer Orientierungsrahmen,* ROPOrient) and the Regional Development Plan (LEPeV) EVR Brandenburg-Berlin, all of the PPPs were from Noord-Holland. In this region, the Second Transport Structure Plan (SVVII) was frequently mentioned as the document from which targets were taken, reflecting the planning approach in The Netherlands (society consensus-led, quasi-top-down). None of the 36 PPPs considered all of the targets formulated in the Fifth Environmental Action Programme. None of them therefore met all of the requirements. Noord-Holland transport policies, however, addressed a comparatively wide range of sustainability targets, mainly for its widespread application of policy-SEA. Some authorities also said that reduction targets of the Fifth Environmental Action Programme were implicitly considered (Table 7.2). Implicit targets were considered in 16 PPPs (including 14 in the transport sector), all of which were from Noord-Holland.

Table 7.1: *Reduction targets of the Fifth Environmental Action Programme considered in PPPs*

Target type	Reduction target	Target acknowledged by
Emission levels	CO_2	• Second Transport Structure Plan, SVVII • Regional Plans (*streekplannen*) Noord-Holland (SVVII target) • Transport Plan INVERNO (regional target) • RVVP Transport Plan Noord-Holland Noord (SVVII target) • RVVP Transport Plan ROA (regional target) • RVVP Transport Plan Haarlem-IJmond (INVERNO target) • Spatial Orientation Framework (ROPOrient)
	NO_x	• Second Transport Structure Plan, SVVII • Transport Plan INVERNO (regional target) • RVVP Transport Plan Noord-Holland Noord (SVVII target) • RVVP Transport Plan ROA (regional target) • RVVP Transport Plan Haarlem-IJmond (INVERNO target)
	VOC	–
	SO_2	• RVVP ROA (regional target)
Noise levels	55 dB(A) to 65 dB (A): no increase; < 55 dB(A): not over 55 dB(A)	• Second Transport Structure Plan, SVVII • Transport Plan INVERNO (regional target) • RVVP Transport Plan Noord-Holland Noord (SVVII target) • RVVP Transport Plan Haarlem-IJmond (INVERNO target)
Land-take	maintenance	• Regional Development Plan (LEP) EVR, no decrease of forested areas: 40% share of total area

Local land use PPPs

General remarks

Targets within local land use PPPs were usually considered rather qualitatively, including, for example, a general intention to reduce certain emissions. Furthermore, a number of restrictions were included, such as the use of a certain proportion of brownfield sites or the location of transport infrastructure at certain distances away from residential or protection areas. SEAs in EVR Brandenburg-Berlin (landscape plans, *Landschaftspläne*) proposed compensation for expected land use impacts (according to the Federal Environment Protection Act, *Bundesnaturschutzgesetz*).

Figure 7.21 portrays the extent to which local land use PPPs considered emission and land use targets in a general and in a transport-specific manner. Significantly more general and transport-specific targets were considered in EVR Brandenburg-Berlin than in the other two regions (P<.01). This is explained

Table 7.2: *Implicit consideration of targets from the Fifth Environmental Action Programme*

Targets	PPPs
Emission targets:	• National Spatial Plan (VINEX) review (NMP target)*
	• Structure Plan (*structuurplan*) ROA (NMP target)
	• Structure Plan (*structuurplan*) Amsterdam
Noise targets:	• National Spatial Plan (VINEX) review
	• Structure Plan (*structuurplan*) ROA
	• Structure Plan (*structuurplan*) Amsterdam
Land-take targets:	• National Transport Structure Plan, SVVII
	• National Spatial Plan (VINEX) review
	• Structure Plan (*structuurplan*) ROA
	• Structure Plan (*structuurplan*) Amsterdam
	• RVVP Transport Plan Haarlem-IJmond
Waste/consumption targets:	• National Spatial Plan (VINEX) review
	• Structure Plan (*structuurplan*) ROA
	• Structure Plan (*structuurplan*) Amsterdam

Note: * National Environment Policy Plan, *nationaal milieubeleidsplan,* NMP.

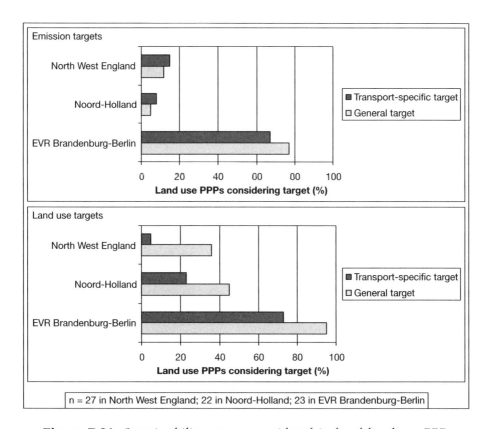

Figure 7.21: *Sustainability targets considered in local land use PPPs*

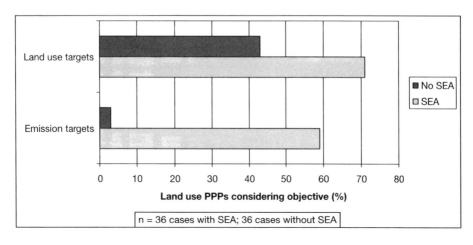

Figure 7.22: *SEA application and the consideration of sustainability targets in local land use PPPs*

mainly by the larger extent of SEA application in EVR Brandenburg-Berlin. Furthermore, it was found that in North West England, SEA led to the consideration of significantly more emission targets (P<.05).

SEA application

Figure 7.22 portrays the influence of SEA on the extent to which sustainability targets were considered in local land use PPPs. SEA was indeed able to improve performance and there was significant correlation for SEA with both emission targets (P<.01) and land use targets (P<.05).

MEASURES FOR SUSTAINABILITY

This section describes and analyses the measures proposed in PPPs in order to meet previously defined sustainability objectives and targets. Similar to the previous sections, it deals firstly with the cross-section of 36 PPPs at all administrative levels (interview results) and secondly with local land use PPPs (postal questionnaire results).

Cross-section of PPPs

General remarks

Figure 7.23 shows the total numbers of measures proposed in the cross-section of 36 PPPs at all administrative levels. Two considered all eight measures, namely the Integrated Transport Plan (IVP) Brandenburg and the Second Transport Structure Plan (SVVII), both of which were policy-SEAs. Seven measures were proposed in the Integrated Transport Plan INVERNO. On average, 4.5 measures were proposed in Noord-Holland, 3.4 measures in EVR

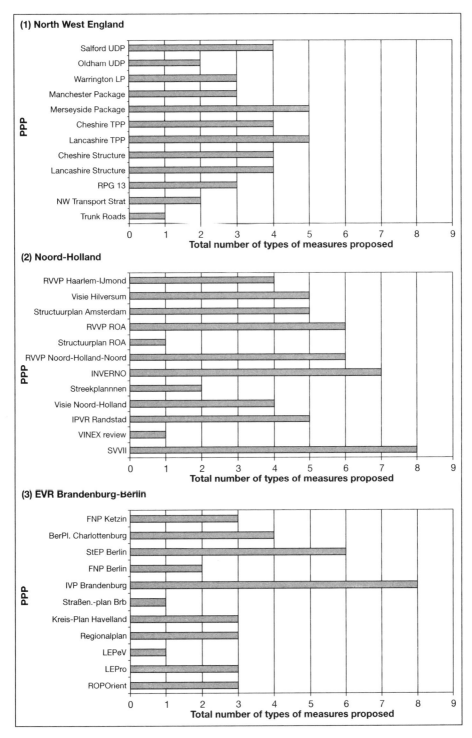

Figure 7.23: *Sustainability measures considered in the individual PPP*

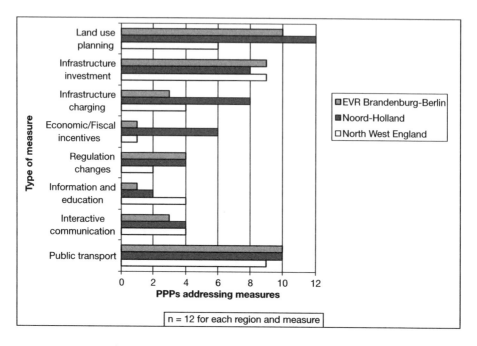

Figure 7.24: *The consideration of sustainability measures in the cross-section of PPPs*

Brandenburg-Berlin and 3.3 measures in North West England (of the total maximum number of 8 measures).

Figure 7.24 shows the number of individual sustainability measures considered in each of the three sample regions. Out of a total possible number of 96 measures (12 PPPs and 8 possible measures for each region), 54 were set in Noord-Holland, 42 in EVR Brandenburg-Berlin and 39 in North West England. Public transport was the measure that was most frequently considered, namely in 29 of the 36 PPPs, including 10 in each of Noord-Holland and EVR Brandenburg-Berlin and 9 in North West England. Public transport included measures on service, infrastructure and fares. Furthermore, land use planning and infrastructure investment were frequently considered.

PPPs in Noord-Holland considered land use planning (P<.01) and economic incentives (P<.05) to a significantly larger extent than those in North West England. PPPs in Noord-Holland also considered infrastructure charging (P<.05) and economic incentives (P<.05) to a significantly greater extent than those in EVR Brandenburg-Berlin. The main reason for the better performance in Noord-Holland was the large extent of policy-SEA application and the consideration of environmental policy plans (NMPs) at all administrative levels.

Figure 7.25 shows the consideration of measures in spatial/land use and transport PPPs. On average, in the transport sector significantly more sustainability measures were considered than in the spatial/land use sector (P<.05). Three sustainability measures were considered to a significantly greater extent in the transport sector than in the spatial/land use sector, namely,

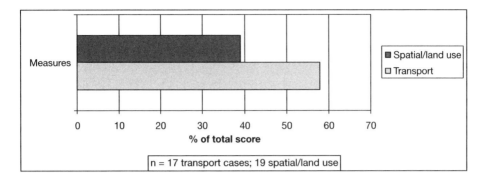

Figure 7.25: *Sustainability measures by sector*

interactive communication (P<.01), infrastructure investment (P<.01) and infrastructure charging (P<.01). This could be expected, as all three measures are clearly transport related. Land use planning (P<.01), on the other hand, was considered to a significantly greater extent in spatial/land use PPPs.

SEA application

Figure 7.26 shows the extent to which sustainability measures were considered according to whether SEA was conducted. PPPs with SEA considered significantly more measures than those without SEA (P<.05). This is partially explained by a more extensive consideration of sustainability measures in policy-SEAs. Those measures that were considered to a significantly greater extent in PPPs with SEA include, infrastructure charging (P<.05) and economic/fiscal incentives (P<.05), both of which were policy-oriented measures that were considered in policy-SEA in particular.

Figure 7.27 shows the differences between the three sample regions. In contrast to sustainability objectives and targets, SEA had a positive effect on the consideration of sustainability measures in all three regions. Differences, however, were not statistically significant. The greater differences were observed in Noord-Holland and the smallest differences were found in North

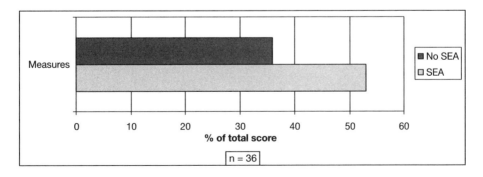

Figure 7.26: *Sustainability measures and SEA application*

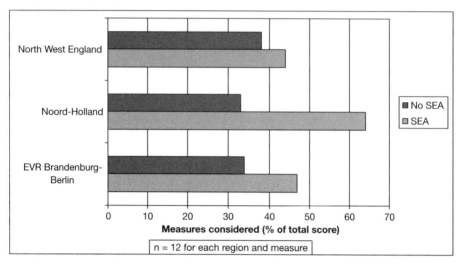

Figure 7.27: *The impact of SEA on the consideration of sustainability measures*

West England. Differences were mainly due to the extent to which policy-SEA was applied. This is discussed further below.

Regarding the differences between the transport and spatial/land use sectors, Figure 7.28 shows that SEA was more effective in transport than in spatial/land use PPPs. While SEA in the transport sector led to the consideration of a significantly greater number of sustainability measures ($P<.05$), there were no significant differences for spatial/land use PPPs. The observed patterns are explained by the greater extent of policy-SEA application in the transport sector.

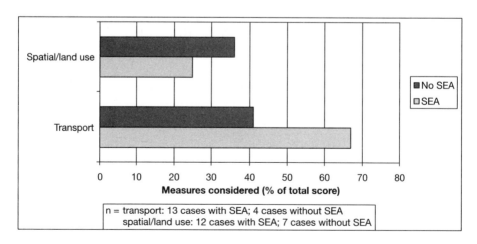

Figure 7.28: *The impact of SEA on the consideration of sustainability measures by sector*

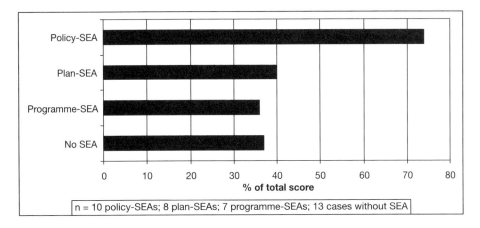

Figure 7.29: *Measures considered in the three SEA types and in PPPs without SEA*

SEA types

Figure 7.29 shows the differences in the consideration of sustainability measures for PPPs involving one of the three SEA types and for those not involving SEA at all. Differences were statistically significant for policy-SEAs, plan-SEAs (P<.01), programme-SEA (P<.01) and those PPPs not involving SEA at all (P<.01).

Regarding individual sustainability measures, policy-SEAs considered two measures significantly more frequently than plan-SEAs and programme-SEAs, including infrastructure charging (P<.01) and economic incentives (P<.01 and P<.05). This is not unexpected, as both measures were policy-oriented and eight of the ten policy-SEAs, but none of the plan-SEAs, were undertaken in the transport sector. Plan-SEAs considered land use measures to a larger extent than policy-SEAs and programme-SEAs (P<.01). Economic and fiscal incentives were considered significantly more frequent in policy-SEAs than in plan-SEAs (P<.01) and PPPs without SEA (P<.01).

Local land use PPPs

General remarks

Figure 7.30 shows the number of local land use PPPs that considered measures for addressing the four sustainability objectives of climate change, air quality, nature/biodiversity and urban environment. Measures for improving the urban environment were most frequently mentioned. While in EVR Brandenburg-Berlin all four measures were significantly more frequently considered than in Noord-Holland (P<.01), in North West England three measures were considered to a significantly greater extent than in Noord-Holland, namely, urban environment (P<.01), nature/biodiversity (P<.05) and air quality (P<.01). Furthermore, in EVR Brandenburg-Berlin significantly more nature/biodiversity measures were considered than in North West England (P<.05). The main reasons for the regional differences are the more extensive application of SEA in

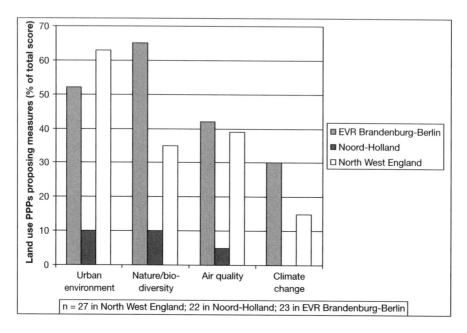

Figure 7.30: *Measures considered in local land use PPPs*

EVR Brandenburg-Berlin and in North West England, and the different planning approaches in the three regions.

Authorities that specified measures mostly mentioned land use measures (eight in North West England, two in Noord-Holland and ten in EVR Brandenburg-Berlin). Furthermore, infrastructure investment and public transport measures

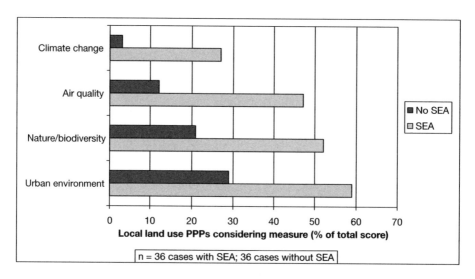

Figure 7.31: *SEA and the consideration of sustainability measures in local land use PPPs*

were frequently mentioned. In North West England, education and information measures were also proposed.

SEA application

Figure 7.31 shows the effect SEA had on the extent to which sustainability measures were considered in local land use PPPs. Differences for PPPs with and without SEA were significant for all four measures (P<.01).

OVERALL EVALUATION OF SUSTAINABILITY OBJECTIVES, TARGETS AND MEASURES

Individual PPPs

Figure 7.32 shows the overall sustainability scores for the individual PPPs. The overall sustainability scores are calculated by summing up explicit objectives, explicit targets and measures and adding 50 per cent of the values for implicit objectives and implicit targets. The sum is divided by 3, resulting in a total possible score of 6.67 (7 objectives + 5 targets + 8 measures ÷ 3).

Noord-Holland, on average, obtained the highest and North West England the lowest sustainability scores. The highest sustainability scores were obtained by the Second Transport Structure Plan (SVVII) and the Integrated Transport Plan (IVP) Brandenburg. The highest score in North West England was obtained by the Lancashire TPP.

Table 7.3 shows the overall scores to be used in the statistical analysis (derived from Figure 7.32). Scores vary between 1.5 (23 per cent) (Road Development Plan, *Landesstraßenbedarfsplan* Brandenburg) and 5.8 (87 per cent) (SVVII).

Regions, SEA types, sectors and general SEA application

Figure 7.33 shows the average scores for the regions, SEA types, sectors and SEA application. It is found that Noord-Holland obtained a significant higher sustainability score than North West England (P<.05). Even though the PPPs with SEA obtained slightly higher scores than those without SEA, differences failed to be statistically significant. Differences between the transport and spatial/land use sectors were also not significant. Regarding the differences between the SEA types, policy-SEAs obtained significantly higher scores than plan-SEAs (P<.01) and programme-SEAs (P<.01) and those PPPs not involving SEA at all (P<.01).

Regarding local land use PPPs, only regional differences were compared, as 34 of the 35 SEAs were plan-SEAs. EVR Brandenburg-Berlin and North West England considered significantly more sustainability aspects than Noord-Holland (P<.01). Furthermore, the cases with SEA obtained significantly higher scores than those without SEA (P<.01).

Only a few of the explanatory variables were found to be significantly correlated with the overall sustainability score. Most importantly, there was

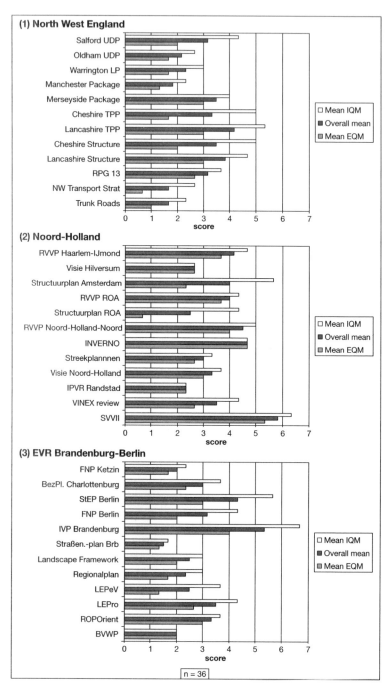

Key: mean IQM: mean value of all (explicit and implicit) objectives, targets and measures
mean EQM: mean value of explicit objectives, quantitative targets and measures
overall mean: overall sustainability score

Figure 7.32: *Sustainability scores for the individual PPP*

Table 7.3: *Overall ranking and evaluation for all PPPs*

PPPs	Sustainability score	Evaluation
Trunk Roads Programme	1.7	○
North West Transport Strategy	1.7	○
Regional Planning Guidance RPG 13	3.2	○
Lancashire Structure Plan	3.8	⊙
Cheshire Structure Plan	3.5	⊙
Lancashire TPP	4.2	⊙
Cheshire TPP	3.3	⊙
Merseyside Package Bid	3.5	⊙
Greater Manchester Package Bid	1.8	○
Warrington Local Plan	2.3	○
Oldham Unitary Development Plan	2.2	○
Salford Unitary Development Plan	3.2	○
Second Transport Structure Plan (SVVII)	5.8	●
National Spatial Plan (VINEX) review	3.5	⊙
Inter-Provincial Urbanisation Vision (IPVR)	2.3	○
Development Vision (*Ontwikkelingsvisie*) Noord Holland	3.3	○
Regional Plans (*Streekplannen*)	3.0	○
Integrated Transport Vision Randstad North (INVERNO)	4.7	⊙
Transport Plan (RVVP) Noord-Holland-Nord	4.5	⊙
Structure Plan (*Structuurplan*) ROA	2.5	○
Transport Plan (RVVP) ROA	4.0	⊙
Structure Plan (*Structuurplan*) Amsterdam	4.0	⊙
Future Vision (*Toekomstvisie*) Hilversum	2.7	○
Transport Plan (RVVP) Haarlem-IJmond	4.2	⊙
Federal Transport Infrastructure Plan (BVWP)	2.0	○
Spatial Orientation Framework (RopOrient)	3.3	○
Land Development Programme (LEPro)	3.5	⊙
Land Development Plan EVR Brb (LEPeV)	2.3	○
Regional Plan (*Regionalplan*) Havelland-Fläming	2.3	○
Development Concept (*Kreisentwicklungskonzept*) Havelland	2.5	○
Road Development Plan (*Landesstraßenplan*) Brandenburg	1.5	▫
Integrated Transport Plan (IVP) Brandenburg	5.3	●
Local Land Use Plan (FNP) Berlin	3.3	○
City Development Plan (StEP) Transport Berlin	4.3	⊙
District Development Plan (*Bereichsplan*) Charlottenburg	3.0	○
Local Land Use Plans (FNPs) Ketzin	2.0	○

▭ policy-SEA ▭ plan-SEA ▭ programme-SEA ▭ no SEA

Overall evaluation: ⊙ = 50% to under 75%
■ = 100% ○ = 25% to under 50%
● = 75% to under 100% ▫ = 0% to under 25%

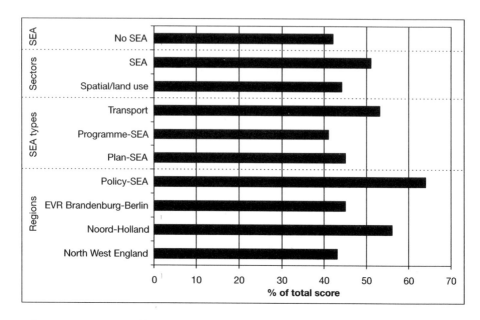

Figure 7.33: *Overall average scores for the regions, SEA types, sectors and PPPs with and without SEA*

significant correlation with the extent to which the associated PPPs considered inter-modal alternatives (P<.01). Furthermore, the extent to which the associated PPPs covered procedural stages explained the overall sustainability scores (P<.05). This underlines the importance for an integrated process in support of sustainable development, as presented in Figure 1.1.

SUMMARY

Policies, plans and programmes considered sustainability objectives to a greater extent than sustainability targets and measures. Sustainability objectives and targets that were particularly well considered include the urban environment, nature/biodiversity, emission levels and land use targets. Those measures that were most frequently proposed in PPPs included land use planning, infrastructure investment and public transport.

Regarding the cross-section of 36 PPPs at all administrative levels, if all of the objectives and targets (explicit and implicit) were considered, results for the three sample regions were similar. Explicit objectives and targets, however, were more extensively considered in Noord-Holland than in the other two regions. SEA application for the cross-section of PPPs did not lead to a significantly better consideration of sustainability objectives and targets. It was, however, able to lead to a better consideration of sustainability measures.

The three SEA types had different effects on the consideration of sustainability aspects. Policy-SEA usually led to a significantly better consideration of sustainability aspects than plan-SEA and programme-SEA. Furthermore, SEA application tended to be more successful in the transport sector than in the spatial/land use sector. Thus, in the transport sector, SEA was able to lead to a better consideration of explicit objectives and targets.

SEA application in local land use PPPs was clearly able to lead to a better consideration of sustainability aspects. While 21 of the 23 local land use plans in EVR Brandenburg-Berlin involved SEA application, only 1 of the 22 in Noord-Holland did so. In contrast to the cross-section of PPPs, EVR Brandenburg-Berlin local land use plans considered the largest number of sustainability aspects and the performance of Noord-Holland was particularly poor.

A number of explanations were provided for the observed patterns. The procedural coverage was able to explain the overall extent to which sustainability aspects were considered. In addition, a better consideration of inter-modal aspects was accompanied by a better consideration of environmental sustainability objectives, targets and measures.

The society consensus-led, quasi-top-down planning approach in The Netherlands led to a better consideration of sustainability aspects for the cross-section of 36 PPPs at all administrative levels than the centrally guided plan making approach in North West England and the public administration, consensus-led, counter-current approach in EVR Brandenburg-Berlin. For local land use PPPs, however, North West England and EVR Brandenburg-Berlin scored higher than Noord-Holland.

Potential benefits from SEA application

Chapter 8 refers to objective 5 and determines the extent to which SEA results in the potential SEA benefits. For this purpose, the evaluation framework provided in Chapter 2 is used. Interview results are presented for the cross-section of 36 PPPs at all administrative levels that were identified in Chapter 4. Chapter 8 is divided into nine sections. The first provides an overall picture of the extent to which current assessment practice results in the five potential SEA benefits. These benefits are then described and analysed in further detail. The extent to which those aspects were met is determined as, required by the EC SEA Directive. Finally, the main results of this chapter are summarized.

OVERALL PICTURE

Figure 8.1 shows the extent to which assessments in the three sample regions resulted in the five potential SEA benefits. Included were seven SEAs from North West England and nine SEAs, from each of Noord-Holland and EVR Brandenburg-Berlin. While SEAs scored comparatively well for the potential benefit 5, 'consultation and participation on SEA related issues' (80 per cent of the total score), SEAs scored comparatively poorly for the potential benefit 3 'strengthening project EIA – increasing the efficiency of tiered decision making' (44 per cent of the total score). The second highest score was reached by benefit 2, 'pro-active assessment – SEA as a supporting tool for PPP formulation for sustainable development' (64 per cent of the total score). The remaining potential SEA benefits 1, 'wider consideration of impacts and alternatives' and 4, 'systematic and effective consideration of the environment at higher tiers of decision making' obtained 59 per cent and 58 per cent of the total scores, respectively.

Figure 8.2 shows the average scores for the five potential SEA benefits in the three sample regions. For the potential benefit 1, 'wider consideration of impacts and alternatives', Noord-Holland SEAs scored significantly higher than North West England SEAs (P<.01) and EVR Brandenburg-Berlin SEAs (P<.05). As will be shown later, this is mainly caused by the large number of policy-SEAs applied in this region. For the potential benefit 2, 'proactive assessment – SEA as a supporting tool for PPP formulation for sustainable development', EVR Brandenburg-Berlin SEAs scored significantly lower than the SEAs in North West England (P<.05) and in Noord-Holland (P<.01). This is explained by a low level of public participation at higher tiers and a comparatively large number

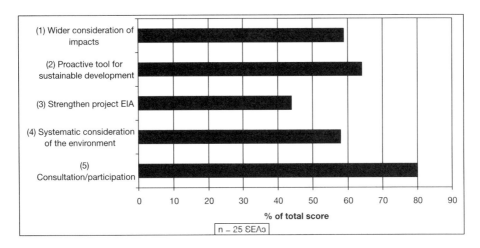

Figure 8.1: *Extent to which SEAs for the cross-section of PPPs result in the potential SEA benefits*

of programme-SEAs in the cross-section of 36 PPPs at all administrative levels in EVR Brandenburg-Berlin. For the potential SEA benefit 3, 'strengthening project EIA – increasing the efficiency of tiered decision making', Noord-Holland SEAs scored significantly higher than those in North West England (P<.05) and EVR Brandenburg-Berlin (P<.05). This was mainly due to the ability of Noord-Holland SEAs to assess different issues from project EIA and to substitute project EIA partly or altogether. For the remaining potential benefits, 4 'systematic and effective consideration of the environment at higher tiers of

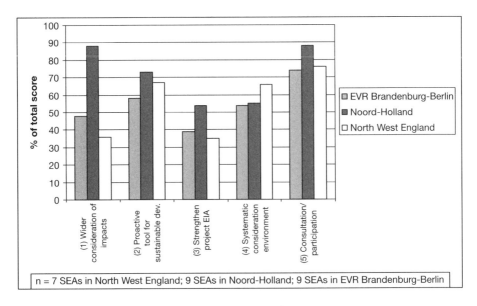

Figure 8.2: *Regional average scores by potential SEA benefit*

decision making' and 5, 'consultation and participation on SEA related issues', the differences between the three regions were not significant.

The overall SEA benefits score was significantly correlated with the context variable of PPP inter-modality (P<.05). This is explained by the comparatively good performance of policy-SEA, which inherently considered inter-modal aspects. There was also significant correlation of the overall SEA benefits score with three SEA variables, namely, SEA methods and techniques (P<.01), SEA procedure (P<.01) and the quantitative assessment (P<.05) of impacts. It is therefore suggested that a comprehensive and extensive SEA process, involving impact maps and calculating impact magnitudes is able to result in potential SEA benefits. Consultation (P<.01), public participation (P<.01) and initiation (scoping)(P<.05) had a particular importance for the overall potential SEA benefits score.

WIDER CONSIDERATION OF IMPACTS AND ALTERNATIVES

This section describes, analyses and explains the results for the potential SEA benefit 1, 'wider consideration of impacts and alternatives'. It is divided into two sub-sections, one of which deals with regional characteristics and the other one with SEA-type and sectoral characteristics.

The extent to which SEAs resulted in the potential benefit 1 was significantly negatively correlated with the context variable of PPP relevance (P<.05). The more a PPP was statutory, mandatory and binding for further planning, the less likely the associated SEA was to therefore consider a wider range of impacts and alternatives. This is possibly explained by a reluctance on the part of authorities to consider more impacts and alternatives than necessary as opposition and delays in PPP preparation are expected, caused by the NIMBY (not in my backyard phenomenon (see Chapter 1). There was significant correlation between the consideration of impacts and alternatives with the extent to which SEA methods and techniques were applied (P<.01), and the coverage of SEA procedural stages (P<.05). A greater extent of the coverage of SEA procedural stages and the widespread use of methods and techniques therefore led to a wider consideration of the impacts and alternatives. Consideration of scenarios and expert consultation were significantly correlated with the potential SEA benefit 1 (P<.01).

Regional characteristics

Table 8.1 shows the overall scores for the individual SEAs. It is observed that Noord-Holland scored significantly higher than both North West England (P<.01) and EVR Brandenburg-Berlin (P<.05). Regional characteristics are described in further detail.

North West England

Six of the seven SEAs in North West England scored poorly, with four SEAs obtaining scores of between 25 per cent and 50 per cent, and two SEAs obtaining the lowest score of under 25 per cent. Only the underlying integrated transport strategy of the Merseyside Package Bid, the only policy-SEA in the region, received 100 per cent of the total score. It was the only SEA in North West England that considered policy-wide, cumulative impacts, impacts on transport, inter-modal alternatives and the zero alternative. The low scores

Table 8.1: *SEA-specific evaluation of the potential SEA benefit 1, 'wider consideration of impacts and alternatives'*

North West England (average score)	36%
Environmental Appraisal for the Lancashire Structure Plan	O
Environmental Appraisal for the Cheshire Structure Plan	O
Cheshire TPP	▫
Merseyside Package Bid	▫
Merseyside Package Bid underlying strategy	■
Environmental Appraisal for the Warrington Local Plan	O
Environmental Appraisal for the Oldham UDP	O
Noord-Holland (average score)	**88%**
Second Transport Structure Plan (SVVII)	■
SEA for the National Spatial Plan (VINEX) review	⊙
Vision (*visie*) Noord-Holland	●
Transport Plan (RVVP) INVERNO	■
Transport Plan (RVVP) Noord-Holland-Noord	■
Transport Plan (RVVP) ROA	■
Environment Matrix (*milieumatrix*) for the Structure Plan Amsterdam	⊙
Vision (*visie*) Hilversum	●
Transport Plan (RVVP) Haarlem-IJmond	■
EVR Brandenburg-Berlin (average score)	**48%**
Federal Transport Infrastructure Plan (BVWP)	O
Ecological Risk Assessment (*ökologische Risikoanalyse)* for the BVWP	⊙
Landscape Framework Plan (*Landschaftsrahmenplan*) Havelland-Flaming	▫
Road Development Plan (*Landesstraßenbedarfsplan*) Brandenburg	O
Integrated Transport Plan (IVP) Brandenburg	■
Ecological Conflict Analysis for the Land Use Plan (FNP) Berlin	O
Landscape Programme (*Landschaftsprogramm*) for the FNP Berlin	▫
Integrated Transport Plan (StEP) Berlin	■
Landscape Plan (*Landschaftsplan*) for the Land Use Plan (FNP) Ketzin	⊙

▨ policy-SEA ▢ plan-SEA ▢ programme-SEA

Overall evaluation:
■ = 100%
● = 75% to under 100% of total score
⊙ = 50% to under 75% of total score
O = 25% to under 50% of total score
▫ = 0% to under 25% of total score

obtained by the four environmental appraisals are explained by a failure to include accumulated or global effects in the guidance used by the authorities to conduct SEA (DoE, 1993). The evaluation matrices for the transport programme-SEAs only considered project-related impacts (following DoT, 1995).

Noord-Holland

Noord-Holland SEAs, on average, scored higher than the SEAs in the other two regions, which was mainly due to the large number of policy-SEAs. The maximum score was reached by five of the nine SEAs, all of which were transport policy-SEAs. Furthermore, two SEAs obtained high scores of between 80 per cent and 100 per cent, namely the spatial/land use policy-SEAs, the visions Noord-Holland (*ontwikkelingsvisie*) and Hilversum (*toekomstvisie*). The lowest score in Noord-Holland was obtained by the Environment Matrix (*milieumatrix*) Amsterdam, not considering any plan-wide, cumulative impacts, scenarios, the zero alternative or inter-modal alternatives.

EVR Brandenburg-Berlin

Two SEAs in EVR Brandenburg-Berlin obtained the maximum score, namely the transport policy-SEAs in the region, IVP Brandenburg and StEP Berlin. Two SEAs obtained moderate scores of between 50 per cent and 75 per cent and three SEAs obtained scores of between 25 per cent and 50 per cent, which were all programme-SEAs. The two SEAs that obtained the lowest score of under 25 per cent were plan-SEAs, namely the Landscape Framework Plan (*Landschaftsrahmenplan*) Havelland-Fläming and the Landscape Programme (*Landschaftsprogramm*) Berlin. Neither of these directly assessed impacts, but defined environmental development objectives and provided authorities with land suitability maps, thus acting as instruments of the precautionary principle (see Table 5.1).

SEA type and sectoral characteristics

Figure 8.3 shows the results for the potential SEA benefit 1, 'wider consideration of impacts and alternatives', for the three SEA types. As expected, policy-SEA scored significantly higher than plan-SEA and programme-SEA (P<.01). Eight of the ten policy-SEAs (all transport) obtained the highest score of 100 per cent and two policy-SEAs (both spatial/land use) obtained high scores of between 75 per cent and 100 per cent.

Scores for plan-SEAs and programme-SEAs varied between moderate (50 per cent to 75 per cent) and lowest scores (0 per cent to 25 per cent). The good performance of policy-SEA is mainly explained by a lower PPP relevance. In particular, the unclear connection with project preparation provided authorities with the opportunity to regard a much wider range of impacts and alternatives without having to fear public opposition due to NIMBYism (see Chapter 1).

Figure 8.4 shows sectoral differences for the potential SEA benefit 1. It is observed that transport SEAs scored significantly higher than spatial/land use

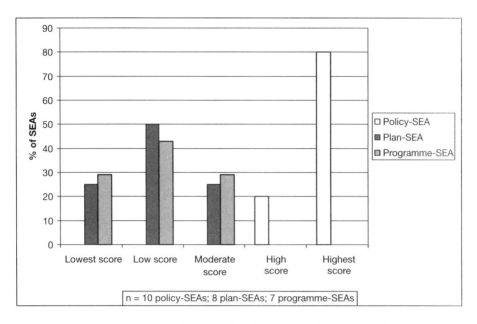

Figure 8.3: *SEA-type evaluation for the potential SEA benefit 1, 'wider consideration of impacts and alternatives'*

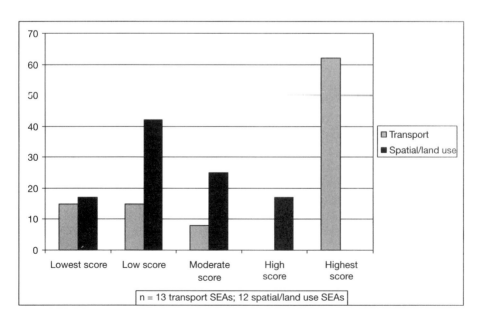

Figure 8.4: *Sector-specific evaluation for the potential SEA benefit 1, 'wider consideration of impacts and alternatives'*

SEAs (P<.01), which is explained by the greater extent of policy-SEA application in the transport sector. While all transport policy-SEAs obtained the highest
score of 100 per cent, transport programme-SEAs obtained only moderate to
the lowest scores. Furthermore, spatial/land use policy-SEAs obtained high scores
and plan-SEAs and programme-SEAs only obtained moderate to the lowest
scores.

PROACTIVE ASSESSMENT: SEA AS A SUPPORTING TOOL FOR PPP FORMULATION FOR SUSTAINABLE DEVELOPMENT

This section describes, analyses and explains the results for the potential SEA
benefit 2 'proactive assessment: SEA as a supporting tool for PPP formulation
for sustainable development'. Regional, sectoral and SEA-type characteristics
are addressed.

Potential SEA benefit scores were significantly correlated with the context
variables PPP accountability and PPP inter-modality (P<.05). This underlines
the importance of external inputs for being proactive and supporting PPP
formulation for sustainable development. There was also significant statistical
correlation with the SEA variable, SEA procedure (P<.05), which was to be
expected, as both were sharing some similar underlying criteria. Thus, the
criteria of screening, scoping and monitoring were used to describe the potential SEA benefit 2 and they were also part of the variable SEA procedure.

Regional characteristics

Table 8.2 shows the extent to which assessments in the three sample regions
resulted in the potential SEA benefit 2. Noord-Holland SEAs obtained the highest average score and EVR Brandenburg-Berlin SEAs obtained the lowest average
score. EVR Brandenburg-Berlin SEAs scored significantly lower than the SEAs in
North West England (P<.05) and Noord-Holland (P<.01). Regional characteristics are described in further detail below and reasons are given for the
differences.

North West England

The plan-SEAs, environmental appraisals for the Cheshire and Lancashire structure plans, were the only SEAs that obtained high scores of between 75 per
cent and 100 per cent. All other SEAs only obtained moderate scores of between 50 per cent and 75 per cent. Screening with external participation was
not undertaken in any of the SEAs. Furthermore, monitoring and follow-up
were not SEA-specific and none of the SEAs were used to structure the PPP
process or ran parallel to it.

Noord-Holland

Six of the nine SEAs obtained high scores of between 75 per cent and 100 per
cent, five of which were transport policy-SEAs. The only spatial/land use SEA

Table 8.2: *SEA-specific evaluation of the potential SEA benefit 2,*
'proactive assessment: SEA as a supporting tool for PPP formulation
for sustainable development'

North West England (average score)	**67%**
Environmental Appraisal for the Lancashire Structure Plan	●
Environmental Appraisal for the Cheshire Structure Plan	●
Cheshire TPP	⊙
Merseyside Package Bid	⊙
Merseyside Package Bid underlying strategy	⊙
Environmental Appraisal for the Warrington Local Plan	⊙
Environmental Appraisal for the Oldham UDP	⊙
Noord-Holland (average score)	**73%**
Second Transport Structure Plan (SVVII)	●
SEA for the National Spatial Plan (VINEX) review	●
Vision (*visie*) Noord-Holland	⊙
Transport Plan (RVVP) INVERNO	●
Transport Plan (RVVP) Noord-Holland-Noord	●
Transport Plan (RVVP) ROA	●
Environment Matrix (*milieumatrix*) for the Structure Plan Amsterdam	⊙
Vision (*visie*) Hilversum	⊙
Transport Plan (RVVP) Haarlem-IJmond	●
EVR Brandenburg-Berlin (average score)	**52%**
Federal Transport Infrastructure Plan (BVWP)	O
Ecological Risk Assessment (*ökologische Risikoanalyse*) for the BVWP	O
Landscape Framework Plan (*Landschaftsrahmenplan*) Havelland-Flaming	⊙
Road Development Plan (*Landesstraßenbedarfsplan*) Brandenburg	O
Integrated Transport Plan (IVP) Brandenburg	⊙
Ecological Conflict Analysis for the Land Use Plan (FNP) Berlin	⊙
Landscape Programme (*Landschaftsprogramm*) for the FNP Berlin	⊙
Integrated Transport Plan (StEP) Berlin	⊙
Landscape Plan (*Landschaftsplan*) for the Land Use Plan (FNP) Ketzin	⊙

▨ policy-SEA ☐ plan-SEA ☐ programme-SEA

Overall evaluation:
- ■ = 100%
- ● = 75% to under 100% of total score
- ⊙ = 50% to under 75% of total score
- O = 25% to under 50% of total score
- ▫ = 0% to under 25% of total score

that obtained a high score was the programme-SEA for the National Spatial Plan (VINEX) review, which closely followed a project EIA procedure as laid out in the national EIA Decree of 1994. All other SEAs in Noord-Holland only obtained moderate scores of between 50 per cent and 75 per cent. All SEAs were undertaken during the PPP process, except the Transport Environment Map (*verkeersmilieukaart*) ROA, which was undertaken after policy preparation. The plan-SEA for the Structure Plan (*structuurplan*) Amsterdam, Environment Matrix (*milieumatrix*), did not include screening, scoping or monitoring, and was used for determining land suitability, thus acting as an instrument of the precautionary principle.

EVR Brandenburg-Berlin

Six SEAs obtained moderate scores of between 50 per cent and 75 per cent. Furthermore, three SEAs obtained low scores of between 25 per cent and 50 per cent, all of which were transport programme-SEAs. Highest scores were obtained by the plan-SEAs, landscape plans and programmes (*Landschaftspläne und -programme*) for the land use plans (FNPs) Berlin and Ketzin, considering all types of objectives and environmental standards in a qualitative manner, according to the *Federal* and *Land* environmental protection acts. Scoping was done with simple checklists, based on legislative requirements formulated in the construction law book (*Baugesetzbuch*, BauGB), and the environmental protection acts. It is still unclear whether the Integrated Transport Plan (IVP) Brandenburg will involve any specific monitoring provisions. Screening in the Ecological Risk Assessment (*ökologische Risikoanalyse*) for the Federal Transport Infrastructure Plan (BVWP) was based on the sole criterion of road length (all projects with a length of over 5km were included). In contrast to the other two regions, sustainable development strategies were not considered at all in any of the SEAs in EVR Brandenburg-Berlin.

SEA type and sectoral characteristics

Figure 8.5 shows the results for the potential SEA benefit 2 for the three SEA types. Policy-SEA, on average, scored slightly better than plan-SEA and programme-SEA.

Differences between the three SEA types were not statistically significant. Following the results of Chapter 7, however, it needs to be stressed that substantive environmental sustainability objectives, targets and measures were considered to a larger extent in policy-SEA than in the other two SEA types.

While spatial/land use SEAs scored slightly better than transport SEAs (66 per cent compared with 62 per cent), sectoral differences were not statistically significant. Most spatial/land use SEAs obtained moderate scores of between 50 per cent and 75 per cent. Only the environmental appraisals for the Cheshire and Lancashire structure plans obtained high scores of between 75 per cent and 100 per cent.

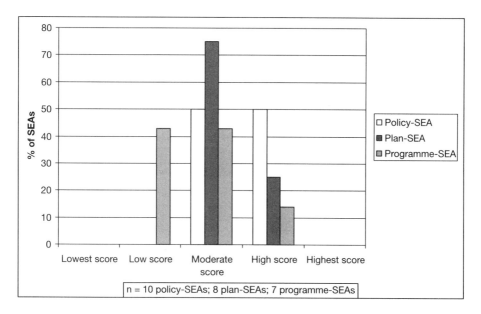

n = 10 policy-SEAs; 8 plan-SEAs; 7 programme-SEAs

Figure 8.5: *SEA-type evaluation for the potential SEA benefit 2, 'proactive assessment: SEA as a supporting tool for PPP formulation for sustainable development'*

STRENGTHENING PROJECT EIA: INCREASING THE EFFICIENCY OF TIERED DECISION MAKING

This section describes, analyses and explains the results for the potential SEA benefit 3, 'strengthening project EIA – increasing the efficiency of tiered decision making'. It is divided into two sub-sections dealing with regional characteristics, SEA-types and sectoral characteristics.

SEA benefit 3 was significantly correlated with the SEA variable of SEA procedure (P<.01). An extensive coverage of the SEA procedural stages was therefore potentially leading to a strengthening of project EIA and to an increased efficiency of tiered decision making. The individual procedural stages of the initiation of SEA, external participation and public consultation were of particular importance and were all significantly correlated with the potential SEA benefit 3 (P<.01).

Regional characteristics

Table 8.3 shows the overall scores for the individual SEAs. Noord-Holland SEAs obtained significantly higher scores than the SEAs in North West England (P<.05).[1]

Table 8.3: *SEA-specific evaluation of the potential SEA benefit 3,*
'strengthening project EIA, increasing efficiency of tiered decision making'

North West England (average score)	36%
Environmental Appraisal for the Lancashire Structure Plan	O
Environmental Appraisal for the Cheshire Structure Plan	⊙
Cheshire TPP	▫
Merseyside Package Bid	▫
Merseyside Package Bid underlying strategy	▫
Environmental Appraisal for the Warrington Local Plan	O
Environmental Appraisal for the Oldham UDP	⊙
Noord-Holland (average score)	**54%**
Second Transport Structure Plan (SVVII)	⊙
SEA for the National Spatial Plan (VINEX) review	●
Vision (*visie*) Noord-Holland	⊙
Transport Plan (RVVP) INVERNO	⊙
Transport Plan (RVVP) Noord-Holland-Noord	⊙
Transport Plan (RVVP) ROA	⊙
Environment Matrix (*milieumatrix*) for the Structure Plan Amsterdam	▫
Vision (*visie*) Hilversum	⊙
Transport Plan (RVVP) Haarlem-IJmond	⊙
EVR Brandenburg-Berlin (average score)	**39%**
Federal Transport Infrastructure Plan (BVWP)	O
Ecological Risk Assessment (*ökologische Risikoanalyse)* for the BVWP	▫
Landscape Framework Plan (*Landschaftsrahmenplan*) Havelland-Flaming	⊙
Road Development Plan (*Landesstraßenbedarfsplan*) Brandenburg	O
Integrated Transport Plan (IVP) Brandenburg	O
Ecological Conflict Analysis for the Land Use Plan (FNP) Berlin	▫
Landscape Programme (*Landschaftsprogramm*) for the FNP Berlin	⊙
Integrated Transport Plan (StEP) Berlin	O
Landscape Plan (*Landschaftsplan*) for the Land Use Plan (FNP) Ketzin	⊙

▨ policy-SEA   ▧ plan-SEA   ☐ programme-SEA

Overall evaluation:
- ■ = 100%
- ● = 75% to under 100% of total score
- ⊙ = 50% to under 75% of total score
- O = 25% to under 50% of total score
- ▫ = 0% to under 25% of total score

North West England

Three of the seven SEAs in North West England obtained the lowest score of under 25 per cent, all of which were transport SEAs. Two of the remaining four spatial/land use SEAs obtained moderate scores of between 50 per cent and 75 per cent and two SEAs obtained low scores of between 25 per cent and 50 per cent. No assessment was able to lead to project acceleration or to substitute parts of project EIA. While only the Environmental Appraisal for the Cheshire Structure Plan explicitly addressed mitigation. The Environmental Appraisal for the Oldham UDP mentioned the need to mitigate impacts.

Noord-Holland

All seven policy-SEAs in Noord-Holland obtained moderate scores of between 50 per cent and 75 per cent. While the programme-SEA for the National Spatial Plan (VINEX) review obtained the highest score of all SEAs (between 75 per cent and 100 per cent), the plan-SEA, Environment Matrix (*milieumatrix*) for the Structure Plan (*structuurplan*) Amsterdam obtained the lowest score with under 25 per cent. Only one assessment entirely substituted project EIA, namely the SEA for the National Spatial Plan (VINEX) review, thus being able to accelerate project preparation. All of the other SEAs were said to be potentially able to accelerate subsequent projects by providing comprehensive environmental information for lower tiers of decision making. Furthermore, all of the assessments addressed issues that were different from those of project EIA, except the Amsterdam Environment Matrix (*milieumatrix*), which was used as an instrument of the precautionary principle for determining land suitability. Only two SEAs explicitly addressed mitigation measures, namely the policy-SEAs, Second Transport Structure Plan (SVVII) and Vision (*toekomstvisie*) Hilversum.

EVR Brandenburg-Berlin

Only three of the nine SEAs in EVR Brandenburg-Berlin obtained moderate scores of between 50 per cent and 75 per cent, all of which were plan-SEAs. Four SEAs obtained low scores and two SEAs obtained very low scores, all of which were transport programme-SEAs. None of the assessments were able to substitute for project EIA. All of the SEAs, however, assessed issues different from project EIA. Only three SEAs were potentially able to accelerate project preparation by providing comprehensive environmental information, namely all landscape plans and programmes (*Landschaftspläne- und programme*). Mitigation measures were proposed in the Landscape Programme (*Landschaftsprogramm*) Berlin and the Landscape Plan (*Landschaftsplan*) Ketzin. The need for mitigation was also addressed in the Landscape Framework Plan (*Landschaftsrahmenplan*) Havelland-Fläming.

SEA type and sectoral characteristics

Figure 8.6 shows the results for the potential SEA benefit 3 for the three SEA types. Policy-SEA and plan-SEA, on average, scored higher than programme-SEA. Furthermore, spatial/land use SEAs, on average, scored higher than transport SEAs. There was, however, no significant statistical correlation between any of the SEA types or between the sectors. While four of the seven programme-SEAs obtained the lowest scores of under 25 per cent, one programme-SEA

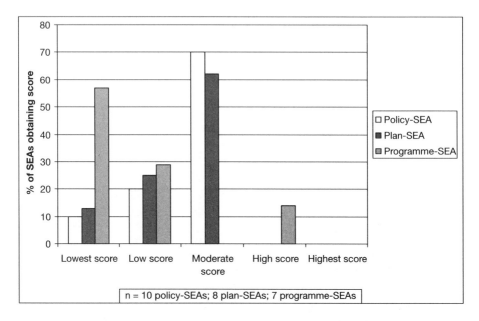

Figure 8.6: *SEA-type evaluation for the potential SEA benefit 3, 'strengthening project EIA: increasing the efficiency of tiered decision making'*

obtained the highest score of all of the SEAs, namely, the National Spatial Plan (VINEX) review, which closely followed a project EIA procedure as laid out in the Dutch EIA Decree of 1994.

SYSTEMATIC AND EFFECTIVE CONSIDERATION OF THE ENVIRONMENT AT HIGHER TIERS OF DECISION MAKING

This section describes, analyses and explains the results for the potential SEA benefit 4, 'systematic and effective consideration of the environment at higher tiers of decision making'. Two sub-sections deal with regional characteristics and with SEA-type and sectoral characteristics. The potential SEA benefit 4 was correlated in a significant manner with the context variable of PPP procedure ($P<.05$). This underlines the importance of a full coverage of the procedural stages for supporting sustainable development (see Figure 1.1).

Regional characteristics

This section describes the regional characteristics, referring to the individual SEAs. In contrast to all of the other potential SEA benefits, on average, SEAs in North West England obtained the highest scores and Noord-Holland SEAs obtained the lowest scores. None of the regional differences were statistically significant.

North West England

Two of the seven SEAs obtained high scores of between 75 per cent and 100 per cent, namely, the programme-SEAs for the Merseyside Package Bid and the Cheshire TPP. These are SEAs that scored comparatively poorly on most

Table 8.4: *SEA-specific evaluation for the potential SEA benefit 4, 'systematic and effective consideration of the environment at higher tiers of decision making'*

North West England (average score)	**66%**
Environmental Appraisal for the Lancashire Structure Plan	⊙
Environmental Appraisal for the Cheshire Structure Plan	⊙
Cheshire TPP	●
Merseyside Package Bid	●
Merseyside Package Bid underlying strategy	⊙
Environmental Appraisal for the Warrington Local Plan	⊙
Environmental Appraisal for the Oldham UDP	⊙
Noord-Holland (average score)	**55%**
Second Transport Structure Plan (SVVII)	⊙
SEA for the National Spatial Plan (VINEX) review	●
Vision (*visie*) Noord-Holland	▫
Transport Plan (RVVP) INVERNO	⊙
Transport Plan (RVVP) Noord-Holland-Noord	⊙
Transport Plan (RVVP) ROA	⊙
Environment Matrix (*milieumatrix*) for the Structure Plan Amsterdam	⊙
Vision (*visie*) Hilversum	▫
Transport Plan (RVVP) Haarlem-IJmond	⊙
EVR Brandenburg-Berlin (average score)	**54%**
Federal Transport Infrastructure Plan (BVWP)	○
Ecological Risk Assessment (*ökologische Risikoanalyse)* for the BVWP	○
Landscape Framework Plan (*Landschaftsrahmenplan*) Havelland-Flaming	●
Road Development Plan (*Landesstraßenbedarfsplan*) Brandenburg	⊙
Integrated Transport Plan (IVP) Brandenburg	○
Ecological Conflict Analysis for the Land Use Plan (FNP) Berlin	⊙
Landscape Programme (*Landschaftsprogramm*) for the FNP Berlin	⊙
Integrated Transport Plan (StEP) Berlin	○
Landscape Plan (*Landschaftsplan*) for the Land Use Plan (FNP) Ketzin	●

▭ policy-SEA   ▭ plan-SEA   ▭ programme-SEA

Overall evaluation:
- ■ = 100%
- ● = 75% to under 100% of total score
- ⊙ = 50% to under 75% of total score
- ○ = 25% to under 50% of total score
- ▫ = 0% to under 25% of total score

other potential SEA benefits. All of the other assessments obtained moderate scores of between 50 per cent and 75 per cent, as there were either formal or quasi-formal requirements. Package bids/TPPs had quasi-formal requirements, as it would have been impossible to secure any government funding without their preparation. Furthermore, guidance was used (local authority circulars; DoT, 1995) and all of the authorities preparing environmental appraisals used the *Good Practice Guide* (DoE, 1993). While authorities responsible for PPP preparation were usually not the same as the approving bodies, most SEA approving bodies were also SEA initiating bodies, except those for the Cheshire TPP and the Merseyside Package Bid (approved by central government). All of the SEAs were reasonably well considered in decision making.

Noord-Holland

The programme-SEA for the National Spatial Plan (VINEX) review was the only SEA that obtained a high score of between 75 per cent and 100 per cent. Six SEAs obtained moderate scores of between 50 per cent and 75 per cent. The only two spatial/land use policy-SEAs in the sample regions, the visions Noord-Holland (*ontwikkelingsvisie*) and Hilversum (*toekomstvisie*) obtained the lowest scores of under 25 per cent. While none of the PPPs had clear legal provisions to conduct SEA, regional transport policies had quasi-formal provisions, as no government funding allocation would have been possible without their preparation. The requirements for conducting SEA for all regional transport plans (RVVPs) were based on the Second Transport Structure Plan (SVVII).

For most PPPs in Noord-Holland, the approving body was not the initiating body. Exceptions were the visions Noord-Holland (*Ontwikkelingsvisie)* and Hilversum (*Toekomstvisie*) and the Structure Plan Amsterdam (*Structuurplan*). Regarding the regional transport plans (RVVPs) ROA and Haarlem-IJmond, only parts of the SEAs were approved by a different body than the initiating body, namely, the transport environment maps (*verkeersmilieukaarten*) by the national government. The Second Transport Structure Plan (SVVII) involved a quasi-outside review, with the Ministry of Spatial Planning, Environment and Water Management (VROM) being involved.

EVR Brandenburg-Berlin

Two SEAs in EVR Brandenburg-Berlin obtained high scores of over 75 per cent, namely, the plan-SEAs, Landscape Plan (*Landschaftsplan*) Ketzin and Landscape Framework Plan (*Landschaftsrahmenplan*) Havelland-Fäming. While there was no official approval, a review was conducted by the Upper Land Environment Authority (*Landesumweltamt*, LUA). The third highest score in EVR Brandenburg-Berlin was also obtained by a plan-SEA, namely, the Landscape Programme (*Landschaftsprogramm*) Berlin. All of the other SEAs obtained moderate and low scores.

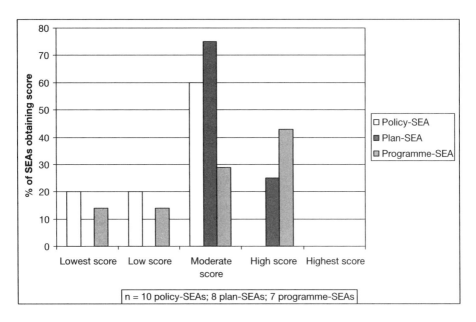

Figure 8.7: *SEA-type evaluation for the potential SEA benefit 4, 'systematic and effective consideration of the environment at higher tiers of decision making'*

SEA type and sectoral characteristics

Figure 8.7 shows the results for the potential SEA benefit 4, 'systematic and effective consideration of the environment at higher tiers of decision making', for the three SEA types. In contrast to all of the other potential SEA benefits, policy-SEA obtained the lowest average score (significantly lower than plan-SEA; P< 05). This is not unexpected, as policy-SEA is applied in a more flexible manner than the other two SEA types. While spatial/land use SEAs scored slightly higher than transport SEAs, there were no significant differences between the two sectors.

CONSULTATION AND PARTICIPATION ON SEA-RELATED ISSUES

This section describes, analyses and explains the results for the potential SEA benefit 5, 'consultation and participation on SEA-related issues'. As done in the previous sections, regional characteristics are firstly described. This is followed by a description of SEA-type and sectoral characteristics.

There was significant statistical correlation with two context variables, namely, PPP accountability (P<.05) and PPP procedure (P<.01) and with two SEA variables, namely, SEA procedure and SEA methods and techniques (P<.01). A comprehensive and extensive SEA process that is conducted parallel to, or integrated with, an open and extensive PPP process is therefore seen to be potentially able to result in high benefits from consultation and participation.

Regional characteristics

Table 8.5 shows the scores for the potential SEA benefit 5 for all SEAs. SEAs Noord-Holland, on average, obtained higher scores than the SEAs of the other two sample regions. None of the regional differences, however, were statistically significant.

North West England

The Environmental Appraisal for the Cheshire Structure Plan obtained the highest score. Three SEAs obtained high scores of between 75 per cent and 100 per cent, namely the plan-SEAs, environmental appraisals for the Warrington Local Plan and the Oldham UDP and the only policy-SEA in North West England, the Transport Strategy for the Merseyside Package Bid. While there was usually both external consultation and public participation in PPP preparation, in SEA preparation only the Transport Strategy for the Merseyside Package Bid as well as the Cheshire Structure Plan included public participation. The Oldham UDP only involved the public in the Environmental Appraisal after the underlying plan was approved.

Noord-Holland

Five of the nine SEAs obtained the highest score. Two of these were transport policy-SEAs and two were spatial/land use policy-SEAs. Furthermore, it also included the only programme-SEA in Noord-Holland, the National Spatial Plan (VINEX) review. While two of the remaining SEAs obtained high scores of between 75 per cent and 100 per cent, the integrated transport plans INVERNO and (RVVP) Noord-Holland-Noord obtained only moderate scores as the public was not involved in its preparation.

EVR Brandenburg-Berlin

Two of the nine SEAs obtained the highest score of 100 per cent, namely the two plan-SEAs, Landscape Programme (*Landschaftsprogramm*) Berlin and the Landscape Plan (*Landschaftsplan*) Ketzin. The third plan-SEA in the region, the Landscape Framework Plan (*Landschaftsrahmenplan*) Havelland-Fläming and the policy-SEA, Integrated Transport Plan (StEP) Berlin obtained high scores of between 75 per cent and 100 per cent. All of the SEAs that obtained high scores were therefore either undertaken at local or at *Kreis* levels and all of the remaining SEAs obtained moderate scores of between 50 per cent and 75 per cent. The Federal Transport Infrastructure Plan (BVWP), the Roads Development Plan (*Landesstraßenbedarfsplan*) Brandenburg and the Integrated Transport Plan (IVP) Brandenburg involved expert participation (however, this was only rather informal and sporadic), but no public participation, either in PPP or in SEA preparation. It is suggested that this is mainly due to a fear of

Table 8.5: *SEA-specific evaluation of the potential SEA benefit 5, 'consultation and participation on SEA-related issues'*

North West England (average score)	76%
Environmental Appraisal for the Lancashire Structure Plan	⊙
Environmental Appraisal for the Cheshire Structure Plan	■
Cheshire TPP	⊙
Merseyside Package Bid	⊙
Merseyside Package Bid underlying strategy	●
Environmental Appraisal for the Warrington Local Plan	●
Environmental Appraisal for the Oldham UDP	●
Noord-Holland (average score)	**88%**
Second Transport Structure Plan (SVVII)	■
SEA for the National Spatial Plan (VINEX) review	■
Vision (*visie*) Noord-Holland	■
Transport Plan (RVVP) INVERNO	⊙
Transport Plan (RVVP) Noord-Holland-Noord	⊙
Transport Plan (RVVP) ROA	●
Environment Matrix (*milieumatrix*) for the Structure Plan Amsterdam	●
Vision (*visie*) Hilversum	■
Transport Plan (RVVP) Haarlem-IJmond	■
EVR Brandenburg-Berlin (average score)	**74%**
Federal Transport Infrastructure Plan (BVWP)	⊙
Ecological Risk Assessment (*ökologische Risikoanalyse)* for the BVWP	⊙
Landscape Framework Plan (*Landschaftsrahmenplan*) Havelland-Flaming	●
Road Development Plan (*Landesstraßenbedarfsplan*) Brandenburg	⊙
Integrated Transport Plan (IVP) Brandenburg	⊙
Ecological Conflict Analysis for the Land Use Plan (FNP) Berlin	⊙
Landscape Programme (*Landschaftsprogramm*) for the FNP Berlin	■
Integrated Transport Plan (StEP) Berlin	●
Landscape Plan (*Landschaftsplan*) for the Land Use Plan (FNP) Ketzin	■

☐ policy-SEA   ☐ plan-SEA ☐ programme-SEA

Overall evaluation:
- ■ = 100%
- ● = 75% to under 100% of total score
- ⊙ = 50% to under 75% of total score
- ○ = 25% to under 50% of total score
- ▫ = 0% to under 25% of total score

public opposition to the projects proposed in the Federal Transport Infrastructure Plan (BVWP). The Ecological Conflict Analysis (*ökologische Konfliktanalyse*) for the Land Use Plans (FNP) Berlin involved neither the public, nor any other external statutory and non-statutory bodies in SEA preparation.

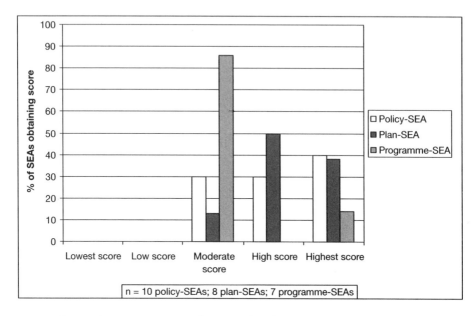

Figure 8.8: *SEA-type evaluation for the potential SEA benefit 5,*
'consultation and participation on SEA-related issues'

SEA type and sectoral patterns

Figure 8.8 shows the results for the potential SEA benefit 5, 'consultation and participation on SEA-related issues' for the three SEA types. While policy-SEA and plan-SEA scored highly (85 per cent and 89 per cent, respectively), programme-SEA obtained the lowest average score (62 per cent). Differences between programme-SEA and policy-SEA as well as between programme-SEA and plan-SEA were statistically significant (P<.01). Most programme-SEAs obtained moderate scores of between 50 per cent and 75 per cent, except the National Spatial Plan (VINEX) review, which obtained the highest score of 100 per cent. Comparatively low scores for consultation and participation in programme-SEA are related to the project-oriented character of this SEA type. As the projects ranked in programme-SEA can usually be geographically located, public opposition is likely (NIMBYism likely, see Chapter 1).

Differences between spatial/land use and transport SEAs were statistically significant (P<.01). Figure 9.9 shows that while most transport SEAs only obtained moderate scores, most spatial/land use SEAs either obtained the highest score or at least a high score of between 75 per cent and 100 per cent. On average, transport SEAs obtained 71 per cent of the total score and spatial/land use SEAs obtained 90 per cent of the total score. This is particularly due to the comparatively large number of transport programme-SEAs that did not involve any public participation.

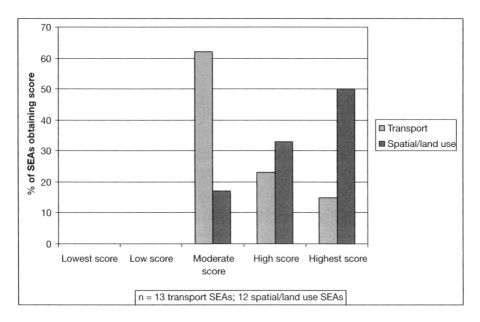

Figure 8.9: *Sector-specific evaluation for the potential SEA benefit 5, 'consultation and participation on SEA-related issues'*

OVERALL EVALUATION OF THE POTENTIAL SEA BENEFITS

Individual SEAs

Table 8.6 shows the overall evaluation for the individual SEAs (average scores for the five potential SEA benefits). Only three SEAs achieved over 75 per cent of the total score, all of which were from Noord-Holland. They include the policy-SEA for the Second Transport Structure Plan (SVVII) (85 per cent), the programme-SEA for the National Spatial Plan (VINEX) review (80 per cent) and the policy-SEA for the regional Transport Plan (RVVP) Haarlem-IJmond (78 per cent). SEAs with the highest scores in the other two regions include plan-SEAs, the Landscape Plan (*Landschaftsplan*) Ketzin (73 per cent) and the Environmental Appraisal for the Cheshire Structure Plan (69 per cent).

Regions, SEA types and sectors

Figure 8.10 shows the average scores for the five potential SEA benefits for the regions, SEA types and sectors. Noord-Holland SEAs, policy-SEAs and spatial/land use SEAs obtained the highest scores. Average scores in Noord-Holland were significantly higher than average scores in North West England and in EVR Brandenburg-Berlin ($P<.01$). Furthermore, policy-SEA scored significantly higher than plan-SEA ($P<.05$) and programme-SEA ($P<.01$). Plan-SEAs also obtained significantly higher scores than programme-SEAs ($P<.05$). Differences between transport and spatial/land use SEAs failed to be statistically significant.

Table 8.6: *Overall evaluation of the potential SEA benefits for the individual SEAs*

North West England (average score)	**56%**
Environmental Appraisal for the Lancashire Structure Plan	⊙
Environmental Appraisal for the Cheshire Structure Plan	⊙
Cheshire TPP	○
Merseyside Package Bid	○
Merseyside Package Bid underlying strategy	⊙
Environmental Appraisal for the Warrington Local Plan	⊙
Environmental Appraisal for the Oldham UDP	⊙
Noord-Holland (average score)	**72%**
Second Transport Structure Plan (SVVII)	●
SEA for the National Spatial Plan (VINEX) review	●
Vision (*visie*) Noord-Holland	⊙
Transport Plan (RVVP) INVERNO	⊙
Transport Plan (RVVP) Noord-Holland-Noord	⊙
Transport Plan (RVVP) ROA	⊙
Environment Matrix (*milieumatrix*) for the Structure Plan Amsterdam	⊙
Vision (*visie*) Hilversum	⊙
Transport Plan (RVVP) Haarlem-IJmond	⊙
EVR Brandenburg-Berlin (average score)	**53%**
Federal Transport Infrastructure Plan (BVWP)	○
Ecological Risk Assessment (*ökologische Risikoanalyse)* for the BVWP	○
Landscape Framework Plan (*Landschaftsrahmenplan*) Havelland-Flaming	⊙
Road Development Plan (*Landesstraßenbedarfsplan*) Brandenburg	○
Integrated Transport Plan (IVP) Brandenburg	⊙
Ecological Conflict Analysis for the Land Use Plan (FNP) Berlin	○
Landscape Programme (*Landschaftsprogramm*) for the FNP Berlin	⊙
Integrated Transport Plan (StEP) Berlin	⊙
Landscape Plan (*Landschaftsplan*) for the Land Use Plan (FNP) Ketzin	⊙

▭ policy-SEA   ▭ plan-SEA ▭ programme-SEA

Overall evaluation:
■ = 100%
● = 75% to under 100% of total score
⊙ = 50% to under 75% of total score
○ = 25% to under 50% of total score
▫ = 0% to under 25% of total score

REQUIREMENTS OF THE EC SEA DIRECTIVE

Figure 8.11 shows the extent to which the SEAs were able to meet the requirements of the EC SEA Directive, as laid down in the proposal of 1999.

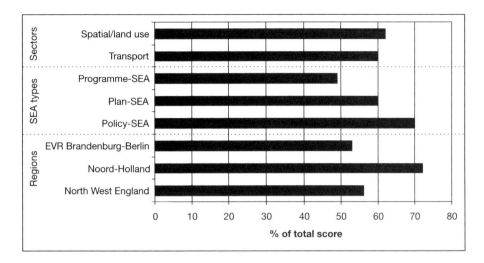

Figure 8.10: *Average potential SEA benefit scores for the regions, SEA types and sectors*

These were identified in terms of the SEA principles describing five potential SEA benefits. Detailed evaluation scores are found in Appendix 4. While none of the SEAs were able to meet the requirements of the proposed EC Directive fully, five SEAs were able to obtain overall scores of over 70 per cent. The highest score was obtained by the plan-SEA, Landscape Plan (*Landschaftsplan*) for the Land Use Plan (FNP) Ketzin. Over 70 per cent of the total score was also reached by three SEAs in Noord-Holland, namely, the policy-SEAs, Second Transport Structure Plan (SVVII) and Regional Transport Plan (RVVP) Haarlem-IJmond, and the programme-SEA for the National Spatial Plan (VINEX) review. Furthermore, over 70 per cent of the requirements were reached by the Environmental Appraisal for the Cheshire Structure Plan.

Six SEAs obtained scores of under 50 per cent, four from EVR Brandenburg-Berlin and two from North West England. All of the six SEAs that obtained the lowest scores were programme-SEAs and the only programme-SEA that was able to obtain a comparatively high score was the National Spatial Plan (VINEX) review, which is not surprising as it followed a formal project EIA procedure as laid out in the Dutch EIA decree of 1994.

If the scores for the PPPs that involved the preparation of two SEAs are summarized (that is the Merseyside Package Bid, involving a policy-SEA and a programme-SEA, and the Land Use Plan, FNP Berlin, involving a plan-SEA and a programme-SEA), over 70 per cent of the total possible score were also reached for the Land Use Plan (FNP) Berlin and the Merseyside Package Bid.

Figure 8.12 shows the extent to which individual requirements of the EC SEA Directive were considered in the SEAs in the three sample regions (see also Appendix 4). Five criteria were considered in over 75 per cent of the SEAs, namely environmental impacts, reporting of the final SEA results, sustainable development, consultation of external bodies and alternatives. Three SEAs did not directly assess environmental impacts, but were used as instruments of

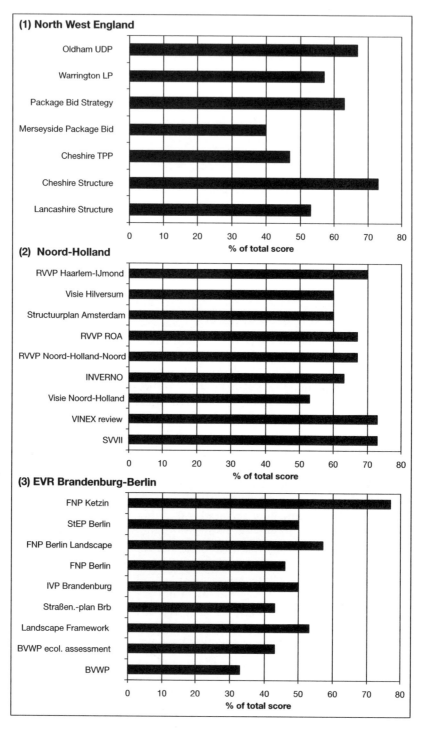

Figure 8.11: *Extent to which individual SEAs meet the requirements of the EC SEA Directive proposal*

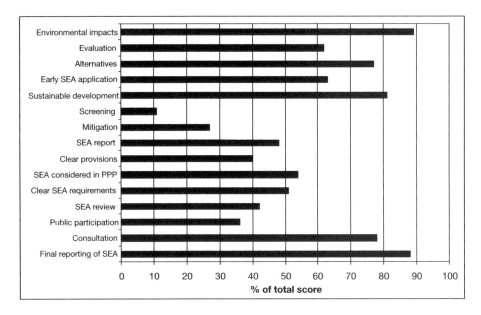

Figure 8.12: *Extent to which the criteria of the EC SEA Directive proposal are considered*

the precautionary principle, identifying land suitability maps. These include the Environment Matrix (*milieumatrix*) Amsterdam, the Landscape Framework Plan (*Landschaftsrahmenplan*) Havelland-Fläming and the Landscape Programme (*Landschaftsprogramm*) Berlin. Reporting of the final SEA results was not done for the Cheshire TPP and the Merseyside Package Bid. While sustainable development was considered in all of the SEAs in North West England and Noord-Holland, it was only acknowledged in three SEAs in EVR Brandenburg-Berlin, namely, in the plan-SEA, Landscape Framework Plan (*Landschaftsrahmenplan*) Havelland-Fläming and the policy-SEAs, integrated transport plans (IVP) Brandenburg and (StEP) Berlin.

Six criteria were considered in less than 50 per cent of the SEAs. These include screening, mitigation, public participation, clear provisions, review by an external body and the preparation of a separate SEA report. While none of the SEAs had screening provisions, public participation was more extensive in Noord-Holland than in EVR Brandenburg-Berlin and in North West England.[2] Mitigation, on the other hand, was particularly poorly considered in North West England. External review was conducted to the largest extent in Noord-Holland and separate SEA reports were most frequently prepared in North West England.

Figure 8.13 shows the average scores for the three regions, SEA types and the two sectors. SEAs in Noord-Holland obtained the highest overall score and SEAs in EVR Brandenburg-Berlin the lowest overall score (P<.01). Both policy-SEA and plan-SEA obtained the same score, which was significantly higher than the score for programme-SEA (P<.05). Plan-SEA and to some extent programme-SEA in the spatial/land use sector, are most likely to be subject to

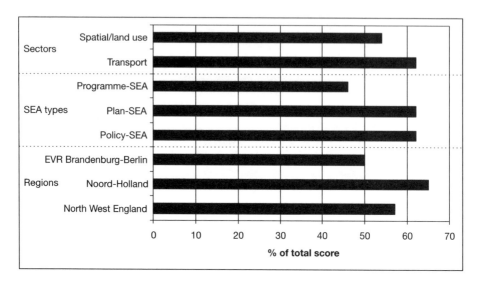

Figure 8.13: *Average scores for the SEA Directive proposal requirements by region, SEA type and sector*

formalized SEA under an SEA Directive. As policy-SEA fulfils certain tasks that are not covered by the other two SEA types (particularly a wider consideration of impacts and alternatives and an extensive consideration of sustainability aspects), it is, however, suggested that SEA should be applied within a tiered SEA system, applying all of these types.

Summary

The 25 SEAs for the cross-section of 36 PPPs at all administrative levels in the three sample regions resulted in the five potential SEA benefits to varying extents. While the potential benefit of consultation and participation on SEA-related issues was comparatively well considered, the potential benefit of 'strengthening project EIA: increasing the efficiency of tiered decision making' was comparatively poorly considered.

The extent to which assessments resulted in the potential SEA benefits depended on the region and the SEA type. While Noord-Holland SEAs and policy-SEAs mostly resulted in high potential SEA benefits scores, programme-SEAs obtained comparatively poor scores, in particular, for the potential SEA benefit of 'wider consideration of impacts and alternatives'.

The variable SEA procedure was of particular importance for explaining the observed patterns and there is significant correlation of the extent to which SEA procedural stages were covered with all SEA benefits. Of all of the context variables, PPP accountability played the most important role, partly explaining the extent to which assessments resulted in three of the potential SEA benefits, namely, 'proactive assessment: SEA as a supporting tool for PPP formulation for sustainable development', 'systematic and effective consideration of the environment at higher tiers of decision making' and 'consultation and participation on SEA-related issues'.

Policy-SEA resulted in high potential SEA benefit scores, involving a comparatively comprehensive, extensive and open SEA process. Most of the SEAs in Noord-Holland were policy-SEAs, which is explained by the overall planning approach in this region (society, consensus-led, quasi-top-down). The use of programme-SEAs was comparatively widespread in EVR Brandenburg-Berlin. Projects were clearly ranked and there was no public participation, particularly for fear of public opposition (NIMBYism – see Chapter 1).

It was found that SEAs were not able to fully meet the requirements of the SEA Directive proposal of the EC. While some policy-SEAs and plan-SEAs were able to obtain comparatively high scores, most programme-SEAs only obtained under 50 per cent of the total score. On average, for a cross-section of 36 PPPs at all administrative levels, Noord-Holland's SEAs were better able to meet the SEA Directive requirements than the SEAs in North West England and EVR Brandenburg-Berlin.

Summary and Conclusions

Introduction to Part 4

Part 4 is divided into two chapters. Chapter 9 provides an overview and a synthesis of the results for the seven SEA aspects analysed, namely, SEA procedure, SEA impact range, SEA methods and techniques, opinions of PPP makers, attitudes of PPP makers, sustainability aspects and potential SEA benefits. Furthermore, a summary of the findings of the correlation analysis is presented and the results are interpreted in the light of current theoretical SEA understanding.

Chapter 10 draws the conclusions, referring to the research questions formulated in Chapter 1. Furthermore, suggestions for improving current SEA practice in transport and spatial/land use planning are made.

Chapter 9

Overview and synthesis

Chapter 9 draws together the main results of Chapters 5 to 8, and explains and interprets observed results in the context of wider research. Reference is made to the 25 SEAs for the cross-section of 36 PPPs at all administrative levels (interview results) and to the 35 SEAs for the 78 local land use PPPs (postal questionnaire results) in the three sample regions. Explanation and interpretation of the results is provided. This fulfils objective 6 of the book, 'to summarize and interpret research results and to suggest improvements to current practice'.

The chapter is divided into four sections. The first presents an overall picture of the results, referring to the regions, SEA types and sectors. The results for the individual SEAs are presented and good practice SEAs are identified. This is followed by an analysis of the correlation between context variables, SEA variables and the other examined SEA aspects (using Spearman's rank order test). Finally, the research results are interpreted with reference to the five statements, reflecting common understanding of SEA, and to the requirements of the EC SEA Directive proposal.

OVERALL RESULTS

This section presents the overall results from Chapters 5 to 8 in a cross-thematic manner. The following seven SEA aspects are covered:

- SEA procedure.
- SEA impact range.
- SEA methods and techniques.
- authorities' attitudes.
- authorities' opinions.
- Consideration of sustainability objectives, targets and measures.
- Potential benefits from SEA application.

While the cross-section of 36 PPPs at all administrative levels covered all seven aspects, local land use PPPs covered only three, namely, the examination of authorities' attitudes and opinions and the consideration of sustainability aspects. The next section has five sub-sections, dealing with the results in terms of the regions, SEA types and sectors, cases with and without SEA, and local land use PPPs.

Regions

Figure 9.1 shows the overall results for the seven SEA aspects in a region-specific manner. While Noord-Holland SEAs obtained high scores for all of the aspects, the SEAs in North West England and in EVR Brandenburg-Berlin scored comparatively poorly on a number of them. Regional differences were statistically significant for all aspects, except for the SEA impact range.

For two aspects, SEAs in Noord-Holland obtained significantly higher scores than SEAs from the other two regions – the potential SEA benefits (P<.01) and the consideration of sustainability aspects (P<.05). This is explained by the more extensive use of policy-SEA in Noord-Holland, which led to a better consideration of two potential SEA benefits, namely, a wider consideration of impacts and alternatives and proactive assessment – SEA as a supporting tool for PPP formulation for sustainable development. Furthermore, policy-SEAs considered explicit sustainability objectives and targets, as well as sustainability measures, to a larger extent than the other two SEA types as well as PPPs without SEA.

SEAs in North West England obtained significantly lower scores on two aspects than SEAs in the other two regions, including the range of SEA methods and techniques (P<.01 for Noord-Holland; P<.05 for EVR Brandenburg-Berlin) and opinions of authorities (P<.05 for Noord-Holland; P<.01 for EVR Brandenburg-Berlin). The smaller range of SEA methods and techniques used in North West England was caused by the use of central government guidance, which mainly promoted the use of matrices and checklists (DoE, 1993; DoT, 1995). While opinions on the quality of SEAs were similar in the three regions, opinions on the influence of SEA in the policy, plan or programme process were compara-

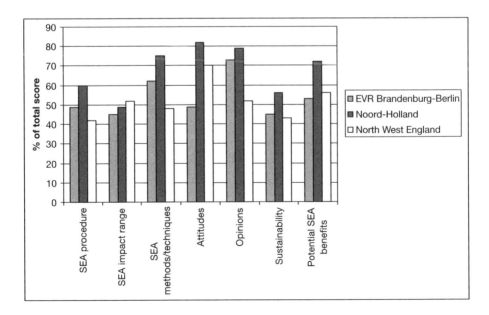

Figure 9.1: *Results for seven SEA aspects by region*

tively low in North West England. This was related to the short SEA preparation times, which were all under one person-year. Finally, SEAs in North West England also obtained a significantly lower score on the coverage of SEA procedural stages than Noord-Holland SEAs (P<.05). Stages that were particularly poorly considered were SEA initiation (scoping) and monitoring. EVR Brandenburg-Berlin SEAs obtained significantly lower scores than the other two regions on the attitudes of authorities towards formalized SEA (P<.05). This is not unexpected, as other studies on SEA and EIA all indicated negative attitudes of decision makers in Germany (see Chapter 1).

Overall, the comparatively poor performance of EVR Brandenburg-Berlin SEAs is principally explained by the comparatively frequent application of programme-SEA. Thus, programme-SEA did not include public participation and only limited external consultation, both aspects previously found to have been of high importance for overall SEA success. Furthermore, public participation in plan-SEA in EVR Brandenburg-Berlin was only conducted at the local level.

These research results confirm the findings of Thérivel and Partidário (1996a, p12) who indicated that British SEAs were more qualitative and slimmer than German and Dutch SEAs, and that German SEAs emphasize quantification. However, based on the results of this research it is arguable whether Dutch SEAs deal particularly well with hierarchies of decision making (Thérivel and Partidário, 1996a, p12). Thus, relationships between policies and projects in Noord-Holland remain largely unclear.

SEA types

Figure 9.2 shows the overall results for the three examined SEA types, which for convenience, were called policy-SEA, plan-SEA and programme-SEA. Policy-SEA obtained significantly higher scores than the other two SEA types on three aspects – potential SEA benefits, SEA procedure (in both cases P<.05 for plan-SEA and P<.01 for programme-SEA), and sustainability aspects (P<.01 for both plan-SEA and programme-SEA). Policy-SEA also obtained significantly higher scores on attitudes of authorities towards formalized SEA than programme-SEA (P<.05). In addition to these differences, plan-SEA obtained significantly higher scores for the potential SEA benefits than programme-SEA (P<.05), which was mainly caused by the more extensive coverage of SEA procedural stages and a wider use of different methods and techniques. On the SEA impact range, however, plan-SEA obtained a significantly lower score than programme-SEA (P<.05), which was mainly due to the failure of plan-SEA to consider socio-economic impacts.

The good performance of policy-SEA regarding all of the examined SEA aspects is mainly explained by its application at an early stage in the planning cycle. Both plan-SEA and programme-SEA are applied at later stages in the planning cycle and are more project oriented. Public opposition due to the NIMBY phenomenon is therefore more likely (see Chapter 1) and the willingness of authorities to involve the public in SEA preparation as well as to consider a wide range of impacts and alternatives is reduced. Policy-SEA usually involved

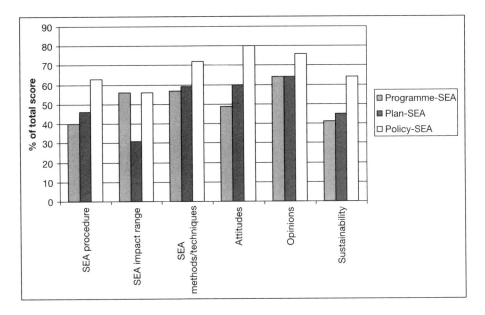

Figure 9.2: *Results for seven SEA aspects by SEA type*

widespread participation and consultation and considered a wide range of impacts and alternatives, factors which proved to be of high importance for good SEA performance.

On average, while most programme-SEAs obtained comparatively poor scores, the programme-SEA for the National Spatial Plan (VINEX) review performed well, following a formal procedure laid out in the Dutch EIA Decree of 1994. The performance of the different plan-SEAs varied considerably, depending on the region and the administrative level of application. In North West England, plan-SEAs (environmental appraisals) mostly obtained moderate scores. In EVR Brandenburg-Berlin, plan-SEAs (landscape plans and programmes, *Landschaftspläne und -programme*), undertaken at the local level obtained higher scores than those undertaken at decision making levels above the project level. This was particularly caused by the fact that public participation in EVR Brandenburg-Berlin SEAs only took place at the local level of decision making.

Sectors

Figure 9.3 summarizes the overall results for the seven main SEA aspects for the two examined sectors.

None of the differences were statistically significant. While transport SEAs, on average, scored slightly higher on the SEA impact range and the consideration of sustainability aspects, spatial/land use SEAs scored slightly higher on SEA methods and techniques and on the attitudes and opinions of authorities. While socio-economic impacts and inter-modal alternatives were considered to a larger extent in transport SEA, public participation and impact mapping were more widespread in spatial/land use SEA.

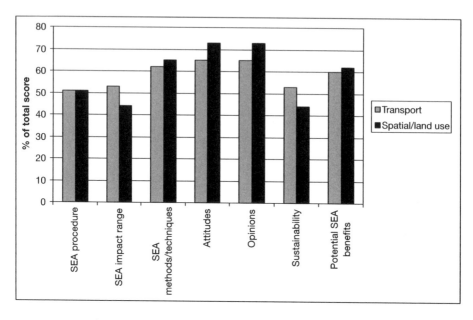

Figure 9.3: *Results for seven SEA aspects by sector*

Comparison of PPPs with and without SEA

Policies, plans and programmes with and without SEA are compared for the consideration of sustainability objectives, targets and measures, and the attitudes of authorities towards an application of formalized SEA. Figure 9.4 shows the overall results.

While SEA application led to a slightly better consideration of sustainability aspects, the results were not statistically significant. Only sustainability measures were considered to a significantly larger extent in PPPs involving SEA

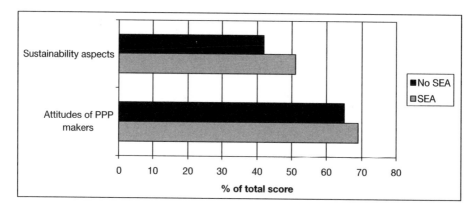

Figure 9.4: *Sustainability aspects and attitudes in PPPs with and without SEA*

(P<.05). While SEA in the transport sector led to the consideration of a significantly larger number of explicit objectives, explicit targets and measures (P<.05), SEA in the spatial/land use sector did not lead to a better consideration of any of these aspects. Only policy-SEAs considered sustainability objectives, targets and measures to a larger extent than PPPs without SEA.

There were no significant differences in attitudes towards the application of formalized SEA between authorities undertaking SEA and authorities not undertaking SEA. It was, however, observed that those authorities that either undertook policy-SEA or that did not undertake SEA at all had more positive attitudes towards formalized SEA than those undertaking plan-SEA and programme-SEA. As policy-SEA was integrated into the PPP process, there was no fear of a process delay. The positive attitudes of authorities that did not undertake SEA are explained by a perception that without formal requirements SEA would be more difficult to conduct. Very long preparation times of plan-SEA and programme-SEA were an important reason for overall negative attitudes, which were particularly observed in EVR Brandenburg-Berlin.

Local land use PPPs

At the local level, three SEA aspects were analysed, namely the attitudes of authorities and opinions of authorities and the consideration of sustainability aspects. Of the 35 SEAs undertaken for local land use PPPs, 34 were of the plan-SEA type. Figure 9.5. shows the overall results. As only one SEA was undertaken at the local level in Noord-Holland, opinions on the quality and the influence of SEA can only be shown for North West England and EVR Brandenburg-Berlin.

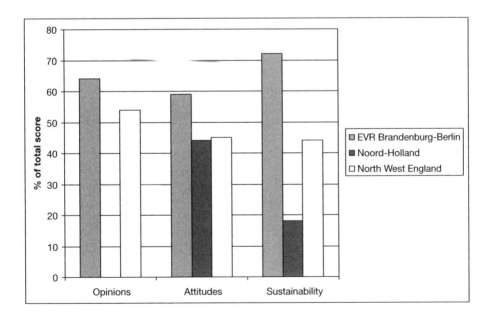

Figure 9.5: *Regional overall scores for local land use PPPs*

Results for local land use PPPs differed considerably from those of the cross-section of 36 PPPs at all administrative levels, particularly for Noord-Holland and EVR Brandenburg-Berlin. While Noord-Holland SEAs obtained the highest scores on all of the examined aspects for the cross-section of PPPs, it obtained the lowest scores on the attitudes towards formalized SEA and the consideration of sustainability aspects at the local level. EVR Brandenburg-Berlin SEAs, on the other hand, scored the highest on all of the SEA aspects at the local level. The only region for which results for the cross-section of PPPs and local land use PPPs were similar was North West England, mainly because most authorities included were from the local and county levels, using similar planning instruments and the same kinds of SEAs (environmental appraisals for development plans and TPPs/package bids).

Differences between the cross-section of PPPs and local land use PPPs in Noord-Holland and EVR Brandenburg-Berlin are explained by the varying extent of SEA application and by the different planning approaches. While only one of 22 local land PPPs in Noord-Holland involved SEA application, this number rose to 21 of 23 in EVR Brandenburg-Berlin (13 of 27 in North West England involved SEA application). The planning approach in Noord-Holland (society, consensus-led, quasi-top-down approach) is the reason that policy objectives and targets are identified at higher tiers for consideration at the local level. Furthermore, attitudes towards formalized SEA were found to be negative at the local level in Noord-Holland, where authorities thought that SEA was inappropriately applied. In EVR Brandenburg-Berlin, the perception that SEA could be based on the existing landscape plans led to local authorities having more positive attitudes towards formalized SEA.

EVALUATION OF INDIVIDUAL SEAS

Table 9.1 shows the scores for the seven SEA aspects examined in Chapters 5 to 8 for each individual SEA (and associated PPP). Overall good practice SEAs were identified for each of the three SEA types, also covering the two sectors. All of the aspects other then attitudes towards formalized SEA were used to identify good practice cases which include:

- the policy-SEA for the Second Transport Structure Plan (SVVII);
- the plan-SEA (Landscape Plan, *Landschaftsplan*) for the Land Use Plan (FNP) Ketzin; and
- the programme-SEA for the National Spatial Plan (VINEX) review.

The overall good practice SEAs scored highly on most aspects with two exceptions, namely, a poor consideration of sustainability aspects in the Landscape Plan (*Landschaftsplan*) Ketzin and a small SEA impact range in the Second Transport Structure Plan (SVVII). All good practice SEAs started before, or at the beginning of, PPP formulation and accompanied, or were integrated into, the process.

In addition to the three overall good practice SEAs, region-specific good practice was identified for each of the three SEA types and the two sectors. In

North West England and EVR Brandenburg-Berlin, no good practice cases for the programme-SEA type were identified, as all of the programme-SEAs obtained comparatively poor scores. In Noord-Holland, no overall good practice plan-SEA was identified, as only one plan-SEA was undertaken. Regional good practice included:

- North West England: the plan-SEA – Environmental Appraisal for the Cheshire Structure Plan; and the policy-SEA – underlying Transport Strategy for the Merseyside Package Bid;
- EVR Brandenburg-Berlin: the plan-SEA – Landscape Plan (*Landschaftsplan*) Ketzin; and the policy-SEA – Integrated Transport Plan (StEP) Berlin.
- Noord-Holland: the policy-SEA – Second Transport Structure Plan (SVVII); the programme-SEA – National Spatial Plan (VINEX) review; and the spatial/land use policy-SEA – Vision (*visie*) Hilversum.

Previously reviewed SEAs

Three assessments representing the three SEA types had been previously reviewed by other authors on a number of occasions. These were:

- the Federal Transport Infrastructure Plan (BVWP) – Integrated Assessment and Ecological Risk Assessment (EC, 1999a; ECMT, 1998; Steer Davies Gleave, 1996; Lee and Hughes, 1995, part B).
- the Lancashire Structure Plan/Environmental Appraisal (Sadler and Verheem, 1996a; EC, 1994).
- the Second Transport Structure Plan, SVVII/integrated assessment (EC, 1999a; ECMT, 1998; Steer Davies Gleave, 1996; and OECD, 1994).

While the Second Transport Structure Plan (SVVII) was identified as an overall good practice SEA, in terms of the SEA types, the sectors and the regions, the Environmental Appraisal for the Lancashire Structure Plan is a moderate SEA example, both in terms of the SEA type and the sector. The Federal Transport Infrastructure Plan (BVWP) – Integrated Assessment and Ecological Risk Assessment scored similarly to the other transport programme-SEAs in the three sample regions, all of which, on average, obtained comparatively poor scores. It is therefore regarded as an average programme-SEA example.

If the three SEAs were evaluated based on their overall performance without taking the SEA type into account, the Federal Transport Infrastructure Plan would have been judged to perform poorly. The SEA categorization put forward in this research therefore helps to evaluate SEA performance based on the specific SEA-type requirements.

CORRELATION ANALYSIS OF SEA ASPECTS

Table 9.2 shows the statistical correlation between the context variables, SEA variables and the other SEA aspects for the cross-section of 36 PPPs at all

Table 9.1: *Results for the seven main comparative aspects for individual SEA and the identification of good practice cases*

SEA	Attitude	Procedure	Impact assessment	Methods and techniques	Opinions	Sustainability aspects	Potential SEA benefits	Good practice SEA
Lancashire Structure Plan, Environmental Appraisal	●	○	⊙	○	⊙	⊙	⊙	
Cheshire Structure Plan, Environmental Appraisal	●	⊙	⊙	⊙	⊙	⊙	⊙	✓
Cheshire TPP	⊙	○	⊙	○	○	⊙	○	
Merseyside Package Bid	n/a	○	⊙	○	○	⊙	○	✓
Merseyside Package Bid, underlying strategy	●	⊙	○	⊙	⊙	○	⊙	
Warrington Local Plan, Environmental Appraisal	●	○	⊙	○	⊙	○	⊙	
Oldham UDP, Environmental Appraisal	⊙	○	⊙	⊙	⊙	○	⊙	
Second Transport Structure Plan (SVVII)	■	●	○	⊙	■	●	●	✓✓
National Spatial Plan (VINEX) - review	●	●	●	■	■	⊙	●	✓✓
Development Vision Noord-Holland	⊙	⊙	⊙	⊙	n/a	○	⊙	
Transport Vision (INVERNO)	■	⊙	⊙	⊙	⊙	⊙	⊙	
Transport Plan (RVVP) Noord-Holland-Nord	■	⊙	○	⊙	○	⊙	⊙	
Transport Plan (RVVP) ROA	○	⊙	○	⊙	●	⊙	⊙	
Structure Plan Amsterdam, Environment Matrix	⊙	□	□	⊙	⊙	⊙	⊙	
Future Vision (*visie*) Hilversum	●	⊙	●	⊙	■	○	⊙	✓
Transport Plan (RVVP) Haarlem-IJmond	■	⊙	⊙	⊙	■	⊙	●	
Federal Transport Plan (BWWP) Ecological Risk Assessment	○	□	○	⊙	⊙	○	○	
Federal Transport Plan (BWWP)	○	○	⊙	⊙	⊙	○	○	

Table 9.1: *Continued*

SEA	SEA stage	Attitude	Procedure	Impact assessment	Methods and techniques	Opinions	Sustainability aspects	Potential SEA benefits	Good practice SEA
Regional Plan Havelland-Fläming }Landscape Framewk Plan		◉	◉				○	◉	
Development Concept Havelland		◉	□	□	◉	●	○	◉	
Road Development Plan Brandenburg		◉		◉	○	◉	□	○	
Integrated Transport Plan, IVP Brandenburg		●	◉	●	◉	n/a	●	◉	
Land Use Plan (FNP) Berlin, Ecological Conflict Analysis		□	○	◉	◉	n/a	○	○	
Land Use Plan (FNP) Berlin, Landscape Programme			◉	□	◉	n/a		◉	
Development Plan (StEP) Transport		○	◉	●	●	n/a	◉	◉	✓
Local Land Use Plan (FNP) Ketzin, Landscape Plan		◉	●	◉	●		○	◉	✓✓

policy-SEA ☐   plan-SEA ☐   programme-SEA ☐   ✓✓ = overall good practice SEA   ✓ = other regional good practice SEA

Overall evaluation:
■ = 100%
● = 75% to under 100% of total score
◉ = 50% to under 75% of total score
○ = 25% to under 50% of total score
□ = 0% to under 25% of total score

administrative levels as defined in Chapters 4 to 8. The observed patterns are then described and discussed in further detail.

Context variables

The context variable PPP relevance was correlated in a negative manner with the SEA impacts. Policies, plans and programmes with a high PPP relevance included, in particular, statutory spatial/land use plans for which plan-SEAs were mostly undertaken. The low score of the SEA impacts is explained by a general failure of plan-SEAs to assess socio-economic impacts (see Table 5.1).

The context variable PPP inter-modality was significantly correlated with the overall sustainability and the potential SEA benefits scores. Furthermore, there was also significant correlation with the SEA procedure. These results were particularly due to policy-SEA application, which systematically considered inter-modal aspects and obtained high sustainability and potential SEA benefits scores (Chapters 7 and 8).

The context variable PPP procedure was significantly correlated with the extent to which sustainability aspects were considered, thus supporting the procedural framework for PPP formulation for sustainable development, portrayed in Figure 1.1. The PPP procedure was significantly correlated with the opinions of authorities. An extensive PPP process is therefore thought to provide greater chances for SEA to be effective in this process.

SEA variables

Among the four SEA variables, SEA procedure and SEA methods and techniques were correlated with the largest number of other aspects. Procedural stages that were of particular importance include public participation and the consultation of external bodies. Furthermore, those methods and techniques that were identified to be most relevant include quantitative impact assessment and impact mapping.

SEA preparation times were correlated with the extent to which SEA methods and techniques were used. This is mainly explained by regional differences. Thus, in North West England short SEA preparation times were accompanied by an application of only a few SEA methods and techniques.[1] There was no correlation of SEA preparation times with the potential SEA benefits, indicating that SEA is not always applied effectively in terms of time input and benefits output.

SEA procedure was correlated with the extent to which sustainability aspects were considered. Furthermore, SEA procedure was correlated with the overall scores for the potential SEA benefits, and also with the opinions and attitudes of authorities. Thus, an extensive coverage of procedural stages in SEA meant that authorities did not expect formal SEA provisions to result in many changes and had rather positive attitudes towards formalized SEA. There was not only correlation of the SEA procedure with those individual potential SEA benefits that shared some of the underlying procedural stages, but also with those potential benefits that did not. These included a wider consideration of impacts and alternatives and strengthening project-EIA, increasing the efficiency of tiered decision making.

Table 9.2: Correlation of context and SEA variables and the other SEA aspects

	Other SEA aspects				SEA variables				Context variables			
	SEA benefits	Sustain-ability	Attit-udes	Opin-ions	SEA time	SEA meth. & techn.	SEA im-pacts	SEA proce-dure	PPP proce-dure	PPP inter-modality	PPP account-ability	PPP rele-vance
Context variables — PPP relevance											**	■
PPP accountability											■	
PPP inter-modality	*	**							**	■		
PPP procedure		*		*				**	■			
SEA variables — SEA procedure	**	*	*	**			**	■				
SEA impacts						**	■					
SEA methods & techniques	**			**	**	■						
SEA time				**	■							
Other SEA aspects — Opinions				■								
Attitudes	**	*	■									
Sustainability	**	■										
SEA benefits	■											

Note: *   P<.05, Spearman's rank order test
     ** P<.01, Spearman's rank order test
     [ ] correlation not significant

SEAs that included monitoring tended to consider sustainability objectives, targets and measures well, in other words monitoring provisions show commitment to achieving previously defined objectives and targets.

The overall SEA impact range was not significantly correlated with any of the examined SEA aspects. However, the extent to which impacts were quantitatively assessed was correlated with the overall potential SEA benefits score, that is quantitative assessment has more positive effects than qualitative assessment. SEA methods and techniques were significantly correlated with the opinions of authorities on the quality and the influence of current assessments. Those methods and techniques that appeared to have been of particular importance included simulation, expert consultation, impact mapping, mitigation, the consideration of inter-modal alternatives and scenarios. All of these methods and techniques were used in policy-SEA, which scored highly on all of the examined SEA aspects (see Figure 9.2).

Other SEA aspects

The extent to which existing assessments resulted in the potential SEA benefits was correlated with all context and SEA variables, except for the SEA preparation times. The attitudes of authorities towards an application of formalized SEA were dependent on the extent to which current assessments considered sustainability aspects and resulted in the potential SEA benefits, that is those authorities that undertook high quality SEAs did not think an introduction of formal requirements would change current practice and had positive attitudes. Furthermore, sustainability aspects were significantly correlated with the overall scores for the potential SEA benefits, and particularly strongly with the benefit proactive assessment – SEA as a tool for PPP making for sustainable development.

INTERPRETATION OF THE RESULTS

This section interprets the results of comparative research presented in the book. In this context, five statements are discussed that reflect current SEA understanding. Furthermore, the likely extent of SEA application in the three sample regions after the implementation of an SEA Directive in the EU is discussed.

Interpretation of the research results in the light of current SEA understanding

This section interprets the research results in the light of five statements, reflecting current SEA understanding. While some statements were found to be confirmed, others were not and are, therefore, rejected.

Statement 1: 'SEA experience is only limited'

Based on a broad definition of SEA (encompassing any kind of assessment of the environmental impacts of a PPP), this research identified a minimum number of 80 assessments in the three regions that, if broadly defined, can be called SEA. These include 17 SEAs in the transport sector and 63 SEAs in the spatial/land use sector. While none of the assessments included in this research were officially called 'SEA', many obtained high scores on the various SEA aspects examined. When considering the combined population (3.5 per cent of total EU population) and area size (0.5 per cent of total EU area) of the regions examined, as well as the fact that only transport and spatial/land use PPPs were examined, the potential number of SEAs in the EU appears to be quite high. It is therefore suggested that SEA experience is more extensive than is often suggested.

Statement 2: 'SEA should develop more independently of project EIA'

This research found that successful SEA application (SEA that results in the potential SEA benefits and scores highly on a large range of examined SEA aspects) is correlated with the extent to which procedural stages, similar to those for project EIA, were covered (NEPA-based process, see Box 1.1). Procedural stages that were of particular importance included public participation and the consultation of external bodies. Furthermore, methods and techniques that were found to be of importance for successful SEA included those that were also known to be used in project EIA, namely, expert involvement, workshops and the quantitative assessment of impacts (calculating impact magnitudes), impact mapping and the consideration of inter-modal alternatives.

While different authors suggested that SEA was particularly difficult to apply early in the planning cycle, this is not confirmed here. In fact, the SEA type that was applied at the earliest stage in the planning cycle (policy-SEA) on average obtained the highest scores of all SEA types. It is therefore suggested that, at least for the kinds of PPPs considered in this research, SEA principles are not different from project EIA principles and the statement in its general sense needs to be rejected.[2]

Statement 3: 'SEA ensures sustainable development is considered in PPP making'

Three aspects that were said to be of importance for PPP making for sustainable development were examined, including procedural aspects, the assessment of environmental and socio-economic impacts and the consideration of sustainability objectives, targets and measures. Figure 5.1 showed that procedural stages for PPP making for sustainable development were indeed considered to a larger extent in those cases that involved SEA. While none of the cases without SEA assessed environmental and socio-economic impacts, all policy-SEAs and programme-SEAs considered both. It appears therefore that SEA can indeed lead to a better coverage of procedural stages and to a better consideration of both environmental and socio-economic aspects.

Regarding the consideration of sustainability objectives, targets and measures, more detailed comments can be made, referring to the results of Chapter 7. Overall, it was found that SEA was not always able to result in higher overall sustainability scores. Substantial differences were observed between the two sectors. Thus, while SEA was able to lead to a significantly larger consideration of explicit objectives, explicit targets and measures in the transport sector, differences in the spatial/land use sector were not statistically significant. Furthermore, it was found that only one SEA type was clearly able to lead to a better consideration of sustainability objectives, targets and measures, namely, the policy-SEA type. Policy-SEA covered SEA procedural stages to a comparatively large extent. Furthermore, inter-modal alternatives as well as environmental and socio-economic impacts were considered, and cumulative impacts were assessed, frequently involving public participation and the consultation of external bodies. It is therefore suggested that only a tiered SEA approach is likely to ensure that the sustainability aspects defined at higher levels will be passed on to lower levels.

Statement 4: 'A tiered approach ensures SEA only addresses those matters and at that level of detail, which are appropriate to it'

Tiering in SEA currently takes place, both between different administrative levels (vertical integration) as well as within administrative levels (horizontal integration). Tiering between different administrative levels was found to consist of the formulation of policy objectives at higher levels that were to be considered at lower levels. Tiering within administrative levels was conducted particularly between policy-SEA and programme-SEA, and between plan-SEA and programme-SEA.[3] While policy-SEA was applied early in the planning cycle and focused on scenarios, inter-modal alternatives and cumulative impacts, programme-SEA prioritized projects and was conducted at a later stage in the planning cycle. Plan-SEAs mainly referred to spatial alternatives. While no tiering between policy-SEA and plan-SEA was observed, consideration of the tasks of the three SEA types indicates that plan-SEA is applied after policy-SEA and before programme-SEA. This research suggests that the tiering of policy-SEA, plan-SEA and programme-SEA can potentially lead to a simplification of current planning practice by fulfilling clearly identified tasks. Statement 4 is therefore supported by the findings of the research.

Statement 5: 'SEA that is well founded and based on the application of clear SEA principles is most likely to be influential'

It was found that the existence of SEA provisions or guidance was not necessarily leading to improved SEA performance in terms of the resulting potential SEA benefits (see Chapter 8) and in a more extensive consideration of sustainability objectives, targets and measures (see Chapter 7). It is indicated that the influence of SEA in PPP making was related, in particular, to SEA preparation times, that is SEAs with long preparation times were said to have been of greater influence in PPP making than SEAs with shorter preparation times. Furthermore, the extent to which SEA methods and techniques were applied, and the extent to which SEA procedural stages were covered, was of importance. It is therefore concluded that the influence of SEA in PPP formulation is only likely to be high if provisions and requirements are based on SEA principles, ensuring that SEA procedural stages are covered and methods and techniques are extensively applied.

Likely extent of SEA application in the three sample regions after the introduction of an SEA Directive

The EC 1996/1999 SEA Directive proposal (COM(96)511; COM(99)073 final) does not differentiate between SEA types. The explanatory memorandum to COM(96)511, however, indicated that probably only those assessments that were classified in this book as plan-SEAs and to some extent programme-SEAs in the spatial/land use sector might be subject to formal SEA provisions.

This research identified that the plan-SEA, Landscape Plan (*Landschaftsplan*) for the Land Use Plan (FNP) Ketzin met the requirements of the SEA Directive proposal to the largest extent (see Chapter 8). Three other SEAs, however, were also able to meet the requirements of the SEA directive to a large extent, including a policy-SEA (Second Structure Transport Plan, SVVII), a plan-SEA (Environmental Appraisal for the Cheshire Structure Plan) and a programme-SEA (National Spatial Plan, VINEX review). This indicates that all SEA types are potentially able to meet the SEA Directive requirements to a similar extent.

It is suggested that if the EC SEA Directive only covered plan-SEA and programme-SEA in the spatial/land use sector, proportionally more PPPs in the UK and Germany would be subject to formalized SEA than in The Netherlands (see Chapter 8). Thus, while most of the local authorities in EVR Brandenburg-Berlin and all of the local authorities in North West England prepared formal land use plans that would most likely be subject to SEA, only one-third of the responding authorities in Noord-Holland were preparing local land use plans (in the form of structure plans, *structuurplannen*), that would require SEA. Furthermore, this research showed that local authorities in Noord-Holland increasingly prepare policies (visions – *visies*) that would not require formalized SEA preparation under the proposed SEA Directive. Therefore, policy-SEA should be included in a future revision of the SEA Directive.

Chapter 10

Conclusions

The main aim of this book was to report on the findings of a systematic comparative analysis of SEA in three EU countries. Furthermore, the patterns observed were to be explained and improvements to SEA practice suggested. Four research questions were addressed through six objectives in Chapters 3 to 9 (following Figure 1.2). The research questions are answered in this chapter, namely:

1. What is the extent of SEA application, and is it possible to classify SEA types based on current practice?
2. What are authorities opinions on current SEA, and what are their attitudes towards formalized SEA?
3. What is the role of SEA in considering sustainability objectives, targets and measures?
4. To what extent do assessments result in the five potential SEA benefits?

In accordance with the main aim of this book, suggestions are made for improving current practice.

EXTENT OF SEA APPLICATION AND SEA CLASSIFICATION

Extent of SEA application

The extent of SEA application (including any type of assessment of the environmental impacts of a PPP) at all administrative levels was systematically identified in the three sample regions of North West England (UK), Noord-Holland (The Netherlands) and EVR Brandenburg-Berlin (Germany). All of the authorities responsible for the preparation of transport and spatial/land use PPPs in the three regions were contacted. Comprehensive interviews were conducted on 12 PPPs in each region, representing all administrative levels (referred to as the cross-section of PPPs). Postal questionnaires were sent to 178 mostly local authorities ie in total, 214 authorities were contacted.

A minimum number of 80 SEAs was identified (see Appendix 3). These included 23 SEAs in North West England, 23 SEAs in Noord-Holland and 34 SEAs in EVR Brandenburg-Berlin. Of these, 17 SEAs were undertaken in the transport sector and 63 SEAs were undertaken in the spatial/land use sector.[1]

In North West England, SEAs were undertaken at only two administrative levels, the county and district levels. In Noord-Holland and EVR Brandenburg-Berlin, SEAs were undertaken at all of the main administrative levels, including national, regional (combined with *provincie* and *Land*), city regional and local levels. While in North West England and EVR Brandenburg-Berlin, SEA was conducted to the largest extent at the local level, only a few local level SEAs were conducted in Noord-Holland. Local level SEAs included 23 of the 34 SEAs in EVR Brandenburg-Berlin, 16 of the 23 SEAs in North West England, but only 6 of the 23 SEAs in Noord-Holland (see Table 5.2). The different focus of SEA application regarding the administrative level in the three regions is explained by the different planning approaches (see Chapter 3). The society, consensus-led, quasi-top-down approach in Noord-Holland identified policy objectives at higher tiers that were to be considered and implemented at lower tiers. Planning approaches in North West England (centrally guided, local plan-making approach) and EVR Brandenburg-Berlin (public administration, consensus-led, counter-current approach) apparently gave the local level more discretion to identify and implement their own environmental policy objectives.

SEA type classification

Three SEA types were identified, based on sectoral and procedural characteristics, the stage of PPP formulation in the planning cycle, the impact coverage and other methodological characteristics (methods and techniques) (Table 5.1). For convenience, they were named according to existing terminology:

- Policy-SEA (16 of which were identified in the three sample regions).
- Plan-SEA (48 of which were identified in the three sample regions).
- Programme-SEA (8 of which were identified in the three sample regions).

Furthermore, eight big-project SEAs/EIAs were applied in Noord-Holland for regional plans (*streekplannen*), following national (project) EIA legislation. The key findings for policy-SEA, plan-SEA and programme-SEA are set out in the following sections. While tiering was conducted by authorities in a planned manner between policy-SEA and programme-SEA and between plan-SEA and programme-SEA within the same administrative level (horizontal tiering), tiering between different administrative levels (vertical tiering) mainly consisted of policy objectives being passed on in a top-down manner.

Policy-SEA

Policy-SEA was undertaken at all administrative levels at an early stage in the planning cycle and was integrated into the PPP process. Environmental impacts (in particular, air and climate) and socio-economic impacts (in particular, social and public service impacts) were considered to a similar extent and SEA procedural stages were covered to a large extent (Table 5.3). Policy-SEA frequently included public participation. Furthermore, scenarios (simulations of possible developments), inter-modal alternatives and cumulative impacts were considered. Spatial/land use policy-SEA identified the impacts of the development options on transport infrastructure.

Of the 16 policy-SEAs[2], 13 were undertaken in Noord-Holland, 8 at decision making levels above the local level, thus reflecting the overall planning approach in The Netherlands. Only one policy-SEA was undertaken in North West England at the county level and two policy-SEAs were undertaken in EVR Brandenburg-Berlin at the city regional and *Land* levels.

Plan-SEA

Plan-SEA was undertaken at a later stage in the planning cycle than policy-SEA for statutory spatial/land use plans at regional, county/*Kreis* and local levels.[3] Plan-SEA focused on environmental impacts and usually started before the plan process. While in EVR Brandenburg-Berlin, SEA procedural stages were covered to a large extent and always involved public participation (see Chapter 5), in North West England and Noord-Holland, procedural stages were poorly covered and the public was usually not involved. No scenarios were considered and no overall cumulative impacts and inter-modal alternatives were assessed (see Table 5.1).

Of the 48 plan-SEAs, 47 were applied in North West England and EVR Brandenburg-Berlin.[4] Plan-SEA is therefore typical for these two regions, applying traditional statutory planning instruments more frequently than in Noord-Holland, where non-statutory PPPs are of increasing importance. Plan-SEA was most frequently applied at the local level of decision making – 40 of the 48 plan-SEAs were undertaken for local land use plans.

Programme-SEA

Programme-SEA was applied at the latest stage in the planning cycle before project preparation. All programme-SEAs used either multi-criteria analysis or cost–benefit analysis and ranked potential projects. Both environmental and socio-economic impacts were assessed in a combined manner (see Chapter 5). On average, programme-SEA covered SEA procedural stages to a lesser extent, with the exception of the spatial/land use programme-SEA for the National Spatial Plan (VINEX) review (Table 5.3). No overall cumulative impacts, inter-modal alternatives or scenarios were considered. All of the eight transport programme-SEAs were undertaken in North West England and in EVR Brandenburg-Berlin. In Noord-Holland, only one spatial/land use programme-SEA was applied (National Spatial Plan, VINEX review).[5]

AUTHORITIES' OPINIONS ON CURRENT SEA AND THEIR ATTITUDES TOWARDS FORMALIZED SEA

Opinions of authorities

While the opinions of authorities on the quality of SEA were similar in the three sample regions, their opinions on the influence of SEA in PPP making were significantly more negative in North West England than in the other two regions (Figure 6.2). These negative opinions were connected with shorter SEA preparation times, the use of a comparatively small number of methods and techniques and a poor coverage of SEA procedural stages. Those methods, techniques and procedural stages that were found to have had a positive impact on authorities' opinions were used to a comparatively small extent in SEAs in North West England, including impact mapping, the consideration of mitigation measures, quantitative impact assessment, scoping and the consultation of external bodies. In North West England, impacts were mainly assessed in a qualitative manner and usually only matrices and checklists were used (based on government guidance, DoE, 1993; see also DoT, 1995).

Of all of the SEA types, policy-SEA was said to have been the most influential. This is not surprising, as policy-SEA and the associated policy were integrated. Also, the influence of EVR Brandenburg-Berlin plan-SEAs was said to have been high. This is explained by a comparatively extensive coverage of SEA procedural stages, involving widespread public participation and the use of a wide range of methods and techniques. Furthermore, in contrast to North West England and Noord-Holland, plan-SEAs in EVR Brandenburg-Berlin were statutory, which also had a positive impact on the influence on plan making. On average, spatial/land use SEAs were thought to have been of significantly higher quality than transport SEAs (see Figure 6.8). In this context, the greater extent of public participation in spatial/land use SEAs was of particular importance.

Attitudes of authorities

Overall findings

Most authorities believed that an integration of SEA into the PPP process was possible, but also thought that SEA would probably delay PPP preparation. Overall, attitudes on whether formalized SEA would lead to project acceleration and to a better consideration of the environment were quite positive (Figure 6.1). The attitudes of authorities preparing policy-SEA were most positive. This was caused by a perception that formal requirements would not change existing practice to any large extent, as SEA procedural stages were extensively covered, environmental and socio-economic impacts were assessed in a cumulative manner and assessment methods and techniques were used extensively. While authorities preparing plan-SEA and programme-SEA, on average, had more negative attitudes, those authorities not undertaking SEA had comparatively positive attitudes. They argued that only formal requirements would ensure that SEA was conducted, and as long as there were no such requirements, there would always be resistance towards the use of SEA.

Attitudes were positively influenced by the extent to which procedural stages were covered in current SEA. Thus, there was a perception that current practice would not need to be changed to any large extent after the introduction of formal SEA requirements, if procedural stages were well covered. Two stages were of particular importance for positive attitudes, namely the consultation of external bodies and the SEA report review. Long preparation times of SEA had a negative impact on authorities' attitudes towards formalized SEA, in other words the time efficiency of current SEA plays an important role in the attitudes of authorities.

Differences between the cross-section of PPPs and local land use PPPs

There were considerable differences between the attitudes of authorities of the cross-section of 36 PPPs at all administrative levels, and of local land use PPPs (see Chapter 6). While the attitudes of authorities representing the cross-section of PPPs were most positive in Noord-Holland and most negative in EVR Brandenburg-Berlin, at the local level the opposite was observed: attitudes were most positive in EVR Brandenburg-Berlin and most negative in Noord-Holland. There were no substantial differences in North West England between the two sets.

Differences within Noord-Holland and EVR Brandenburg-Berlin are most likely explained by the different planning approaches (referring particularly to public participation) and the extent of SEA application at the local level. While there was widespread public participation and consultation of external bodies in SEA in Noord-Holland at all decision making levels, in EVR Brandenburg-Berlin, public participation in SEA only took place at the local level. Current practice at all administrative levels above the local level therefore will need to change after an introduction of formalized SEA requirements. At the local level, authorities in Noord-Holland did not think that SEA was necessary, as local activities were perceived to only have minor impacts which, it was thought, need not be assessed by SEA. As a consequence, SEA was seen to be appropriately applied only at higher tiers (in particular, at the regional level) and attitudes at the local level were more negative. In EVR Brandenburg-Berlin, local authorities had the view that formal SEA requirements would not change existing practice to any great extent.

The current extent of SEA application at the local level had a positive impact on authorities' attitudes towards formalized SEA. Thus, while 21 of the 23 local land use plans in EVR Brandenburg-Berlin involved SEA application, only 1 of the 21 local land use PPPs in Noord-Holland involved the application of SEA. Attitudes at the local level were significantly more positive in EVR Brandenburg-Berlin than in Noord-Holland (see Chapter 6). Furthermore, it was found that in North West England, those 13 authorities preparing SEA at the local level had more positive attitudes than the 14 authorities not preparing SEA.

CONSIDERATION OF SUSTAINABILITY OBJECTIVES, TARGETS AND MEASURES AND THE ROLE OF SEA

The EC Fifth Environmental Action Programme

Overall, it was observed that general sustainability objectives were considered to a greater extent than the more specific targets and measures. However, the requirements of a decision making framework in support of sustainable development (Figure 1.1), indicate that objectives, targets and measures should be considered to the same extent. Current practice therefore fails to consider sustainability aspects consistently.

Objectives on nature/biodiversity and the urban environment were comparatively well considered in the three sample regions as were measures on land use, public transport and infrastructure investment. Targets were not as well considered as objectives and measures. At the local level, there was widespread consideration of land use and emission targets, which is mainly due to EVR Brandenburg-Berlin local land use plans, most of which involved the preparation of plan-SEAs – landscape plans (*Landschaftspläne*). None of the examples included in the research were able to fully meet the requirements of the Fifth Environmental Action Programme. Some of the Noord-Holland PPPs, however, performed comparatively well.

In the cross-section of PPPs, sustainability objectives, targets and measures were clearly considered to the greatest extent in Noord-Holland. For local land use PPPs, on the other hand, they were considered to the greatest extent in EVR Brandenburg-Berlin. The observed patterns are explained by the different planning approaches in the three regions, as well as by the different extent of SEA application. Thus, higher-tier PPPs in Noord-Holland focused on the identification of policy objectives that were to be considered and implemented at lower tiers. In the other two regions, the local level had more discretion to identify environmental objectives.

The extent to which PPPs considered the sustainability objectives, targets and measures of the Fifth Environmental Action Programme was correlated with the extent to which socio-economic issues were considered. This is a surprising finding, as the EC Fifth Environmental Action Programme focused on the environment and did not consider any socio-economic issues. The extent to which the the stages of the procedural framework in support of sustainable development were covered (see Figure 1.1) was also correlated with the extent to which sustainability objectives, targets and measures were considered. This supports the suggested connection of substantive aspects and procedural stages (see Box 2.2).

Influence of SEA

While SEA application for the cross-section of PPPs did not have a significant impact on the consideration of sustainability objectives or targets, it was able to lead to a better consideration of sustainability measures (see Figure 7.25). SEA was observed to be more effective in the transport sector, leading to a significantly better consideration of explicit objectives and targets and measures (Figures 7.10, 7.19 and 7.28). For the cross-section of PPPs, SEA was more effective in leading to a better consideration of sustainability aspects in North West England and in Noord-Holland than in EVR Brandenburg-Berlin.[6] Furthermore, policy-SEA had the most positive impact on the consideration of explicit objectives and targets and measures.

At the local level, current SEA application had a positive effect, as 21 of the 23 EVR Brandenburg-Berlin plans that considered sustainability aspects to the greatest extent involved SEA application. Only 1 of the 21 Noord-Holland PPPs that considered sustainability aspects to the smallest extent involved SEA application. Furthermore, the 13 local land use plans in North West England with SEA considered sustainability objectives, targets and measures to a larger extent than the 14 plans that did not involve SEA. The consideration of sustainability aspects was correlated with the extent to which procedural stages were covered. Those procedural stages that appeared to have been of particular importance included consultation and public participation as well as monitoring.

EXTENT TO WHICH ASSESSMENTS RESULT IN THE FIVE POTENTIAL SEA BENEFITS

The extent to which assessments resulted in the following five potential SEA benefits was analysed (see Box 2.7):[7]

1. Wider consideration of impacts and alternatives.
2. Proactive assessment – SEA as a supporting tool for PPP formulation for sustainable development.
3. Strengthening project EIA: increasing the efficiency of tiered decision making.
4. Systematic and effective consideration of the environment at higher tiers of decision making.
5. Consultation and participation on SEA-related issues.

Overall, while potential benefit 5 ('consultation and participation on SEA-related issues') was found to have been considered to a comparatively large extent – 80 per cent of the possible score – potential benefit 3 ('strengthening project EIA: increasing the efficiency of tiered decision making') was comparatively poorly considered – 43 per cent of the possible score. On average, the other three potential SEA benefits were met to a moderate extent – around 60 per cent of possible score.

Regional differences were statistically significant for three potential SEA benefits, namely for benefit 1 ('wider consideration of impacts and alternatives'), benefit 2 ('proactive assessment – SEA as a supporting tool for PPP formulation for sustainable development') and benefit 3 ('strengthening project EIA: increasing the efficiency of tiered decision making'). For all of the three potential benefits, SEAs in Noord-Holland obtained higher scores than the SEAs in the other two regions. The high score for potential SEA benefit 1 was caused by the high degree of policy-SEA application in Noord-Holland. Thus, being applied at an early stage in the planning cycle, strategic choices for considering alternatives and options were still numerous (see Chapter 8). Furthermore, in policy-SEA application, public opposition due to NIMBYism was less likely (see Chapter 1), and authorities were more inclined to consider a wider range of impacts and alternatives.

The extent to which assessments resulted in the five potential SEA benefits was explained, in particular, by the coverage of SEA procedural stages, the
extent to which methods and techniques were used and the inter-modality of
the underlying PPP. Public participation and external consultation were found
to be of particular importance. Furthermore, the extent to which impacts were
assessed in a quantitative manner (ie calculating impact magnitudes and
impact mapping) was also an important aspect that increased the likelihood of
SEA resulting in the potential SEA benefits.

EC SEA Directive

The 1999 SEA Directive proposal of the EC did not require all of the principles that underlie the five potential SEA benefits to be met (Box 2.4).
Therefore, only a selected number of principles were used to identify the
extent to which SEA was meeting its requirements.

While most of the SEAs in Noord-Holland were able to meet the SEA
Directive requirements to a comparatively large extent (mainly caused by the
large extent of policy-SEA application), the variation in SEA scores in North
West England and, particularly in EVR Brandenburg-Berlin was considerable.
While the average extent to which the SEA Directive requirements were met
in EVR Brandenburg-Berlin was smallest in the cross-section of PPPs, it was
largest in local land use PPPs. Current practice needs to be improved, particularly regarding screening, mitigation and public participation. While policy-SEA
and plan-SEA, on average, met the SEA Directive requirements to the same
moderate extent, programme-SEA, on average, scored comparatively poorly.

Suggestions for improving current practice

This section suggests improvements to current SEA practice and is divided
into four sub-sections. Firstly, specific tasks for the three SEA types are recom-
mended within a tiered system and improvements are suggested to current
tiering practice. This is followed by an identification of the general ingredients
for SEA success. Improvements to the existing SEA instruments currently used
in the three regions are suggested and finally, other SEA improvement measures are also examined.

Developing tiered SEA systems

The identification of SEA type-specific tasks

In order to be an effective decision making tool and to meet overall SEA
principles, SEA should be applied in a tiered manner, with a specific SEA type
with clearly identified tasks used at each tier. In the three sample regions,
tiering between different administrative levels (vertical tiering) mainly took
the form of policy objectives being passed on from higher tiers to lower tiers.
A clear tiering structure consisting of different SEA types was only identified
within the same administrative level (horizontal tiering). The structure of

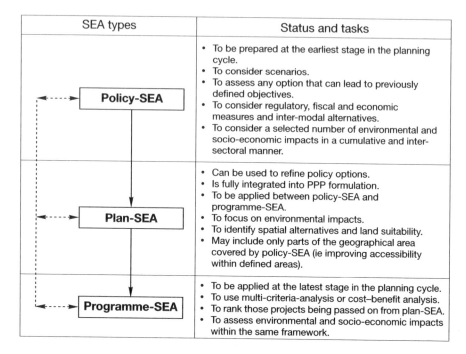

SEA types	Status and tasks
Policy-SEA	• To be prepared at the earliest stage in the planning cycle. • To consider scenarios. • To assess any option that can lead to previously defined objectives. • To consider regulatory, fiscal and economic measures and inter-modal alternatives. • To consider a selected number of environmental and socio-economic impacts in a cumulative and inter-sectoral manner.
Plan-SEA	• Can be used to refine policy options. • Is fully integrated into PPP formulation. • To be applied between policy-SEA and programme-SEA. • To focus on environmental impacts. • To identify spatial alternatives and land suitability. • May include only parts of the geographical area covered by policy-SEA (ie improving accessibility within defined areas).
Programme-SEA	• To be applied at the latest stage in the planning cycle. • To use multi-criteria-analysis or cost–benefit analysis. • To rank those projects being passed on from plan-SEA. • To assess environmental and socio-economic impacts within the same framework.

Note: only plan-SEA and, to some, extent programme-SEA in the spatial/land use sector are likely to be required after the introduction of the SEA Directive.

Figure 10.1: *Status and tasks of SEA types*

horizontal tiering is characterized by three stages, consisting of policy-SEA at the highest level, followed by plan-SEA and programme-SEA. While examples for the three SEA types are found in each of the regions, tiering is currently rarely undertaken. In order to improve SEA performance, it is therefore suggested that SEA tiering be used more frequently. The three SEA types should fulfil specific tasks. These are outlined in Figure 10.1.

Improving current SEA tiering

Table 10.1 shows experience with the application of the three SEA types in the three regions at national, regional (including *Provincie, Land,* county and *Kreis* levels) and local levels, indicating where improvement in current practice is needed. Individual examples for each of the SEA types are listed in Appendix 3 and overall good practice examples are found in Table 10.1. Suggestions are made for improving current tiering practice for the three regions.

For North West England, current SEA tiering could be improved greatly by a more widespread use of policy-SEA for the spatial/land use and transport sectors at all administrative levels. As long as the emphasis is put on the application of plan-SEA and programme-SEA, it is unlikely that a wider consideration of impacts and alternatives (see Chapter 8) and a better inclusion of sustainability aspects (see Chapter 7) in PPP formulation can be achieved.

Table 10.1: *Current SEA type practice for the transport and spatial/land use sectors at national, regional and local levels in the three sample regions*

SEA type	North West England(1)			Noord-Holland			EVR Brandenburg-Berlin		
	National (2)	Region-al	Local	Nation-al	Region-al	Local (3)	Nation-al	Region-al	Local (3)
Transport									
Policy-SEA	–	⊙		■	■	?	–	■	?
Plan-SEA	(⊙)	○		○	○	?	(⊙)	○	?
Programme-SEA	■	●		○	○	?	■	■	?
Spatial/land use									
Policy-SEA	–	–	–	■	■	⊙	○	–	(⊙)
Plan-SEA	–	■	■	○	○	⊙	–	■	■
Programme-SEA	–	○	○	⊙	○	○	–	○	⊙

Note: (1) It is not possible to clearly distinguish between local and county levels in transport planning in North West England, as local TPPs are combined for metropolitan or county areas.
(2) Planning policy guidance is not regarded as equivalent to a national spatial plan.
(3) Following the *Regionalisierungsgesetz* in Germany and the *planwet verkeer en vervoer* in The Netherlands, local authorities will need to prepare local transport PPPs.

■   All of the identified PPPs involved SEA.
●   Most of the identified PPPs involved SEA.
⊙   Sporadic SEA application.
(⊙) Research studies (for local policy-SEA in EVR Brandenburg-Berlin, see Bunge, 1998).
○   PPP prepared, but no SEA application (plan-SEA and programme-SEA are regarded as having the same underlying PPPs; in Noord-Holland, policy-SEAs often include specific projects that can be the basis for further SEA application).
?   PPPs to be prepared under new legislation, scope unclear.
–   No PPP prepared.

Furthermore, programme-SEA could be conducted for development plans (possibly integrated into environmental appraisal) in order to rank proposed developments according to their environmental and socio-economic benefits. If plan-SEA was applied in the transport sector (package bids and TPPs), environmentally suitable options within larger geographical areas could be identified for achieving the desired degree of accessibility.

For Noord-Holland, current practice can be improved by applying plan-SEA and programme-SEA more widely than is currently done. Resulting from the current failure to apply these two SEA types, it remains largely unclear how the findings of policy-SEA are passed on to the project level, that is without the use of other SEA instruments, the connection between policies and project implementation is unclear.

For EVR Brandenburg-Berlin, there is a need for more frequent application of policy-SEA at all administrative levels of decision making to both spatial/land use and transport sectors. Without the application of policy-SEA, it will remain unclear how the projects included in plan-SEA and programme-SEA fit into the overall policy framework, and how they are able to help to achieve the overall aims and objectives.

General ingredients for SEA success

Based on the findings of this book, general ingredients are identified for enhancing SEA performance and overall SEA success. It needs to be stressed that no individual SEA is likely to meet all of the SEA principles and result in all of the potential SEA benefits, but that a tiered SEA approach is needed for securing success, using the SEA types identified in this research. SEA success ingredients include the following.

Complete coverage of procedural stages

The extent to which procedural stages were covered was positively correlated with all of the examined SEA themes, including opinions on current SEA, attitudes towards formalized SEA, the consideration of sustainability aspects and the extent to which assessments resulted in the overall potential SEA benefits. Procedural stages to be covered include screening, scoping, the main impact assessment stage with the preparation of an SEA report and SEA report review, participation and consultation, as well as monitoring (Figure 1.1). Monitoring and auditing provisions generally need to be improved in order to learn more about the actual effects of the measures proposed in SEA. Only a clear understanding of causes and effects can improve current practice and ultimately ensure that SEA is successful. General research can also help to achieve this aim.

Integration of SEA into the PPP

SEA that is integrated into the associated PPP has proven to perform well. In this book, examples included policy-SEAs and, in some instances, plan-SEAs.

Early SEA start

Those SEAs that start before or at the beginning of the PPP process and are integrated into PPP making are more likely to be successful. In this research, SEAs with an early application included, in particular, the policy-SEAs and EVR Brandenburg-Berlin landscape plans (*Landschaftspläne*) at the local level.

Consultation with external bodies and public participation

This research concluded that those SEAs involving consultation with external bodies and public participation were more successful. Furthermore, they were perceived by authorities to be of better quality.

Extensive use of methods and techniques

The extent of the use of methods and techniques was correlated with overall SEA performance. Methods and techniques that were of particular importance included workshops and impact mapping. Furthermore, quantitative impact assessment (indicating clear impact magnitudes) was found to be beneficial for the overall SEA success. Mitigation is currently not included in transport SEA, without which different development options cannot be properly compared and alternatives that result in the highest overall benefits cannot be determined.

Appropriate funding and appropriate SEA preparation times

Short SEA preparation times (and associated low funding) were found to lead to a reduced influence of the SEA in PPP making. Longer preparation times were associated with a better coverage of procedural stages and a wider use of methods and techniques. Authorities perceived SEA with longer preparation times to be of higher relevance.

Improving existing SEA instruments

Based on the earlier analysis in this chapter, suggestions for improving existing SEA instruments in the three sample regions are made. Table 10.2 shows 11 improvement aspects, including procedural aspects and some methodological aspects. No suggestions for improvement are made for those instruments that were conducted only once, including policy-SEA for TPPs/package bids in North West England and both plan-SEA and programme-SEA in Noord-Holland. It is found that all instruments could be considerably strengthened if there was better SEA tiering. While there were hardly any aspects to be improved in policy-SEA, plan-SEA and programme-SEA should cover procedural stages more fully and include public participation, external consultation and workshops.

Instruments that need improvement in a large number of aspects include the transport programme-SEAs in North West England and in EVR Brandenburg-Berlin (there was no transport programme-SEA undertaken in Noord-Holland) and the plan-SEAs in North West England (environmental appraisals). In addition to a better tiering and a more complete coverage of procedural stages, transport programme-SEA should consider overall policy objectives. North West England plan-SEAs (environmental appraisals) should also use techniques other than matrices and checklists. Furthermore, impacts should be assessed in a quantitative manner and impact mapping should be applied.

Other SEA improvement measures

Based on the findings of the research, other measures are suggested that aim at improving SEA. These include a better dissemination of existing SEA experience, more research and the need for formal requirements for tiered SEA application.

Table 10.2: *Improving current SEA instruments*

Instrument	Improve tiered SEA	Cover procedural stages more fully	Integrate SEA and PPP better	Conduct public participation	Conduct consultation with external bodies	Use techniques other than checklists & matrices	Use impact mapping	Conduct workshops	Assess impacts quantitatively	Consider overall objectives	Include impact assessment
North West England											
Environmental appraisal development plans	!	!	!	!	!	!	!	!	!	✓	✓
Multi-criteria analysis for TPPs/package bids	!	!	✓	!	!	✓	!	!	✓	!	✓
Policy-SEA for TPPs/package bids	(shaded)	(shaded)	(shaded)	(shaded)	(shaded)	(shaded)	(shaded)	(shaded)	(shaded)	(shaded)	(shaded)
Noord-Holland											
Transport and spatial/land use policy-SEAs,	!	✓	✓	✓	✓	✓	✓	✓	✓	!(1)	✓
plan-SEA and programme-SEA	(shaded)	(shaded)	(shaded)	(shaded)	(shaded)	(shaded)	(shaded)	(shaded)	(shaded)	(shaded)	(shaded)
EVR Brandenburg-Berlin											
Landscape plans and programmes	!	✓	!(2)	✓	✓	✓	✓	!	✓	✓	!(2)
Integrated transport plans	!	!	✓	!	!	✓	✓	✓	✓	✓	✓
Transport programmes (federal and *Länder*)	!	!	✓	!	!	✓	✓	!	✓	!	✓

Key: ! Improvement needed.

✓ While individual cases need to be checked, in a generic sense there is no urgent need for improvement.

(1) Need for improvement only for spatial/land use PPPs.

(2) Improvement needed, except for landscape plans (*Landschaftspläne*) for local land use plans (FNPs) in Brandenburg.

(shaded) Only one SEA found, generic recommendations therefore not made, more frequent use of SEA type is needed.

Dissemination of existing experience

This research has shown that SEA application in the EU is more widespread than is often acknowledged. While there is scope for improving current practice, there is no need to reinvent the wheel. SEA is there and waiting to be applied. Current practice could largely be improved if existing experience and knowledge were used more extensively. Good practice SEA case studies, identified in comparative research therefore need to be disseminated more widely.

More research

Much more of an effort needs to be put into systematic research on existing practice as well as on understanding cause–effect relationships (including monitoring and post-audit) and the impact SEA has in decision making. Case study research is needed, particularly for increasing the effectiveness of tiered SEA, that is policy-SEA, plan-SEA and programme-SEA. A review package should be developed, distinguishing between the three SEA types and allowing for the identification of good quality SEA reports.

Formal requirements for tiered SEA

This research has shown that only a tiered approach is likely to be successful in meeting SEA principles. The EC SEA Directive only includes provisions for plan-SEA and, to some extent, for programme-SEA. In the interest of avoiding the distortion of competition between EU member states, it is, however that it should be amended in order to include provisions for policy-SEA (as used in this book).

Appendix 1

Main source documentation used in the analysis

NORTH WEST ENGLAND

1. Cheshire County Council 1995a. *Cheshire County Structure Plan – New Thoughts for the Next Century*, Chester.
2. Cheshire County Council 1995b. *Cheshire County Structure Plan – New Thoughts for the Next Century: Environmental Appraisal*, Chester.
3. Cheshire County Council 1996a. *Cheshire 2011 – Deposit Draft Plan, Replacement Structure Plan*, Chester.
4. Cheshire County Council 1996b. *Cheshire 2011 – Environmental Appraisal, Replacement Structure Plan*, Chester.
5. Cheshire County Council 1996c. *Transport Policies and Programme, 1996 Submission for the Period 1997–02*, Chester.
6. Cheshire County Council 1996d. *Sustainable Transport Strategy – Moving in a New Direction*, Chester.
7. Cheshire County Council 1996e. *Cheshire's Agenda 21. Strategy and Action Plan*, Chester.
8. Department of Transport (DoT) 1994. *Trunk Roads in England – 1994 Review*, HMSO, London.
9. Government Office for the North West 1996. *Regional Planning Guidance for the North West (RPG 13)*, HMSO, London.
10. Greater Manchester Passenger Transport Authority 1996. *Greater Manchester Transport Package Bid 1997/8*, Manchester.
11. Lancashire County Council 1993. *Report 13: Environmental Appraisal of the 1986–96 Structure Plan*, Preston.
12. Lancashire County Council 1994a. *Lancashire Structure Plan 1991–06*, Preston.
13. Lancashire County Council 1994b. *Report 19: Environmental Appraisal of the 1991–06 Structure Plan*, Preston.
14. Lancashire County Council 1994c. *Report 23: Lancashire Structure Plan 1991–06, Public Attitudes Survey*, Preston.
15. Lancashire County Council 1994d. *Public Transport in Lancashire*, Preston.
16. Lancashire County Council 1996. *Transport Policies and Programme 1997/98*, Preston.
17. Lancashire Environmental Forum 1993. *Lancashire Environmental Action Programme*, Preston.
18. Merseyside Passenger Transport Authority 1993. *MerITS – Merseyside Integrated Transport Study*, Liverpool.
19. Merseyside Passenger Transport Authority 1996. *Package Bid 1997/98*, Liverpool.

20. North West Regional Association 1994. *Greener Growth – Regional Planning Guidance for North West England*, Advice submitted to the Secretary of State for the Environment.
21. North West Regional Association 1996. *Regional Transport Strategy for North West England*, Lancashire County Council, Preston.
22. Oldham Metropolitan Borough Council 1996. *Unitary Development Plan*, Oldham.
23. Salford City Council 1995. *Unitary Development Plan*, Salford.
24. Warrington Borough Council 1994. *Warrington Borough Local Plan – Deposit Draft*, Warrington.

NOORD-HOLLAND

1. Dienst Ruimtelijke Ordening Amsterdam 1994a. *Ontwerp structuurplan*, Amsterdam.
2. Dienst Ruimtelijke Ordening Amsterdam 1994b. *Beleidsnota ruimtelijke ordening en milieu*, Amsterdam.
3. Dienst Ruimtelijke Ordening Amsterdam 1996. *Milieumatrix structuurplan*, Amsterdam.
4. Gemeente Hilversum 1998. *Toekomstvisie Hilversum 2015*, Hilversum.
5. Gewest Zuid-Kennemerland 1994. *Verkeersmilieukaarten Zuid-Kennemerland*, Haarlem.
6. Ministerie van Verkeer en Waterstaat 1989. *Second Transport Structure Plan* (SVVII), *part d: government decision*, Den Haag.
7. Ministerie van Verkeer en Waterstaat 1995. *Beleidseffectmeting verkeer en vervoer, beleidseffectrapportage 1995*, Den Haag.
8. Ministerie van Verkeer en Waterstaat 1996. *Meerjarenprogramma infrastructuur en transport 1997–01*, Den Haag.
9. Ministerie van Volkshuisvesting, Ruimtelijke Ordening en Milieubeheer (VROM) 1993. *Vierde nota over de ruimtelijke ordening Extra, deel 4*, Den Haag.
10. Ministerie van Volkshuisvesting, Ruimtelijke Ordening en Milieubeheer (VROM) 1996a. *Vierde nota over de ruimtelijke ordening Extra, actualisering, deel 1*, Den Haag.
11. Ministerie van Volkshuisvesting, Ruimtelijke Ordening en Milieubeheer (VROM) 1996b. *(Milieu-) effectrapport over de Leidse en de Rotterdamse Regio, deel 1*, Den Haag.
12. Projectteam INVERNO 1993. *Integrale verkeers- en vervoersvisie Noordvleugel –* INVERNO, Haarlem.
13. Provincie Noord-Holland 1987. *Streekplan voor het Amsterdam-Noordzeekanaalgebied*, Haarlem.
14. Provincie Noord-Holland 1991. *Streekplan Waterland*, Haarlem.
15. Provincie Noord-Holland 1992. *Streekplan Gooi en Vechtstreek*, Haarlem.
16. Provincie Noord-Holland 1994. *Streekplan Noord-Holland-Noord*, Haarlem.
17. Provincie Noord-Holland 1995. *Streekplan voor het Amsterdam-Noordzeekanaalgebied – partiele herziening*, Haarlem.
18. Provincie Noord-Holland 1997. *Ontwikkelingsvisie Noord-Holland 2030 – verkenningen*, Haarlem.
19. Regionaal Orgaan Amsterdam 1993. *Regionaal verkeers- en vervoersplan ROA Vervoerregio*, Amsterdam.
20. Regionaal Orgaan Amsterdam 1995a. *Regionale verkeers-milieukaart*, Amsterdam.

21. Regionaal Orgaan Amsterdam 1995b. *Regionaal verkeers- en vervoersplan ROA Vervoerregio – uitvoeringsprogramma 1995–1997*, Amsterdam.
22. Regionaal Orgaan Amsterdam 1995c. *Regionaal structuurplan*, Amsterdam.
23. Regionaal Orgaan Amsterdam 1995d. *ROA milieuverkenning*, Amsterdam.
24. RoRo-Projectteam 1994. *Evaluatienota interprovinciale verstedelijkingsvisie op de Randstad*, Randstad Overleg Ruimtelijke Ordening, Haarlem.
25. RoRo-Projectteam 1995a. *Uitkomsten van nadere discussie over de evaluatienota IPVR*, Randstad Overleg Ruimtelijke Ordening, Haarlem.
26. RoRo-Projectteam 1995b. *Evaluatie interprovinciale verstedelijkingsvisie op de Randstad*, Randstad Overleg Ruimtelijke Ordening, Haarlem.
27. Vervoerregio Haarlem/IJmond 1994. *Ontwerp regionaal verkeers- en vervoersplan*, Amersfoort/Haarlem.
28. Vervoerregio Noord-Holland-Noord 1994. *Ontwerp regionaal verkeers- en vervoerplan*, Overveen.

EVR BRANDENBURG-BERLIN

1. Amt Ketzin 1996a. *Flächennutzungsplan-Entwürfe der Gemeinden Ketzin/Etzin/Falkenrehde/Tremmen/Zachow*, Ketzin.
2. Amt Ketzin 1996b. *Landschaftsplan Gemeinden Ketzin/Etzin/Falkenrehde/Tremmen/Zachow*, Ketzin.
3. Bezirksamt Charlottenburg 1994. *Bezirksentwicklungsplan*, Berlin.
4. Bundesministerium für Raumordnung, Bauwesen und Städtebau 1992. *Raumordnungspolitischer Orientierungsrahmen*, Bonn.
5. Bundesministerium für Verkehr 1992. *Bundesverkehrswegeplan*, Bonn.
6. Bundesministerium für Verkehr 1993a. *Fünfjahresplan für den Ausbau der Bundesfernstraßen in den Jahren 1993 bis 1997*, Bonn.
7. Bundesministerium für Verkehr 1993b. *Gesamtwirtschaftliche Bewertung von Verkehrswegeinvestitionen*, Bonn.
8. Bundesschienenwegeausbaugesetz vom 15. November 1993, BGBl. IS. 2378.
9. Fernstraßenausbaugesetz vom 15. November 1993, BGBl. IS.1878.
10. Gemeinsame Landesplanung 1994. *Landesentwicklungsprogramm Brandenburg-Berlin*, Potsdam.
11. Gemeinsame Landesplanung 1995. *Landesentwicklungsplan für den engeren Verflechtungsraum Brandenburg-Berlin*, Potsdam.
12. Landkreis Havelland 1995. *Landschaftsrahmenplan – Entwurf, Entwicklungskonzept, Band 1*, Rathenow.
13. Landkreis Havelland 1996. *Entwicklungskonzeption Havelland*, Rathenow.
14. Ministerium für Stadtentwicklung, Wohnen und Verkehr 1995a. *Landesstraßenbedarfsplan des Landes Brandenburg*, Potsdam.
15. Ministerium für Stadtentwicklung, Wohnen und Verkehr 1995b. *Integriertes Verkehrskonzept*, Potsdam.
16. Ministerkonferenz für Raumordnung 1995. *Raumordnungspolitischer Handlungsrahmen*, Bonn.
17. Planungsgruppe Ökologie und Umwelt 1992. *Beurteilung der Umwelteffekte von Straßenneubauprojekten des Gesamtdeutschen Verkehrswegeplanes GVWP '92*, Hannover.
18. Regionale Planungsgemeinschaft Havelland-Fläming 1997. *Regionalplan Havelland-Fläming, Arbeitspapier*, Kleinmachnow.

19. Senatsverwaltung für Bauen, Wohnen und Verkehr 1995. *Verkehrspolitisches Strukturkonzept – Grundlagen für den Stadtentwicklungsplan Verkehr*, Berlin.
20. Senatsverwaltung für Bauen, Wohnen und Verkehr 1996. *Stadtentwicklungsplan Verkehr, Arbeitskonzept – Entwurf zur Abstimmung*, Berlin.
21. Senatsverwaltung für Stadtentwicklung und Umweltschutz 1994a. *Landschaftsprogramm 1994*, Berlin.
22. Senatsverwaltung für Stadtentwicklung und Umweltschutz 1994b. *Ökologische Konfliktanalyse im Flächennutzungsplan Berlin*, Berlin.
23. Senatsverwaltung für Stadtentwicklung und Umweltschutz 1994c. *Flächennutzungsplan Berlin*, Berlin.

Appendix 2

Statutes and statutory instruments

Only a selected number of important statutes and statutory instruments mentioned in the main text are listed below.

Statutes and statutory instruments can be found on the Internet:

- European directives: http://europa.eu.int/eur-lex/
- UK (after 1996): www.hmso.gov.uk/acts.htm
- The Netherlands: www.wetten.nu/ *and* www.businessandlaw.nl/fjuridischelinks.html
- Germany (complete since 1949): www.bundesgesetzblatt.makrolog.de

European Directives

Amended Proposal for a Council Directive on Assessment of the Effects of Certain Plans and Programmes on the Environment 1999 (COM(99)073 final), *Document 596PL0511.*

Council Directive amending Directive 85/337/EEC on the Assessment of the Effects of Certain Public and Private Projects on the Environment (97/11/EC), *Official Journal L73, 5.*

Council Directive of 27 June 1985 on the Assessment of the Effects of Certain Public and Private Projects on the Environment (85/337/EEC), *Official Journal L175, 40.*

Habitats Directive 1992 (93/43/EEC), *Official Journal L 107, 1*, amended by *Official Journal L 305, 42.*

Proposal for a Council Directive on Assessment of the Effects of Certain Plans and Programmes on the Environment 1996 (COM(96)511), *Official Journal L129 14–8.*

United Kingdom

Environment Act 1995.

Highways Act 1980.

Land Compensation Act 1997.

Local Authority (Capital Finance and Approved Investments) Regulations 1995.

Local Government Act 1985.

Planning and Compensation Act 1991.

Road Traffic Reduction Act 1997.

Town and Country Planning (Assessment of Environmental Effects) Regulations 1988, last amended 14.03.1999.

Town and Country Planning Act 1990.
Transport Act 1985.

The Netherlands

Algemene wet bestuursrecht of 01.01.1994 (Stb. 315), last amended 01.01.1998.
Besluit milieu-effectrapportage 1994 (EIA decree), last amended 07.05.1999 (Stb. 224).
Grondwet 1815 (Stb. 45; 1987, Stb.458), last amended 10.07. 1995 (Stb. 404).
Kaderwet bestuur in verandering of 21.05.1994.
Planwet verkeer en vervoer of 01.01.1998 (based on 'convenant vervkeer en
    vervoer: regionaal, decentraal, integraal of 24.11.1995).
Wet milieubeheer 1979 (Stb. 442; 1994 Stb. 80), last amended 29/04/1999
    (Stb.208), hoofdstuk 7: milieu-effectrapportage.
Wet op de ruimtelijke ordening 1962 (Stb. 286 and Stb. 1994, 28), last amended
    06.02.1997 (Stb.63).
Woningwet 1991 (Stb. 439), last amended 06.12.1997 (Stb.63).

Germany

Baugesetzbuch (BauGB) vom 27.08.1997 (BGBl. IS. 2141), last amended 1998
    (BGBl. IS. 137).
Brandenburgisches Naturschutzgesetz (BbgNatSchG) vom 29.06.1992 (GVBl. S. 207).
Gemeinsamer Erlaß des Ministeriums für Umwelt, Naturschutz und Raumordnung
    und des Ministeriums für Stadtentwicklung, Wohnen und Verkehr vom
    24.10.1994 (Bauleitplanung und Landschaftsplanung) (Amtsblatt für
    Brandenburg vom 06.12.1994), last amended 29.04.1997 (Amtsblatt für
    Brandenburg vom 23.05.1997).
Gesetz über die Umweltverträglichkeitsprüfung (UVPG) vom 12.02.1990 (BGBl. IS.
    205), last amended 18.08.1997 (BGBl. IS. 2081).
Gesetz über Naturschutz und Landschaftspflege (Bundesnaturschutzgesetz –
    BNatSchG) vom 21.09.1998 (BGBl. IS. 2994).
Gesetz über Naturschutz und Landschaftspflege von Berlin (Berliner
    Naturschutzgesetz – NatSchGBln) vom 30.01.1979 (GVBl. S. 183), last
    amended 30.03.1994 (GVBl. S. 106).
Gesetz vom 09.02.1998 zu dem Staatsvertrag über das gemeinsame
    Landesentwicklungsprogramm der Länder Berlin und Brandenburg
    (Landesentwicklungsprogramm) über die Änderung des Landesplanungsver-
    trages (GVBl. S. 407).
Gesetz zum Staatsvertrag über die Aufgaben und Trägerschaft sowie Grundlagen
    und Verfahren der gemeinsamen Landesplanung zwischen den Ländern Berlin
    und Brandenburg (Landesplanungsvertrag) vom 04.07.1995 (GVBl. S. 407).
Gesetz zur Änderung des Baugesetzbuches und zur Regelung des Rechts der
    Raumordnung (Bau- und Raumordnungsgesetz – BauROG) vom 01.01.98.
Gesetz zur Ausführung des Baugesetzbuchs (AGBauGB) vom 11.12.1987 (GVBl.
    S. 2731), last amended 04.07.1995 (GVBl. S. 407).
Gesetz zur Einführung der Regionalplanung und der Braunkohlen- und
    Sanierungsplanung im Land Brandenburg (RegBkPlG) (Gesetz- und
    Verordnungsblatt für das Land Brandenburg vom 18.05.1993, GVBl. S. 170),
    last amended 20.07.1995 (GVBl. S. 210).
Gesetz zur Regionalisierung des öffentlichen Personennahverkehrs
    (Regionalisierungsgesetz) 1993 (BGBl. IS. 2395).

Gesetz zur Umsetzung der Richtlinie des Rates vom 27.06.1985 über die Umweltverträglichkeitsprüfung bei bestimmten öffentlichen und privaten Projekten (85/337/EWG) vom 12.02.1990 (BGBl. IS. 205).

Grundgesetz für die Bundesrepublik Deutschland vom 23.05.1949 (BGBl. IS. 1), last amended 28.04.1997 (BGBl. IS. 966).

Grundsätze für die Prüfung der Umweltverträglichkeit öffentlicher Maßnahmen des Bundes, Bek. d. BMI vom 12.09.1975 (GMBl. S. 717).

Raumordnungsgesetz (ROG) vom 18.08.1997 (BGBl. IS. 2081), last amended 15.12.1997 (BGBl. IS. 2902).

List of all the SEAs in the three regions

POLICY-SEAs

Transport

National level

Second Transport Structure Plan (SVVII), The Netherlands*

Regional level

Transport Strategy for the Merseyside Package Bid (MerITS), UK*
Transport Plan (RVVP) Noord-Holland-Noord, The Netherlands*
Transport Plan (RVVP) Haarlem-IJmond, The Netherlands*
Transport Plan (RVVP) ROA, The Netherlands*
Transport Plan (RVVP) Gooi en Vechtstreek, the Netherlands***
Integrated Transport Plan for the Northern Wing of the Randstad (INVERNO), The Netherlands*
City Development Plan Transport (*Stadtentwicklungsplan Verkehr*) Berlin, Germany*
Integrated Transport Plan (*Integrierter Verkehrsplan*) Brandenburg, Germany*

Local level

No SEA found.

Spatial/land use

National level

National Vision of The Netherlands (*Visie Nederland*), The Netherlands***

Regional level

Development Vision (*ontwikkelingsvisie*) Noord-Holland, The Netherlands*

---

*   = included in analysis, based on interview results
**   = included in analysis, based on postal questionnaire results
*** = not included in analysis (not accessible, accessible only after data collection, no reply by local authority, research study)

Local level

Future Vision (*Toekomstvisie*) Hilversum, The Netherlands*
Vision (*visie*) Enkhuizen, The Netherlands **
Vision (*visie*) Waterland, The Netherlands ***
Vision (*visie*) Uithoorn, The Netherlands ***
Vision (*visie*) Aalsmeer, The Netherlands ***

PLAN-SEAs

Transport

National level

SEA in the Trans-Pennine Corridor, UK***
Improvement of the Transport Infrastructure within the Triangle Hamburg–
    Hannover–Berlin (Verkehrsuntersuchung Nord-Ost), Germany***

Regional level

No SEA found.

Local level

No SEA found.

Spatial/land use

National level

No SEA found.

Regional level

Environmental Appraisal for the Lancashire Structure Plan, UK*
Environmental Appraisal for the Cheshire Structure Plan, UK*
Landscape Framework Plan (*Landschaftsrahmenplan*) Havelland, Germany*
Landscape Framework Plan (*Landschaftsrahmenplan*) Oberhavel, Germany***
Landscape Framework Plan (*Landschaftsrahmenplan*) Dahmeland, Germany***
Landscape Programme (*Landschaftsprogramm*) Berlin, Germany*

Local level

Environmental Appraisal for the Oldham UDP, UK*
Environmental Appraisal for the Warrington Local Plan, UK*
Environmental Appraisal for the Vale Royal Local Plan, UK**

---

*   = included in analysis, based on interview results
**   = included in analysis, based on postal questionnaire results
***   = not included in analysis (not accessible, accessible only after data collection,
        no reply by local authority, research study)

Environmental Appraisal for the Burnley Local Plan, UK**
Environmental Appraisal for the Chester Local Plan, UK**
Environmental Appraisal for the Halton Local Plan, UK**
Environmental Appraisal for the Pendle Local Plan, UK**
Environmental Appraisal for the South Ribble Local Plan, UK**
Environmental Appraisal for the West Lancashire Local Plan, UK**
Environmental Appraisal for the Crewe Local Plan, UK**
Environmental Appraisal for the Congleton Local Plan, UK**
Environmental Appraisal for the Blackburn Local Plan, UK**
Environmental Appraisal for the Lancaster Local Plan, UK**
Environmental Appraisal for the Macclesfield Local Plan, UK**
Environmental Appraisal for the Liverpool UDP, UK**
Environmental Appraisal for the Sefton UDP, UK***
Landscape Plan (*Landschaftsplan*) for the Land Use Plan (FNP) Ketzin, Germany*
Landscape Plan (*Landschaftsplan*) for the Land Use Plan (FNP) Nauen, Germany**
Landscape Plan (*Landschaftsplan*) for the Land Use Plan (FNP) Fürstenwalde, Germany**
Landscape Plan (*Landschaftsplan*) for the Land Use Plan (FNP) Oranienburg, Germany**
Landscape Plan (*Landschaftsplan*) for the Land Use Plan (FNP) Hohen-Neuendorf, Germany**
Landscape Plan (*Landschaftsplan*) for the Land Use Plan (FNP) Strausberg, Germany**
Landscape Plan (*Landschaftsplan*) for the Land Use Plan (FNP) Unteres Dahmeland, Germany**
Landscape Plan (*Landschaftsplan*) for the Land Use Plan (FNP) Birkenwerder, Germany**
Landscape Plan (*Landschaftsplan*) for the Land Use Plan (FNP) Kleinmachnow, Germany**
Landscape Plan (*Landschaftsplan*) for the Land Use Plan (FNP) Woltersdorf, Germany**
Landscape Plan (*Landschaftsplan*) for the Land Use Plan (FNP) Königs-Wusterhausen, Germany**
Landscape Plan (*Landschaftsplan*) for the Land Use Plan (FNP) Schönefeld, Germany**
Landscape Plan (*Landschaftsplan*) for the Land Use Plan (FNP) Bestensee, Germany**
Landscape Plan (*Landschaftsplan*) for the Land Use Plan (FNP) Schwielosee, Germany**
Landscape Plan (*Landschaftsplan*) for the Land Use Plan (FNP) Neuenhagen, Germany**
Landscape Plan (*Landschaftsplan*) for the Land Use Plan (FNP) Trebbin, Germany**
Landscape Plan (*Landschaftsplan*) for the Land Use Plan (FNP) Stadt Bernau, Germany**

---

*   = included in analysis, based on interview results
**   = included in analysis, based on postal questionnaire results
*** = not included in analysis (not accessible, accessible only after data collection, no reply by local authority, research study)

Landscape Plan (*Landschaftsplan*) for the Land Use Plan (FNP) Petershagen, Germany**

Landscape Plan (*Landschaftsplan*) for the Land Use Plan (FNP) Stahnsdorf, Germany**

Landscape Plan (*Landschaftsplan*) for the Land Use Plan (FNP) Velten, Germany**

Landscape Plan (*Landschaftsplan*) for the Land Use Plan (FNP) Nauen-Land, Germany**

Landscape Plan (*Landschaftsplan*) for the Land Use Plan (FNP) Ludwigsfelde, Germany**

Landscape Plan (*Landschaftsplan*) for the Land Use Plan (FNP) Oranienburg-Land, Germany***

Environment Matrix (*milieumatrix*) for the Structure Plan (*structuurplan*) Amsterdam, The Netherlands*

Programme-SEAs

Transport

National Level

Roads Programme, UK***
Federal Transport Structure Plan (BVWP), Germany*
Federal Transport Structure Plan (BVWP), ecological assessment, Germany*

Regional level

Cheshire TPP, integrated appraisal, UK*
Merseyside Package Bid, integrated appraisal, UK*
Land Road Development Plan (*Landesstraßenbedarfsplan*), integrated appraisal, Germany*

Local level

No SEA found.

Spatial/land use

National level

National Spatial Plan (VINEX) review*

Regional level

Ecological Conflict Assesssment (*Ökologische Konfliktanalyse*) for the Land Use Plan (*FNP*) Berlin, Germany*

---

*   = included in analysis, based on interview results
**   = included in analysis, based on postal questionnaire results
*** = not included in analysis (not accessible, accessible only after data collection, no reply by local authority, research study)

Local level

No SEA found.

BIG-PROJECT SEAs/EIAs

Only for regional level spatial/land use PPPs (*streekplannen*) in The Netherlands:
Residential Area Amsterdam-Nieuw Oost***
Residential Area Amsterdam-Nieuw Oost, 1st stage***
City Extension Amsterdam-Nieuw Oost, 2nd stage***
Residential Area Purmerend***
Residential Area HAL-gebied (Heerhugowaard, Alkmaar, Langedijk) ***
Residential Area Zaanstad***
Residential Area Haarlemmermeer-West***
Airport Schiphol and surrounding area***

---

*   = included in analysis, based on interview results
**   = included in analysis, based on postal questionnaire results
***   = not included in analysis (not accessible, accessible only after data collection, no reply by local authority, research study)

Appendix 4

Conformity of case study SEAs with the requirements of the EC SEA Directive (proposal of 1999)

Conformity of case study SEAs with the requirements of the EC SEA Directive (proposal of 1999)

PPP \ Principles	Environmental impacts	Evaluation	Alternatives	Early application	Sustainable development	Screening	Mitigation	SEA report
North West England								
Lancashire Structure Plan	✓	⇔	✓	⇔	✓	×	×	✓
Cheshire Structure Plan	✓	⇔	✓	⇔	✓	×	✓	✓
Cheshire TPP	✓	×	✓	⇔	✓	×	×	⇔
Merseyside Package Bid	✓	×	×	⇔	✓	×	×	⇔
Merseyside Package Bid Strategy	✓	✓	✓	✓	✓	×	×	⇔
Warrington Local Plan	✓	⇔	✓	⇔	✓	×	×	⇔
Oldham UDP	✓	⇔	✓	⇔	✓	×	⇔	✓
Noord-Holland								
Transport 'Plan', SVVII	✓	✓	✓	⇔	✓	×	✓	×
Spatial Plan, VINEX review	✓	✓	⇔	⇔	✓	×	⇔	✓
Vision, visie Noord-Holland	✓	⇔	✓	⇔	✓	×	⇔	×
Transport Plan INVERNO	✓	✓	✓	✓	✓	⇔	×	×
Transport Plan, RVVP NHN	✓	✓	✓	✓	✓	⇔	×	×
Transport Plan, RVVP ROA	✓	✓	✓	✓	✓	⇔	×	⇔
Structure Plan Amsterdam	✓	✓	✓	⇔	✓	×	×	✓
Vision, *visie* Hilversum	✓	✓	✓	⇔	✓	×	✓	×
RVVP Haarlem-IJmond	✓	✓	✓	✓	✓	⇔	×	⇔
EVR Brandenburg-Berlin								
Transport Plan BVWP	✓	⇔	×	⇔	×	×	×	×
BVWP ecological assessment	✓	⇔	⇔	⇔	×	⇔	×	⇔
Regional Plan/Dev. Concept	×	×	×	✓	✓	×	⇔	✓
Road Development Plan Brandenburg	✓	⇔	✓	⇔	×	×	×	×
Transport Plan, IVP Brandenburg	✓	n/a	✓	⇔	✓	×	×	×
Land Use Plan, FNP Berlin	✓	✓	⇔	⇔	⇔	×	✓	⇔
FNP Berlin, Landscape Programme	×	×	×	⇔	⇔	⇔	⇔	✓
Transport Plan, StEP Berlin	✓	✓	✓	⇔	✓	×	×	×
Land Use Plan, FNP Ketzin	✓	✓	⇔	✓	×	×	⇔	✓
average score of 3 regions (in %)	89	62	77	63	81	11	27	48
Overall Evaluation	●	◉	●	◉	●	□	○	○

Conformity of case study SEAs with the requirements of the EC SEA Directive proposal (Continued)

PPP / Principles	Clear provisions	SEA considered	Clear requirements	SEA review	Public participation	Consultation	Reporting final SEA	Average score (in %)	Overall evaluation
North West England									
Lancashire Structure Plan	⇔	⇔	✓	✗	✗	✗	✓	53	◉
Cheshire Structure Plan	⇔	⇔	✓	✗	✓	✓	✓	73	◉
Cheshire TPP	⇔	⇔	✓	✓	✗	✗	✗	47	○
Merseyside Package Bid	⇔	⇔	✓	✓	✗	✗	✗	40	○
Merseyside Package Bid Strategy	✗	⇔	✗	✓	✓	✓	⇔	63	◉
Warrington Local Plan	⇔	⇔	✓	✗	✗	✓	✓	57	◉
Oldham UDP	⇔	⇔	✓	✗	⇔	✓	✓	67	◉
Noord-Holland									
Transport 'Plan', SVVII	⇔	✓	⇔	⇔	✓	✓	✓	73	◉
Spatial Plan, VINEX review	✗	✓	⇔	✓	✓	✓	✓	73	◉
Vision, visie Noord-Holland	✗	⇔	✗	✗	✓	✓	✓	53	◉
Transport Plan INVERNO	✗	✓	✗	✓	✗	✓	✓	63	◉
Transport Plan, RVVP NHN	⇔	✓	✗	✓	✗	✓	✓	67	◉
Transport Plan, RVVP ROA	⇔	⇔	✗	✓	✗	✓	✓	67	◉
Structure Plan Amsterdam	✗	✓	⇔	✗	✗	✓	✓	60	◉
Vision, *visie* Hilversum	✗	⇔	✗	✗	✓	✓	✓	60	◉
RVVP Haarlem-IJmond	⇔	⇔	✗	✓	⇔	✓	✓	70	◉
EVR Brandenburg-Berlin									
Transport Plan BVWP	⇔	⇔	⇔	✗	✗	⇔	✓	33	○
BVWP ecological assessment	⇔	⇔	⇔	✗	✗	⇔	✓	43	○
Regional Plan/Dev. Concept	⇔	⇔	⇔	✓	✗	✓	✓	53	◉
Road Development Plan Brandenburg	⇔	⇔	⇔	✗	✗	✓	✓	43	○
Transport Plan, IVP Brandenburg	⇔	n/a	⇔	✗	✗	✓	✓	50	◉
Land Use Plan, FNP Berlin	⇔	n/a	✗	✗	✗	✗	✓	46	◯
FNP Berlin, Landscape Programme	✓	n/a	✓	✗	✓	✓	✓	57	◉
Transport Plan, StEP Berlin	⇔	n/a	✗	✗	✗	✓	✓	50	◉
Land Use Plan, FNP Ketzin	⇔	✓	✓	✓	✓	✓	✓	77	●
average score of 3 regions (in %)	40	54	51	42	36	78	88		
Overall Evaluation	○	◉	◉	○	○	●	●		

Scores: ✓ = 2; ⇔ = 1; ✗ = 0;
Overall Evaluation:
◻ = under 25 per cent
○ = over 25 per cent to 50 per cent
◉ = over 50 per cent to 75 per cent
● = over 75 per cent
■ = 100 per cent

Comparison of targets of the Fifth Environmental Action Programme with national sustainable development strategies

Targets of Fifth Action Programme and national sustainable development strategies

Target	EU	UK (DoE, 1994)	The Netherlands (Ministerie van VROM, 1994b) for transport sector	Germany (BMU, 1994)
CO_2	1990–2000: no increase 1990–05/10: progressive reduction	1990–2000: no increase	1986–2000: 0% to –3% 1986–10: –10%	1990–05: –25%
NO_x	1990–94: no increase 1990–2000: –30%	1987–94: no increase	1986–2000: passenger transport (PT): –75 %, goods transport (GT): –35%; 2000–10: PT: –75%, GT: –75%	1986–98: –30%
VOC	1990–96: –10%; 1990–99: –30%	1988–98: –30%	general target acknowledged, but not for transport sector	1988–99: –30%
SO_2	1985–2000: –35%	–	general target acknowledged, but not for transport sector	1980–2000: –83% 1980–05: –87%
N_2O	–	1990–2000: no increase	general target acknowledged, but not for transport sector	–
CxHy	–	–	1986–2000: PT: –75%, GT: –35%; 1986–2010: PT: –75%, GT: –75%	–

Targets of Fifth Action Programme and national sustainable development strategies

Target	EU	UK (DoE, 1994)	The Netherlands (Ministerie van VROM, 1994b) for transport sector	Germany (BMU, 1994)
Noise levels	never > 85 dB(A) > 65 dB(A): to be phased out 55–65 dB(A): no increase areas now below 55 dB (A) not over 55 dB (A) in the future	–	maximum noise production of vehicles restrained; houses > 55dB(A): 2000: –10%, 2010: –50%; total area > 55dB(A): no increase to 1986	maximum noise production of vehicles restrained
Land-take	• maintenance/ restoration of natural habitats • protection and enhancement of historical heritage, provision for green areas	• protect countryside for its landscape, wildlife, agricultural, recreational and natural resource volume	• prevent or reduce further fragmentation of countryside • reduce longer-term fragmentation	• avoid severence • minimization of land take and economic growth
Waste/consump-tion levels	• halt and reverse current trend in waste • recycling paper, glass and plastics at least 50% • sustainable use of resources	• minimize natural resource consumption • minimize amount of travel required	• vehicles made of parts optimally suitable for reuse • mode choice leading to lowest possible energy consumption	• make producer responsible for waste • make producer take back used cars • better recycling • reduce material throughflow
Accident levels	–	1981–85 to 2000: $-\frac{1}{3}$	fatalities: 1986–95: –15%; 1986–10: –40%; injuries: 1986–95: –10% 1986–10: –40%; casualties: 1986 –2000: –25%; hazardous material transport: maintain at least current level of safety	–

EU target stricter or more specific than country targets

Notes

CHAPTER 1

1   Following Elling and Nielsen (1996, p9), a 'strategic action is usually understood to mean a situation in which one or more objectives can be achieved in different ways and in which the strategic element consists of optimizing the achievement of objectives by means of the most appropriate action'. Following Hughes (1994, p168), a strategy 'aims to specify clear goals and objectives; it attempts to move away from routine management tasks to consider, in a *systematic* way, longer-term considerations of the ... future'.

2   The need for the environmental assessment of PPPs, however, was stressed much earlier than 1989, for example, by Lee and Wood in 1978 and O'Riordan and Sewell in 1981.

3   Throughout this book, no distinction is made between the terms 'impacts' and 'effects', as suggested, for example, by Gilpin (1995, p5), as the two terms are frequently used interchangeably and the borders between them are unclear.

4   'Knowledge' has been portrayed as usually not being unbiased, but to be influenced by *ethical,* ie *value-based* principles. Ethical principles for decision making were described by Finsterbusch (1989, pp17–24).

5   The World Commission Report, also stressed the importance of 'integrated decision making' (World Commission on Environment and Development, 1987, p313).

6   Studies in The Netherlands indicated that structured, EIA-based SEAs can be successfully conducted for waste management, electricity supply programmes and land use plans (van Eck, 1996, p8). Case studies from Germany also concluded that EIA-based SEAs can work for the preparation of land use plans (Riehl and Winkler-Kühlken, 1995; Kleffner and Ried, 1995).

7   The EIA Directive of the EC (85/337/EEC) was portrayed as having two main aims (Pro Terra Team, 1995, p8), namely to:
    • avoid environmental impacts and to apply the precautionary principle; and
    • avoid distortion of competition between EU member states.

8   Burris and Canter (1997) suggested that assessments usually do not properly assess cumulative impacts.

9   Sustainable development is a philosophical concept and open to interpretation. In the context of this book, the different interpretations of the concept are not further discussed. The meaning of sustainable development has been widely discussed, for example, by the EC, 1997b; Franks, 1996; Goodland, 1995; Dalal-Clayton et al, 1994; Ekins, 1992; Daly, 1991; Daly and Cobb, 1990. Sustainable development was made known to a broader audience, particularly through the *World Conservation Strategy* and *Caring for Earth – Strategy for Sustainable Living* of the International Union for Conservation of Nature and

Natural Resources (IUCN) et al (1980 and 1991). Furthermore, the *World Commission Report* (World Commission on Environment and Development, 1987) was an important document that helped to raise awareness of sustainable development worldwide.

10 The Fifth Environmental Action Programme (EC, 1993a) is the sustainable development strategy of the EC.

11 On the need, the feasibility and applicability of the integration of economic, environmental and social aspects see University of Manchester (1998), Canadian Environment Assessment Agency (1995), Sadler and Jacobs (1989), Jakimchuk (1989), McNeely (1989), Cornford et al (1985).

12 The possibility of vertically integrating PPPs with the project level was said to depend on its form. Thus, it was suggested that it is easiest when dealing with tiers that initiate or fix projects (Sadler, 1996, p155).

13 The important role of public involvement in decision making was stressed by many authors, in an SEA and EIA specific as well as in a general way, particularly in communicative planning theory (see, for example, Finsterbusch, 1989; Habermas, 1979).

14 Even though the widespread practice of evaluating EIA/SEA effectiveness in procedural terms has been criticized (Swensen, 1997), the importance of decision making procedures for successful policy making has been stressed by social science. Thus, interactive models that underline the role of processes are said to reflect actual decision making better than more substantive, scientific models that do not allow for flexibility (Innes, 1994, p35).

15 Systematic comparative research on project EIA has been more widespread. For example, for EIA quality: Marr (1997); Glasson et al (1996); Lee et al (1994); Lee and Dancey (1993). For other aspects of EIA application: Papoulias and Nelson (1996); Wood (1995), Cupei (1994); Tarling (1991).

CHAPTER 2

1 Administrative regions were used as opposed to functional regions, which often comprise several administrative regions and may stretch across national borders, for example, Randstad in Holland and the Lille area in France and Belgium (further examples are presented by Gemaca, 1996). For a further discussion of the EU regions, see Jones et al (1995).

2 Some authorities, for example, considered building restrictions around roads (to prevent noise nuisance) as quantitative targets. Furthermore, in EVR Brandenburg-Berlin, it is indicated that compensation measures that need to be implemented according to the Brandenburg Environment Protection Act (*Brandenburgisches Naturschutzgesetz*) were regarded as quantitative targets.

3 Attitudes on the introduction of formalized SEA were examined only recently by Devuyst et al (1998) for Belgium.

4 International comparative studies (for non-EU countries) could be based on international conventions, such as Agenda 21 (United Nations Conference on Environment and Development – UNCED, 1992a), the Climate Change Convention (UNCED, 1992b), the Convention on Biological Diversity (UNCED, 1992c) as well as the conventions on long-range, transboundary air pollution (UNECE, 1994; 1991; 1988; 1985).

5 Suggestions on how sustainable development can be measured were made by Reed (1996), Pearce (1993), Rees and Wackernagel (1992). For possibilities on

how to implement sustainable development at the local level see Gibbs et al (1996), Ferrary (1995), Mitlin and Satterthwaite (1994) and Jacobs (1991).

Chapter 3

1 BoN areas include the Regionaal Orgaan Amsterdam (ROA), Stadsregio Rotterdam (SRR), Stadsgewest Haaglanden, Bestur Regio Utrecht (BRU), Knooppunt Arnhem-Nijmegen (KAN), Stadsregio Eindhoven (SRE) and Regio Twente.
2 An important strategic road transport document of the 1980s was the White Paper *Roads for Prosperity* (DoT, 1989), which announced a doubling of the trunk roads programme and defined basic objectives for the Trunk roads programme. The 1998 review of the programme, however, reduced the number of schemes originally proposed considerably (DETR, 1998d).
3 De facto, central government is a major player in all transport infrastructure decisions, as it provides the financial means for many of the transport infrastructure measures.
4 To date, Railtrack has, however, obtained national government funding.
5 Over the past few years, central government has started to address the transport system in a more holistic way, in particular through consultation papers and draft guidance. These include the 1996 White Paper *Transport: The Way Forward* (by the former Conservative government) and consultation papers by the current Labour government, for example, *Developing an Integrated Transport Policy* (DETR, 1997a), *A New Deal for Transport* (DETR, 1998h).
6 The Dutch society is often described as a consensual society (EC, 1999c, p21; see also Van der Heiden et al, 1991).
7 The costs of servicing the low-lying lands in The Netherlands are often too high for developments to be commercially feasible. Central government therefore frequently provides the necessary funding and municipalities service the lands (EC, 1999b, p28).
8 The extra-legal visions (*visies*) are strongly influenced by the concept of communicative, or collaborative planning (see also Voogd and Woltjer, forthcoming).
9 The connection between the policies introduced in the SVVII and the projects appearing in the MIT, however, remains largely unclear.
10 The objective of the precautionary principle is to avoid or to minimize any pollution or damage before it arises. Environmental policy should not only be reactive, but anticipatory; that is to say, not only averting dangers and repairing damages, but also preventing them at source (Bundesministerium für Umwelt, Naturschutz und Reaktorsicherheit, 1992, p74).
11 The VERDI agreement (*verkeer en vervoer: regionaal, decentraal, integraal*) was signed by the national Ministry of Transport and Water Management (MVW), the Ministry of Internal Affairs, the Inter-Provincial Administrative Committee (IPO) and the Association of Dutch Municipalities (VNG) on 29 March 1996. In 1996/7, all financial support of the national government for non-national infrastructure went to provincial authorities. In 1998 this practice was changed and financial support now goes to both, *provincies* as well as municipalities.

CHAPTER 4

1   Postal survey results indicate that 50 per cent of all local authorities in North West England, 17 per cent in Noord-Holland and 4 per cent in EVR Brandenburg-Berlin were aware of Local Agenda 21.

2   The connection between implementation programmes in the underlying regional transport policy, however, often remained unclear.

3   Similar to the Dutch structure plans (*structuurplannen*), German land use plans (FNPs) only have to be prepared in case the specific local circumstances require it. In effect, in contrast to Noord-Holland, in EVR Brandenburg-Berlin most municipalities did prepare FNPs.

CHAPTER 5

1   The German Constitution (*Grundgesetz*) formulates the principle of equivalent living conditions for all parts of the country (article 72, paragraph 2(3)).

2   Formal requirements for public participation in plan-SEA were formulated in EVR Brandenburg-Berlin landscape plans (*Landschaftspläne*) for the statutory local land use plans (FNPs).

3   The results of the subsequent chapters will suggest that quantitative assessment appears to be most effective.

CHAPTER 6

1   Opinions on existing local level SEAs could only be determined for North West England and EVR Brandenburg-Berlin, as information was obtained on only one further assessment at the local level in Noord-Holland (see Chapter 5).

2   It needs to be stressed, however, that SEAs were also conducted in the sample regions for general strategies in the form of policy SEA.

3   Negative attitudes of local authorities were also observed in Belgium by Devuyst et al (1998, p9). A lack of interest in Local Agenda 21 was observed in local authorities in The Netherlands (Broere, 1998).

4   This response therefore does not refer to policy-SEA, which does not assess transport modes separately, but integratively.

CHAPTER 7

1   Climate change, acidification, air quality, nature/biodiversity, water, urban environment and waste/raw material consumption.

2   Emission and noise levels, land-take, waste/consumption and accident levels.

3   Land use planning, infrastructure investment, infrastructure charging, economic incentives, regulation changes, information and education, interactive communication and public transport.

4   Implicit objectives and targets are those that were not explicitly referred to in a clear and quantifiable manner, but that, according to authorities, were still acknowledged.

5   Climate change, air quality, nature/biodiversity and the urban environment.
6   Emission and land use targets.
7   Any measures proposed by local authorities to meet the four objectives.
8   The same environmental/sustainability objectives were shared by the National Environmental Policy Plan (NMP) and the Second Transport Structure Plan (SVVII).

CHAPTER 8

1   However, it needs to be stressed that the connection between policies and projects in reality, often remain unclear.
2   If, however, local land use PPPs are considered, EVR Brandenburg-Berlin SEAs involved public participation to the largest extent.

CHAPTER 9

1   Government spending on planning and environmental issues in general is smaller in the UK than in other EU countries (Eurostat Jahrbuch, 1997, p239). Furthermore, project EIA preparation times in the UK were also found to be smaller than in other EU countries (see, for example, Marr, 1997).
2   It is acknowledged that under different circumstances, SEA might need to be applied more flexibly, for example, 'legislative environmental assessment' (see Marsden, 1999). This, however, needs to be researched in further detail.
3   Note that this terminology was not necessarily reflected in current practice, for example, policy-SEA was applied to the Second Transport Structure Plan and programme-SEA was applied to the Federal Transport Infrastructure Plan.

CHAPTER 10

1   The number of SEAs finally included in the analysis was 25 SEAs for the 36 cross-section of PPPs (analysis based on comprehensive interviews) and 35 SEAs for local land use PPPs (analysis based on postal questionnaires). Twenty SEAs were not analysed, including those that became accessible only after data collection was completed and big-project SEAs/EIAs for Noord-Holland regional plans (*streekplannen*), which were conducted according to the national EIA decree, dealing with 'big' projects, but not with the plan as a whole. PPP makers of three visions (*visies*) in Noord-Holland and one landscape plan in EVR Brandenburg-Berlin did not provide any information on the assessment of environmental impacts, and could therefore not be included.
2   Of the 16 policy-SEAs, 8 were called plans, 7 were called visions and one was called strategy.
3   Two transport SEA research studies, covering parts of North West England and EVR Brandenburg-Berlin, could also be classified as plan-SEAs (see MVA et al, 1999; Ministerium für Wohnungswesen, Städtebau und Verkehr, 1995). These involved assessing transport alternatives for improving accessibility in a larger regional context.

4   Of the 48 plan-SEAs, only 1 was not called a plan, namely, the Landscape Programme Berlin.
5   Of the nine programme-SEAs, six were called plans, two were called programmes and one was called package.
6   This was mainly caused by three examples without SEA at higher tiers, that were said to consider sustainability particularly well (see Chapter 7).
7   The analysis of SEA benefits only referred to the cross-section of PPPs, mainly because the set of questions was too comprehensive for inclusion in a postal questionnaire. Those local land use SEAs included in the cross-section of PPPs, however, allowed an estimation of possible differences between local and higher tiers of decision making.

References

Abaza, H (1996) 'Integration of sustainability objectives in structural adjustment programmes using SEA', *Project Appraisal* 10(4): 217–228

Acutt, M Z and Dodgson, J S (1996) 'Transport and global warming – modelling the impacts of alternative policies', paper presented at the final conference for the ESRC Research Programme *Transport and the Environment*, Regent's College Conference Centre, 22 March, London

Bass, R and Herson, A (1993) *Successful CEQA Compliance: A Step-by-step Approach*, Solano Press, Point Arena, CA

Bonde, J (1998) *Quality of Strategic Environmental Assessments of Land Use Plans – A Review Package for the UK and Sweden*, MA dissertation, EIA Centre, University of Manchester

Booth, P (1986) 'The design and implementation of cross-national research projects – introduction', in: Masser, I and Williams, R (eds), *Learning from Other Countries*, Geo Books, Norwich

Boothroyd, P (1994) 'Policy assessment', in: Vanclay, F and Bronstein, D A (eds), *Environmental and Social Impact Assessment*, John Wiley and Sons, Chichester

Bradley, K (1998) 'Developments in regard to environmental appraisal of regional development plans in the context of the structural fund', *Impact Assessment in the Development Process: Advances in Integrating Environmental Assessment with Economic and Social Appraisal*, Conference Proceedings, University of Manchester, 23–24 October, Manchester

Bregha F, Benedickson, J, Gauble, D, Shillington, T and Weick, E (1990) *The Integration of Environmental Factors in Government Policy Making*, Canadian Environmental Assessment Research Council (CEARC), Hull, Québec

Broere, M (1998) 'Lokale Agenda 21 probeert plaatselijke actie voor duurzaamheid te mobiliseren', *ROM Magazine* 16(3): 18–20

Bundesministerium für Raumordnung, Bauwesen und Städtebau (BfRBS) (1996) *Raumordnung in Deutschland*, BfRBS, Bonn

Bundesministerium für Umwelt, Naturschutz und Reaktorsicherheit (BMU) (1992) *Environmental Protection in Germany*, Economica Verlag, Bonn

Bundesministerium für Umwelt, Naturschutz und Reaktorsicherheit (BMU) (1993) *Landscape Planning*, BMU, Bonn

Bundesministerium für Umwelt, Naturschutz und Reaktorsicherheit (BMU) (1994) *Environmental Policy – German Strategy for Sustainable Development*, BMU, Bonn

Bunge, T (1998) 'SEA in land use planning: the Erlangen case study', in: Kleinschmidt, V and Wagner, D (eds), *SEA in Europe: Fourth European Workshop on EIA*, Kluwer Academic Publishers, Dordrecht

Burris, R K and Canter, L W (1997) 'Cumulative impacts are not properly addressed in environmental assessments', *Environmental Impact Assessment Review* 17: 5–18

Canadian Environment Assessment Agency (CEAA) (1995) *Balancing the Scale: Integrating Environmental and Economic Assessment*, CEAA, Ottawa

Canter, L W (1996) *Environmental Impact Assessment*, second edition, McGraw-Hill, New York

Commissie voor de Mer (cvm) (1996) *Environmental Impact Assessment in The Netherlands, Experiences and Views*, cvm, Utrecht

Cornford, A, O'Riordan, J and Sadler, B (1985) 'Planning, assessment and implementation: a strategy for integration', in: Sadler, B (ed), *Environmental Protection and Resource Development: Convergence for Today*, The University of Calgary Press, Calgary

Counsell, D (1998) 'Sustainable development and structure plans in England and Wales: a review of current practice', *Journal of Environmental Planning and Management* 41(2): 177–194

Cramer, D (1998) *Fundamental Statistics for Social Research*, Routledge, London

Cullinworth, J B and Nadin, V (1994) *Town and Country Planning in Britain*, eleventh edition, Routledge, London

Cullinworth, J B and Nadin, V (1997) *Town and Country Planning in the UK*, twelfth edition, Routledge, London

Cupei, J (1994) *Vermeidung von Wettbewerbsverzerrungen durch UVP? Eine vergleichende Analyse der Umsetzung der UVP – Richtlinie in Frankreich, Großbritannien und den Niederlanden*, Nomos, Baden-Baden

Curran, J M, Wood, C and Hilton, M (1998) 'Environmental appraisal of UK development plans: current practice and future directions', *Environment and Planning B: Planning and Design* 25: 411–433

Dalal-Clayton, B, Bass, S, Sadler, B, Thomson, K, Sandbrook, R, Robins, N and Hughes, R (1994) *National Sustainable Development Strategies: Experience and Dilemmas, Environmental Planning Issues 6,* International Institute for Environment and Development (IIED), London

Daly, H (1991) *Steady State Economics*, Island Press, Washington, DC

Daly, H and Cobb, J B (1990) *For the Common Good – Restricting the Economy Towards Community, the Environment and a Sustainable Future*, Beacon Press, Boston

Davoudi, S, Hull, A and Healy, P (1996) 'Environmental concerns and economic imperatives in strategic plan making', *Town Planning Review* 67(4): 421–436

De Vries, Y and Tonk, J (1997) 'Assessing draft regulations – the Dutch experience', *Environmental Assessment (ea)* 5(3): 37–38

Department of the Environment (DoE) (1989) *Planning Control in Western Europe*, HMSO, London

Department of the Environment (DoE) (1991) *Policy Appraisal and the Environment*, HMSO, London

Department of the Environment (DoE) (1993) *Environmental Appraisal of Development Plans – A Good Practice Guide*, HMSO, London

Department of the Environment (DoE) (1994) *Sustainable Development – The UK Strategy*, HMSO, London

Department of the Environment, Transport and the Regions (DETR) (1997a) *Developing an Integrated Transport Policy*, DETR, London www.detr.gov.uk/itd/consult/objectiv.htm

Department of the Environment, Transport and the Regions (DETR) (1997b) *Press Notice 49, 18/02/97*, DETR, London

Department of the Environment, Transport and the Regions (DETR) (1997c) *A New Approach to Trunk Roads Planning*, DETR, London

Department of the Environment, Transport and the Regions (DETR) (1998a) *Sustainability Appraisal of Regional Planning Guidance, Interim Report*, DETR, London

Department of the Environment, Transport and the Regions (DETR) (1998b) *The Future of Regional Planning Guidance – Consultation Paper*, DETR, London www.planning.detr.gov.uk/consult/future/index.htm

Department of the Environment, Transport and the Regions (DETR) (1998c) *Policy Appraisal and the Environment: Policy Guidance*, HMSO, London

Department of the Environment, Transport and the Regions (DETR) (1998d) *A New Deal for Trunk Roads in England*, HMSO, London

Department of the Environment, Transport and the Regions (DETR) (1998e) *Strategic Environmental Appraisal, Report of the International Seminar, Lincoln 27–29 May 1998*, DETR, London

Department of the Environment, Transport and the Regions (DETR) (1998f) *Modernising Planning*, DETR, London

Department of the Environment, Transport and the Regions (DETR) (1998g) *Experience with the Policy Appraisal and the Environment Initiative*, DETR, London

Department of the Environment, Transport and the Regions (DETR) (1998h) *A New Deal for Transport*, DETR, London

Department of Transport (DoT) (1989) *Roads for Prosperity*, HMSO, London

Department of Transport (DoT) (1994) *Trunk Roads in England*, HMSO, London

Department of Transport (DoT) (1995) *Local Authority Circular 2/95, Transport Policies and Programme Submissions for 1996–97*, DoT, London

Devuyst, D, von Wijngaarden, T and Hens, L (1998) 'The introduction of strategic environmental assessment of provincial and municipal levels in the Flemish region (Belgium): examining attitudes of persons involved, proposals for an SEA system and future challenges', International Association for Impact Assessment (IAIA), Conference Proceedings, 18th Annual Meeting, Auckland 1998, CD-ROM, IAIA, Fargo, ND

Dipper, B, Jones, C and Wood, C (1998) 'Monitoring and post-auditing in environmental impact assessment: a review', *Journal of Environmental Planning and Management*, 41(6): 731–747

Ekins, P (1992) *Wealth Beyond Measure – An Atlas of New Economics*, Gaia, London

Elling, B (1998) 'Environmental assessment in Denmark', *EIA Newsletter 17*, EIA Centre, University of Manchester

Elling, B and Nielsen, J (1996) *Environmental Assessment of Policies, Centre for Environmental Assessment*, Roskilde University

English Nature (1992) *Strategic Planning and Sustainable Development*, English Nature, Peterborough

English Nature (1996) *SEA and Nature Conservation,* English Nature, Peterborough

Environment Australia (1997) *Strategic Environmental Assessment, Final Report of the International Study of the Effectiveness of Environmental Assessment*, Internet Version, Chapter 6, www.erin.gov.au

Eriksson, I-M (1994) 'The SEIA approach', paper presented at the International Seminar on Environmental Impact Assessment of Roads – Strategic and Integrated Approaches, 31 May–2 June, Palermo, OECD, Paris

European Commission (EC) (1992) *Green Paper on the Impact of Transport on the Environment – A Community Strategy for 'Sustainable Mobility'*, Directorate General Environment, Nuclear Safety and Civil Protection (DG XI), Brussels

European Commission (EC) (1993a) *Towards Sustainability – A European Community Programme of Policy and Action in Relation to the Environment and Sustainable Development (Fifth Environmental Action Programme)*, Directorate General Environment, Nuclear Safety and Civil Protection (DG XI), Brussels

European Commission (EC) (1993b) *The European High Speed Train Network, Environmental Impact Assessment, Executive Summary*, Directorate General Transport (DG VII), Brussels

European Commission (EC) (1994a) *Environmental Impact Assessment, Methodology and Research, Third EU workshop on EIA, Delphi 1994*, Directorate General Environment, Nuclear Safety and Civil Protection (DG XI), Brussels

European Commission (EC) (1994b) *Strategic Environmental Assessment, Existing Strategic Environmental Assessment Methodology*, Directorate General Environment, Nuclear Safety and Civil Protection (DG XI), Brussels

European Commission (EC) (1996a) *Progress Report on the Implementation of the European Community Programme of Policy and Action in Relation to the Environment and Sustainable Development 'Towards Sustainability'*, Directorate General Environment, Nuclear Safety and Civil Protection (DG XI), Brussels

European Commission (EC) (1996b) *Environmental Impact Assessment: A Study on Costs and Benefits*, Directorate General Environment, Nuclear Safety and Civil Protection (DG XI), Brussels

European Commission (EC) (1997a) *Case Studies on Strategic Environmental Assessment*, Directorate General Environment, Nuclear Safety and Civil Protection (DG XI), Brussels

European Commission (EC) (1997b) *Optionen für eine dauerhafte Entwicklung in Europa – Politische Empfehlungen des Allgemeinen Beratenden Forums für Umweltfragen*, Directorate General Environment, Nuclear Safety and Civil Protection (DG XI), Brussels

European Commission (EC) (1998a) *Spatial and Ecological Assessment of the TENs*, Directorate General Environment, Nuclear Safety and Civil Protection (DG XI), Brussels

European Commission (EC) (1998b) *SEA Report of the Workshop Semmering, Austria, 5–7 October 1998*. Directorate General Environment, Nuclear Safety and Civil Protection (DG XI), Brussels

European Commission (EC) (1999a) *Manual on SEA of Transport Infrastructure Plans*, Directorate General for Transport (DG VII), Brussels

European Commission (EC) (1999b) *The EU Compendium of Spatial Planning Systems and Policies, The Netherlands*, Directorate General for Regional Planning and Cohesion, Brussels (DG VI), Brussels

European Commission (EC) (1999c) *The EU Compendium of Spatial Planning Systems and Policies, Germany*, Directorate General for Regional Planning and Cohesion, Brussels (DG VI), Brussels

European Conference of Ministers of Transport (ECMT) (1993) *Reducing Transport's Contribution to Global Warming, Conclusions of ECMT Seminar, 30 September–1 October*, ECMT, Paris

European Conference of Ministers of Transport (ECMT) (1995) *Urban Travel and Sustainable Development*, ECMT, Paris

European Conference of Ministers of Transport (ECMT) (1998) *Strategic Environmental Assessment in the Transport Sector*, ECMT, Paris

European Environment Agency (EEA) (1998) *Spatial and Ecological Assessment of the TEN: Demonstration of Indicators and GIS Methods, Second Draft*, EEA, Copenhagen

Eurostat (1997) *Jahrbuch '97*, Eurostat, Luxembourg

Falque, M (1995) 'Environmental assessment in France', *EIA Newsletter 10*, EIA Centre, University of Manchester

Feldmann, L (1998a) Die strategische Umweltprüfung – SUP, in: Hartje, V and Klaphake, A (eds), *Die Rolle der Europäischen Union in der Umweltplanung*, Metropolis Verlag, Marburg

Feldmann, L (1998b) 'The European Commission's proposal for a strategic environmental assessment directive: expanding the scope of environmental impact assessment in Europe', *Environmental Impacts Assessment Review* 18: 3–14

Ferrary, C K (1995) 'Sustainability and transport: helping ensure policies and infrastructure proposals can be sustainable', *Report for the Natural and Built Environmental Professions, no 5*, Stourbridge

Finsterbusch, K (1989) 'How should policy decisions be made?', *Impact Assessment Bulletin* 7: 17–25

Fischer, T B (1998) Die Strategische Umweltprüfung – Vorteile ihrer Anwendung und Klassifizierungsmöglichkeiten, *UVP Report* 12(2+3): 69–73

Fischer, T B (1999a) 'Benefits from SEA application, a comparative review of North West England, Noord-Holland and Brandenburg-Berlin', *Environmental Impact Assessment Review* 19: 143–173

Fischer, T B (1999b) 'The Consideration of "sustainability" aspects in transport infrastructure related policies, plans and programmes', *Journal of Environmental Planning and Management* 42(2): 189–219

Fischer, T B (1999c) 'Comparative analysis of environmental and socio-economic impacts in SEA for transport related policies, plans and programs', *Environmental Impact Assessment Review* 19: 275–303

Fischer, T B, Wood, C and Jones, C (forthcoming) Policy, Plan and Programme Environmental Assessment: Theory and Practice, *Environment and Planning B*

Fischer, T B (2001b) Strategic environmental assessment in the UK, The Netherlands and Germany – some systematic research conclusions, *Impact Assessment and Project Appraisal* 19(1): 41–51

Fischer Weltalmanach (1994) *Fischer Tachenbuchverlag*, Frankfurt/Main

Flynn, R (1993) 'Restructuring health systems: a comparative analysis of England and The Netherlands', in: Hill, M (ed), *New Agendas in the Study of the Policy Process*, Harvester Wheatsheaf, New York

Franks, T R (1996) 'Managing sustainable development: definitions, paradigms and dimensions', *Sustainable Development* 4: 53–60

Friends of the Earth (1995) *Towards Sustainable Europe – A Summary*, Friends of the Earth, Brussels

Gardner, J E (1989) 'The elephant and the nine blind men: an initial review of environmental assessment and related processes in support of sustainable development', in: Jacobs, P and Sadler, B (eds), *Sustainable Development and Environmental Assessment: Perspectives on Planning for a Common Future*, Canadian Environmental Assessment Research Council (CEARC), Hull, Québec

Gemaca (1996) *North-West European Metropolitan Regions – Geographical Boundaries and Economic Structures*, Gemaca, Paris

Gibbs, D, Longhurst, J and Braithwaite, C (1996) 'Moving towards sustainable development? Integrating economic development and the environment in local authorities', *Journal of Environmental Planning and Management* 39(3): 317–332

Gilpin, A (1995) *Environmental Impact Assessment, Cutting Edge for the Twenty-First Century*, Cambridge University Press, Cambridge

Glasson, J (1995a) 'Socio-economic impacts 1: overview and economic impacts', in: Morris, P and Thérivel, R (eds), *Methods of EIA*, UCL Press, London

Glasson, J (1995b) 'Regional planning and the environment: time for a SEA change', *Urban Studies* 32: 713–731

Glasson, J, Thérivel, R and Chadwick, A (1995) *Introduction to Environmental Impact Assessment*, UCL Press, London

Glasson, J, Thérivel, R, Weston, J, Wilson, E and Frost, R (1996) *Changes in the Quality of Environmental Statements for Planning Projects*, HMSO, London

Goodland, R (1995) 'The concept of environmental sustainability', *Annual Review of Ecological Systems* 26: 1–24

Goodland, R (1997) 'The strategic environmental assessment family', *Environmental Assessment* (ea) 5(3): 17–20

Goodland R and Edmundson, V (eds) (1994) *Environmental Assessment and Development*, The World Bank, Washington, DC

Goodland, R and Tillmann, G (1995) *Strategic Environmental Assessment*, Shell International BV, Health, Safety and Environment Division, The Hague

Goodwin, P and Parkhurst, G (1996) 'The real effects of "environmentally friendly" transport policies', paper presented at the final conference for the ESRC Research Programme, 22 March, Regent's College, London

Gordon, I, Lewis, J and Young, K (1993) 'Perspectives on policy analysis', in: Hill, M (ed), *The Policy Process – A Reader*, Harvester Wheatsheaf, New York

Gosling, J A (1999) 'SEA and the planning process: four models and a report?', International Association for Impact Assessment (IAIA), Conference Proceedings, 19th Annual Meeting, Glasgow, CD-Rom, IAIA, Fargo, ND

Habermas, J (1979) *Communication and the Evolution of Society*, Beacon, Boston

Handbuch der Umweltverträglichkeitsprüfung (1999) Erich Schmidt Verlag, Berlin

Hanna, J and Mogridge, M (1992) 'Market forces and transport choices', in: Roberts, J, Cleari, C, Hambleton, C and Hanna, J (eds), *Travel Sickness: The Need for a Sustainable Transport Policy for Britain*, Lawrence and Wishart, London

Hartje, V and Klaphake, A (eds) (1998) *Die Rolle der Europäischen Union in der Umweltplanung*, Metropolis Verlag, Marburg

Hey, C (ed) (1996) *Strengthening the Environmental Dimension – Conclusions and Recommendations from the Research Project 'Environment and Freight Transport Policies'*, Eures, Freiburg

Hill, M (ed) (1993) *The Policy Process – A Reader*, Harvester Wheatsheaf, New York

Holling, C S (ed) (1978) *Adaptive Environmental Assessment and Management*, Wiley, New York

Hübler, K-H, Riehl, C and Winkler-Kühlken, B (1995) *UVP in der Bauleitplanung – Praxisprobleme und Lösungsvorschläge, Band 1: Leitfaden zur UVP in der Bauleitplanung mit dem Schwerpunkt auf der Ebene der Flächennutzungsplanung'*, Reihe Berichte des Umweltbundesamtes 6/95, Umweltbundesamt, Berlin

Hughes, O E (1994) *Public Management and Administration: An Introduction*, The Macmillan Press, London

Hundloe, T, McDonald, G, Ware, J and Wilks, L (1990) 'Cost-benefit analysis and environmental impact assessment', *Environmental Impact Assessment Review* 10: 55–68

Innes, J E (1994) *Knowledge and Public Policy: The Search for Meaningful Indicators*, Transaction Publishers, New Brunswick

Institute for European Environmental Policy (IEEP) (1994) *Strategic Environmental Assessment: Implications for the English Countryside*, IEEP, London

International Association for Impact Assessment (IAIA) (1996) Conference Proceedings, 16th Annual Meeting, Estoril 1996, IAIA, Fargo, ND

International Association for Impact Assessment (IAIA) (1997) Conference Proceedings, 17th Annual Meeting, New Orleans 1997, CD-ROM, IAIA, Fargo, ND

International Association for Impact Assessment (IAIA) (1998) Conference Proceedings, 18th Annual Meeting, Auckland 1998, CD-Rom, IAIA, Fargo, ND

International Association for Impact Assessment (IAIA) (1999) Conference Proceedings, 19th Annual Meeting Glasgow 1999, CD-Rom, IAIA, Fargo, ND

International Union for Conservation of Nature and Natural Resources, United Nations Environment Programme and World Wide Fund For Nature (IUCN, UNEP, WWF) (1980) *World Conservation Strategy*, Gland, Switzerland

International Union for Conservation of Nature and Natural Resources, United Nations Environment Programme and World Wide Fund For Nature (IUCN, UNEP, WWF) (1991) *Caring for Earth: a Strategy for Sustainable Living*, Earthscan, London

Jacobs, M (1991) *The Green Economy: Environment, Sustainable Development and the Politics of the Future*, CPRE, London

Jacobs, P and Sadler, B (eds) (1989) *Sustainable Development and Environmental Assessment: Perspectives on Planning for a Common Future*, Canadian Environmental Assessment Research Council (CEARC), Hull, Québec

Jacoby, C (ed) (1996) *Strategische Umweltvorsorge in der Flächennutzungsplanung*, Analytica Verlag, Essen

Jakimchuk, R D (1989) 'The role of environmental assessment in support of sustainable development', in: Jacobs, P and Sadler, B (eds), *Sustainable Development and Environmental Assessment: Perspectives on Planning for a Common Future*, Canadian Environmental Assessment Research Council (CEARC), Hull, Québec

Jones, B and Keating, M (1995) *The European Union and the Regions*, Clarendon, Oxford

Karas, H H W (1991) *Back from the Brink: Greenhouse Gas Targets for a Sustainable World*, Friends of the Earth, London

Kleffner, U and Ried, W M (1995) 'Programm-UVP in der Flächennutzungs-planung beim Stadtverband Saarbrücken', paper presented at Stadtverband Saarbrücken congress, 30–31 March, Stadtverband Saarbrücken

Kleinschmidt, V and Wagner, D (eds) (1998) *SEA in Europe: Fourth European Workshop on EIA*, Kluwer Academic Publishers, Dordrecht

Knieps, E and Stein, W (1998) 'EU-Richtlinienvorschlag in der Diskussion', *UVP-Report* 12(2+3): 77–80

Koernov, L (1999) 'Integrating SEA in institutional structures', International Association for Impact Assessment (IAIA), Conference Proceedings, 19th Annual Meeting, Glasgow, CD-Rom, IAIA, Fargo, ND

Läpple, D (ed) (1993) *Güterverkehr, Logistik und Umwelt*, Edition Sigma, Berlin

Lawrence, D P (1997) 'Integrating sustainability and environmental impact assessment', *Environmental Management*, 21(1): 23–42

Lee, N, Bonde, J and Simpson, J (1999) *Reviewing the Quality of Environmental Statements and Environmental Appraisals, Occasional Paper 55*, University of Manchester

Lee, N and Colley, R (1992) *Reviewing the Quality of Environmental Statements, Occasional Paper 24*, Department of Planning and Landscape, University of Manchester

Lee, N and Dancey, R (1993) 'The quality of environmental impact statements in Ireland and the United Kingdom: a comparative analysis', *Project Appraisal* 8(1): 31–36

Lee, N and Hughes, J (1995) *Strategic Environmental Assessment, Legislation and Procedures in the Community, Final Report*, EIA Centre, University of Manchester

Lee, N and Walsh, F (1992) 'Strategic environmental assessment: an overview', *Project Appraisal* 7(3): 126–136

Lee, N, Walsh, F and Reeder, G (1994) 'Assessing the performance of the EA process', *Project Appraisal* 9(3): 161–172

Lee, N and Wood, C (1978) 'EIA – a European perspective', *Built Environment* 4(2): 101–110

Leistritz, F L (1995) 'Economic and fiscal impact assessment', in: Vanclay, F and Bronstein, D A (eds), *Environmental and Social Impact Assessment*, Wiley, New York

Marr, K (1997) *Environmental Impact Assessment in the United Kingdom and Germany*, Ashgate, Aldershot

Marsh, S (1997) *Reviewing the Environmental Appraisal of Development Plans: A Critical Assessment of Progress and Best Practice with a Focus upon the North West Region of England*, MSc dissertation, University of Liverpool

Marsden, S (1999) *Legislative Environmental Assessment: An Evaluation of Procedure and Context with Reference to Canada and The Netherlands*, PhD thesis, University of Tasmania, Hobart

Masser, I (1984) 'Cross-national planning studies: a review', *Town Planning Review* 20: 103–108

Masser, I and Williams, R (eds) (1986) *Learning from Other Countries*, Geo Books, Norwich

McNeely, J A (1989) 'Environmental assessment in support of sustainable development: exploring the relationship', in: Jacobs, P and Sadler, B (eds), *Sustainable Development and Environmental Assessment: Perspectives on Planning for a Common Future*, Canadian Environmental Assessment Research Council (CEARC), Hull, Québec

Mikesell, R F (1994) 'Environmental assessment and sustainability at the project and program level', in: Goodland, R and Edmundson, V (eds), *Environmental Assessment and Development*, The World Bank, Washington, DC

Milieudefensie (1992) *Sustainable Netherlands*, Milieudefensie, Amsterdam

Milieudefensie (1996) *Sustainable Europe*, Milieudefensie, Amsterdam

Ministère de l'Environnement, Direction de la Nature et des Paysages (MENP) (1995) *Évaluation Environnementale des Politiques, Plans et Programmes*, MENP, Paris

Ministère de l'Equipement, du Logement et des Transports (MELT) (1992) *L'axe A7–A9 à l'horizon 2010 – Propositions Intermodales*, MELT, Paris

Ministerie van Economische Zaken (ME) (1995) *Nota ruimte voor regios*, ME, Den Haag

Ministerie van Verkeer en Waterstaat (MVW) (1996a) *Nota samenwerken an bereikbarheid*, MVW, Den Haag

Ministerie van Verkeer en Waterstaat (MVW) (1996b) *Nota transport in balans*, MVW, Den Haag

Ministerie van Volkshuisvesting, Ruimtelijke Ordening en Milieubeheer (VROM) (1989a) *National Environmental Policy Plan I*, VROM, Den Haag

Ministerie van Volkshuisvesting, Ruimtelijke Ordening en Milieubeheer (VROM) (1989b) *Derde nota waterhuisvesting*, VROM, Den Haag

Ministerie van Volkshuisvesting, Ruimtelijke Ordening en Milieubeheer (VROM) (1991) *Nota locatiebeleid*, VROM, Den Haag

Ministerie van Volkshuisvesting, Ruimtelijke Ordening en Milieubeheer (VROM) (1994a) *Mer-besluiten voor een leefbaar Nederland – handleiding*, VROM, Den Haag

Ministerie van Volkshuisvesting, Ruimtelijke Ordening en Milieubeheer (VROM) (1994b) *National Environmental Policy Plan II*, VROM, Den Haag

Ministerie van Volkshuisvesting, Ruimtelijke Ordening en Milieubeheer (VROM) (1996a) *Spatial Planning in The Netherlands*, VROM, Den Haag

Ministerie van Volkshuisvesting, Ruimtelijke Ordening en Milieubeheer (VROM) (1996b) *De milieutoets, checklist en toelichting*, VROM, Den Haag

Ministerie van Volkshuisvesting, Ruimtelijke Ordening en Milieubeheer (VROM) (1998a) *Evaluatie digitale discussie Nederland 2030*, Instituut voor Maatschappelijke Innovatie, Leiden

Ministerie van Volkshuisvesting, Ruimtelijke Ordening en Milieubeheer (VROM) (1998b) *Nationaal milieubeleidsplan III*, VROM, Den Haag

Ministerium für Umwelt, Naturschutz und Raumordnung (MUNR) (1995a) *Bauleitplanung und Landschaftsplanung*, MUNR, Potsdam

Ministerium für Umwelt, Naturschutz und Raumordnung (MUNR) (1995b) *Gemeinsamer Landesentwicklungsplan für den engeren Verflechtungsraum Brandenburg-Berlin*, MUNR, Potsdam

Ministerium für Umwelt, Raumordnung und Landwirtschaft (MURL) (1997) *Die UVP für Pläne und Programme – Eine Chance zur Weiterentwicklung von Planungsinstrumenten?*, MURL, Düsseldorf

Ministerium für Wohnungswesen, Städtebau und Verkehr des Landes Sachsen-Anhalt (MWSV) (1995) *Verkehrsuntersuchung Nordost – Kurzfassung*, MWSV, Magdeburg

Ministry of Environment and Energy (MEE) (1995a) *Administrative Order No. 12 of 11 January 1995*, MEE, Copenhagen

Ministry of Environment and Energy (MEE) (1995b) *Guidance on Procedures for Emvironmental Assessments of Bills and Other Government Proposals*, MEE, Copenhagen

Ministry of Transport, Public Works and Water Management (MVW) (1993) *Working Together Towards Greater Accessibility*, MVW, Den Haag

Minogue, M (1993) 'Theory and practice in public policy and administration', in: Hill, M (ed), *The Policy Process – A Reader*, Harvester Wheatsheaf, New York

Mitlin, D and Satterthwaite, D (1994) *Global Forum '94, Cities and Sustainable Development*, International Institute for Environment and Development (IIED), London

MVA, David Simonds Consultancy and Environmental Resources Management (1999) *Strategic Environmental Assessment in the Trans-Pennine Corridor*, MVA, London

Municipal Year Book and Public Services Directory (1996) Newman Books, London

Niekerk, F and Arts, J (1996) 'Impact assessment in Dutch infrastructure planning: towards a better timing and integration?', Integrating Environmental Assessment and Socio-Economic Appraisal in the Development Process, Conference Proceedings, University of Bradford 24–25 May, Bradford

Niekerk, F and Voogd, H (1996) Impact assessment for infrastructure planning: some Dutch dilemmas', Paper prepared for the ACSP-AESOP Congress, July, Toronto

North Atlantic Treaty Organization (NATO) (1996) *Methodology, Focalization, Evaluation and Scope of Environmental Impact Assessment, Fourth report (No. 212), Strategic Environmental Assessment: Theory versus Practice*, Brussels

North Atlantic Treaty Organization (NATO) (1997) *Methodology, Focalization, Evaluation and Scope of Environmental Impact Assessment, Fifth report (No. 218), SEA in Land-use Planning*, Brussels

North West Regional Association (NWRA) (1994) *Greener Growth*, NWRA, Oldham Metropolitan Area Council, Oldham

O'Riordan, T and Sewell, W R D (1981) *Project Appraisal and Policy Review*, John Wiley and Sons, Chichester

O'Riordan, T (1986) 'EIA: dangers and opportunities', *Environmental Impact Assessment Review* 6: 3–6

Organisation for Economic Co-operation and Development (OECD) (1994) *Environmental Impact Assessment of Roads*, Road Transport Research, OECD, Paris

Organisation for Economic Co-operation and Development (OECD) (1995) *10 Recommendations of Monte Pellegrino*, OECD, Paris

Ottersbach, U (1996) 'Die Umweltverträglichkeitsprüfung in der Regionalplanung am Beispiel der Elemente "oberflächennahe Rohstoffe" und "Siedlung"', in: *Handbuch der Umweltverträglichkeitsprüfung*, Erich Schmidt Verlag, Berlin

Papoulias, F and Nelson, P (1996) 'Cost-effectiveness of European EIA Directive', International Association for Impact Assessment (IAIA) Conference proceedings, 16th Annual Meeting, Estoril, IAIA, Fargo, ND

Partidário, M R (1996) 'SEA: key issues emerging from recent practice', *Environmental Impact Assessment Review* 16: 31–55

Partidário, M R (1997) 'Case studies on strategic EA in land-use planning: a comparative review', in: *NATO Report No 218*, NATO, Brussels

Partidário, M R (ed) (2000) *Perspectives on SEA*, Earthscan, London

Pearce, D W (1993) *Blueprint 3 – Measuring Sustainable Development*, Earthscan, London

Petts, J (ed) (1999) *Handbook on EIA*, Blackwell, London

Physical Planning Department (1993) *Amsterdam to Cut Back Cars in Centre*, Information Office of the Physical Planning Department, Amsterdam

Pinfield, G (1992) 'SEA and land-use planning', *Project Appraisal* 7(3):157–163

Popper, F (1981) 'Siting LULUS', *Planning* 47(4): 12–15

Price, A (1998) 'The new approach to appraisal', Impact Assessment in the Development Process: Advances in Integrating Environmental Assessment with Economic and Social Appraisal, Conference proceedings, University of Manchester, 23–24 October, Manchester

Pro Terra Team (1995) *UVP in Brandenburg – Informationsschrift zur Umweltverträglichkeitsprüfung*, Pro Terra Team, Dortmund

Provincie Noord-Holland (1992) *Relatienota natuurontwikkeling op landbouwgrond*, Provincie Noord-Holland, Haarlem

Provincie Noord-Holland (1993) *Provinciale nota locatiebeleid*, Provincie Noord-Holland, Haarlem

Provincie Noord-Holland (1994) *1994/1995 Almanak*, Provincie Noord-Holland, Haarlem

Reed, D (ed) (1996) *Structural Adjustment, the Environment and Sustainable Development*, Earthscan, London

Rees, W E (1988) 'A role for environmental assessment in achieving sustainable development', *Environmental Impact Assessment Review* 8: 273–291

Rees, W E and Wackernagel, M (1992) 'Ecological footprints and appropriated carrying capacity: measuring the natural capital requirements of the human economy', Paper presented to the second meeting of the International Society for Ecological Economics, Investing in Natural Capital, Stockholm

Regionaal Orgaan Amsterdam (ROA) (1993) *Kijk op het ROA*, ROA Amsterdam

Riehl, C and Winkler-Kühlken, B (1995) *Environmental Impact Assessment in Area Master Planning: Practical Problems and Suggested Solutions*, Institut für Stadtforschung und Strukturpolitik GmbH, Berlin

Roberts, J, Cleari, C, Hambleton, C and Hanna, J (1992) *Travel Sickness: The Need for a Sustainable Transport Policy for Britain*, Lawrence and Wishart, London

Rommerskirchen, S (1993) 'The effects of individual measures, and of combinations of measures, on reducing CO_2 emissions of transport in Germany', in: The European Conference of Ministers of Transport (ECMT): *Reducing Transport's Contribution to Global Warming, Conclusions of ECMT Seminar, 30 September–1 October 1992*, ECMT, Paris

Royal Commission on Environmental Pollution (1995) *18th Report: Transport and the Environment*, Oxford University Press, Oxford

Sadler, B (1994) 'Environmental assessment and development policy making', in: Goodland, R and Edmundson, V (eds), *Environmental Assessment and Development*, The World Bank: 3–19, Washington, DC

Sadler, B (1995) *Environmental Assessment: Towards Improved Effectiveness, International Study of the Effectiveness of Environmental Assessment*, Canadian Environmental Assessment Research Council (CEARC), Hull, Québec

Sadler, B (1996) *International Study of the Effectiveness of Environmental Assessment – Final Report: Environmental Assessment in a Changing World: Evaluation Practice to Improve Performance*, International Association for Impact Assessment (IAIA), Canadian Environmental Assessment Agency (CEAA), Ottawa

Sadler, B and Jacobs, P (1989) 'A key to tomorrow: on the relationship of environmental assessment and sustainable development', in: Jacobs, P and Sadler, B, *Sustainable Development and Environmental Assessment: Perspectives on Planning for a Common Future*, Canadian Environmental Assessment Research Council (CEARC), Hull, Québec

Sadler, B and Verheem, R (1996a) *Strategic Environmental Assessment – Status, Challenges and Future Directions*, Ministerie van Volkshuisvesting, Ruimtelijke Ordening en Milieubeheer (VROM), Den Haag

Sadler, B, Verheem, R (1996b) 'Conclusions and recommendations of the international SEA effectiveness study', International Association for Impact Assessment (IAIA), Conference Proceedings, 16th Annual Meeting, Estoril, IAIA, Fargo, ND

Schaenam, P S (1976) *Using an Impact Measurement System to Evaluate Land Development*, The Urban Institute, Washington, DC

Schallaböck (1991) Verkehrsvermeidungspotentiale durch Reduktion von Wegezahlen und Entfernungen, *Informationen zur Raumentwicklung*, Heft 1/2

Sheate, W (1992) 'Strategic environmental assessment in the transport sector', *Project Appraisal* 7(3): 170–174

Sheate, W (1994) *Making an Impact, a Guide to EIA Law and Policy*, Cameron May, London

Sheate, W (1995) 'Transport policy: a critical role for SEA', *World Transport Policy and Practice* 1(4): 17–24

Sheate, W (1996) *Making an Impact II: EIA Law and Policy*, Cameron May, London

Spalding, H, Smit, B and Kreutzwiser, R (1989) 'Evaluating impact assessment: approaches, lessons and prospects', *Environments* 22(1): 63–74

Steer Davies Gleave (1996) *State of the Art on Strategic Environmental Assessment for Transport Infrastructure*, Steer Davies Gleave, London

Swensen, I (1997) 'EIA effectiveness: some methodological questions', International Association for Impact Assessment (IAIA), Conference proceedings, 17th Annual Meeting, New Orleans 1997, CD-Rom, IAIA, Fargo, ND

Tarling, J (1991) *A Comparison of Environmental Assessment Procedures and Experience in the UK and The Netherlands*, MSc Thesis, Department of Environmental Management, University of Stirling

Thérivel, R (1995) 'Environmental appraisal of development plans', *Planning Practice and Research* 10(2): 223–234

Thérivel, R (1996) 'SEA methodology in practice', in: Thérivel, R and Partidário, M R (eds), *The Practice of Strategic Environmental Assessment*, Earthscan, London

Thérivel, R, Wilson, E, Thompson, S, Heaney, D and Pritchard, D (1992) *Strategic Environmental Assessment*, Earthscan, London

Thérivel, R and Partidário, M R (1996a) *The Practice of Strategic Environmental Assessment*, Earthscan, London

Thérivel, R and Partidário, M R (1996b) 'Learning from SEA practice', International Association for Impact Assessment (IAIA), Conference proceedings, 16th Annual Meeting, Estoril, IAIA, Fargo, ND

Thissen, W (1997) 'From SEA to integrated assessment: a policy analysis perspective', *Environmental Assessment* (ca) 5(3): 24–26

Tonk, J and Verheem, R (1998) *Integrating the Environment in Strategic Decision Making – One Concept, Multiple Forms*, Commissie voor de Mer, Utrecht

Tromans, S and Roger-Machart, C (1997) 'Strategic environmental assessment: early evaluation equals efficiency?', *Journal of Planning and Environment Law*, November: 993–996

United Nations Conference on Environment and Development (UNCED) (1992a) *Agenda 21*, UNCED, New York

United Nations Conference on Environment and Development (UNCED) (1992b) *Climate Change Convention*, UNCED, Rio de Janeiro

United Nations Conference on Environment and Development (UNCED) (1992c) *Convention on Biological Diversity*, UNCED, Rio de Janeiro

United Nations Economic Commission for Europe (UNECE) (1985) *Convention on Long-range Transboundary Air Pollution (LRTAP), Sulphur Protocol*, UNECE, New York

United Nations Economic Commission for Europe (UNECE) (1988) *Convention on Long-range Transboundary Air Pollution (LRTAP), NO_x Protocol*, UNECE, New York

United Nations Economic Commission for Europe (UNECE) (1991) *Convention on Long-range Transboundary Air Pollution (LRTAP), VOC Protocol*, UNECE, New York

United Nations Economic Commission for Europe (UNECE) (1992) *Application of Environmental Impact Assessment Principles to Policies, Plans and Programmes*, UNECE, New York

United Nations Economic Commission for Europe (UNECE) (1994) *Convention on Long-range Transboundary Air Pollution (LRTAP), New Sulphur Protocol*, UNECE, New York

University of Manchester (1995a) *Strategic Environmental Assessment*, EIA Centre Leaflet Series 13, University of Manchester

University of Manchester (1995b) *EIA Centres in Europe*, EIA Centre Leaflet Series 1, University of Manchester

University of Manchester (1998) 'Impact Assessment in the Development Process: Advances in Integrating Environmental Assessment with Economic and Social Appraisal', 22–23 October, Conference proceedings, University of Manchester

UVP-Gesellschaft (1999) *UVP Report 1, Main Subject: Cooperative Planning Processes*, UVP-Gesellschaft, Hamm

UVP-Zentrum (1996) UVP und Verkehrssysteme, Conference Proceedings, 13–14 November, UVP-Zentrum, Hamm

Vägverket (1998) *Gothenburg-Jönköping Transport Corridor, Environmental Impact of Strategic Choices*, Swedish National Road Administration, Stockholm

Van der Heiden, N, Kok, J, Postuma, R and Wallagh, G (1991) 'Consensus-building as an essential element of the Dutch planning system', Paper presented at the ACSP-AESOP Joint International Congress, 8–12 July, Oxford

Van Eck, M (1996) *Environmental Impact Assessment for Policy, Plans and Programmes in The Netherlands*, Commissie voor de Mer, Utrecht

Vanclay, F and Bronstein, D A (eds) (1995) *Environmental and Social Impact Assessment*, John Wiley and Sons, Chichester

Verheem, R (1992) 'Environmental assessment at the strategic level in The Netherlands', *Project Appraisal* 7(3): 150–156

Verheem, R (1994) *Toetsing van de LCA – methodiek aan de kentallenmethodiek ten behoeve van de MER – TJPA*. Dutch Waste Management Council

Verheyen, R F (1996) 'Conclusions and recommendations', in: *NATO Report No. 212*, NATO, Brussels

Volkskrant (1997) *Coalities is het eens over stadsprovincies*, Volkskrant Daily Newspaper, 22 May, Amsterdam

Voogd, H (1996) *Facetten van de Planologie*, Samson H D Tjeenk Willink, Alphen aan den Rijn

Voogd, H and Woltjer, J (forthcoming) 'The communicative ideology in spatial planning: some critical reflections based on the Dutch experience', *Environment and Planning B: Planning and Design*

Wagner, J (1990) 'Zweiter Kongreß UVP und kommunale Planung', *Zentrales Verwaltungsblatt*, June: 566–569

Wagner, D (1994) 'Strategic Environmental Assessment for Transport Planning in Germany', in: European Commission, Directorate General Environment, Nuclear Safety and Civil Protection (DG XI), *Third EU Workshop on Environmental Impact Assessment in Delphi*, DG XI, Brussels

Wathern, P (ed) (1988) *Environmental Impact Assessment: Theory and Practice*, Unwin Hyman, London

Wildavsky, A (1979) *The Art and Craft of Policy Making*, The Macmillan Press, London

Williams, R (1986) 'Translation of theory into practice', in: Masser, I and Williams, R (eds), *Learning from Other Countries*, Geo Books, Norwich

Wood, C (1988) 'EIA in plan making', in: Wathern, P (ed), *Environmental Impact Assessment: Theory and Practice*, Unwin Hyman, London

Wood, C (1995) *Environmental Impact Assessment, A Comparative Review*, Longman, Harlow

Wood, C (1997) 'SEA – the way forward', *Environmental Assessment* (es) 5 (3): 5–6

Wood, C and Djeddour, M (1992) 'Strategic environmental assessment: EA of policies, plans and programmes', *Impact Assessment Bulletin* 10(1): 3–22

World Commission on Environment and Development (1987) *Our Common Future*, Oxford University Press, Oxford

Wuppertal Institut für Klima, Umwelt, Energie GmbH (1995) *Zukunftsfähiges Deutschland – Ein Beitrag zu einer global nachhaltigen Entwicklung, Kurzfassung*, Wuppertal Institut, Wuppertal

Yin, R K (1982) *Studying Phenomenon and Context Across Sites*, Sage Publications, London

Yin, R K (1994) *Case Study Research: Design and Methods*, Sage Publications, London

Index

Åarhus convention 33
accelerating project preparation 27,
    141, 231
accountability 13, 31, 33, 71–77, 188,
    197, 206
acidification 28, 152–160
acts *see* Brandenburg Environment Act;
    Environment Act; Environment Act
    Berlin; Federal Nature Protection
    Act; General Administrative Act;
    Highways Act; Land Compensation
    Act; Local Government Act;
    National Transport Environmental
    Policy Act; Public Regionalization
    Act; Regional Planning Act; road
    and rail extension acts; Spatial
    Planning Act; Town and Country
    Planning Act; Transport Act;
    Transport Planning Act
adaptive environmental management 6
administrative areas 22–23
administrative levels 23–26, 92
Agenda 21 259
    see also Local Agenda 21
air impacts 103–104, 140
air quality 28, 152–160
airports 44–52
alternatives 9, 184, 234, 229–230
Amsterdam 22–23
Amsterdam Physical Planning
    Department 52
Amt (authority) 42
assessment report 11
    adequacy 5, 13
    quality 27, 131–133, 230–231
Association of Dutch municipalities
    (VNG) 260
Austria 20
Authority for Construction, Building Tech-
    niques and Settlements (LBBW) 98

Belgium 20
Berlin 22–23
big-project SEA/EIA 87
biodiversity 28, 152–160, 233
Brandenburg 22–23, 42
Brandenburg Environment Act 107
Bundesregierung (Federal Government)
    42
Bundesverkehrswegeplan (Federal
    Transport Infrastructure Plan) 48,
    52, 55

carbon dioxide (CO_2) 28, 163
centrally guided, local plan making
    approach 43, 56–57, 100, 125, 183,
    229
    see also planning, systems
certainty 12
    legal certainty 45, 52
checklists 9, 27, 119, 231, 239
Cheshire 32–33, 89
city district development plans 53
city province 41
climate 103–104
climate change 28, 152–160, 233, 261
Climate Change Convention 259
collaborative planning 260
    see also planning
College van Burgemeester en
    Wethouders 41
Common Land Planning Authority (GL)
    21
communicative planning 260
    see also planning
comparative aspects 221
    see also regions; strategic
        environmental assessment,
        types of
comparative research 14, 15
    criteria 16

identifying sample regions 19–22
   problems 22–25
   studies 19
compensation 27, 116, 166, 259
   see also methods; mitigation
consent-related SEA 7
Construction Lead Planning system 53
Construction Statute Book (BauGB) 55
consultation 13, 197–200, 234
   see also expert consultation;
      participation
consumption 28, 154, 167
context variables 81, 93
   PPP accountability 71
   PPP inter-modality 77
   PPP procedure 78
   PPP relevance 67
Convention on Biological Diversity 259
conventions on long-range,
   transboundary air pollution 259
correlation analysis 219
councillors 40
cultural heritage impacts 27, 103–104
cumulative impacts 185–186, 226, 229–
   230, 258

data availability 23
data collection 34
decision making cycle 100
Denmark 20
Department for Transport, Local
   Government and the Regions
   (DTLR) 43
Department of the Environment (DoE)
   40, 109
Department of the Environment,
   Transport and the Regions (DETR)
   40, 43, 50
Department of Transport (DoT) 43
design of analytical framework 26
Deutsche Bahn (DB) (German Rail) 48
Development Concept (The
   Netherlands) 86
devolution 43
dissemination of SEA experience 239
distortion of competition 241

ecological conflict assessment 90
ecological risk assessment 86
economic
   impacts 27, 105–106
   incentives 172
   objectives 106
effects *see* impacts
efficiency of tiered decision making
   12, 191–194, 234
enforceability 33
Environment Act (UK) 53
Environment Act Berlin 107
environment test (The Netherlands) 9
environmental appraisal 9, 86
   assessment provisions 5
   concerns 145
   impacts 8, 103, 111–112, 142–146
      see also air; climate; cultural
         heritage; fauna; flora;
         noise; soil; waste; water
   objectives 30, 89–90, 138, 233
   policy and plans 97
   targets 89–80, 138, 233
Environmental Matrix Amsterdam 98
European Commission (EC) 8
European Conference of Ministers of
   Transport (ECMT) 12
European Environment Agency (EEA) 8
European High Speed Train Network 8
European Union
   member states 20
   regions 259
evaluation 116
   individual SEAs 218
   methods 120
   sustainability measures 177
   sustainability objectives 177
   sustainability targets 177
   techniques 120
   see also methods
EVR Brandenburg-Berlin 21, 22, 23, 63
expert consultation 76, 118–119, 184,
   200
   see also consultation
external control 3

fauna impacts 27, 103–104
Federal Ministry of Transport
   (BMVBW) 47
Federal Nature Protection Act 49
Federal Parliament (*Bundestag*) 55
Federal Spatial Orientation Framework
   (ROPOrient) 64
Federal Transport Infrastructure Plan
   (BVWP) 48

field research 119
Fifth Environmental Action Programme
    28, 149, 167–168, Annex 5
    measures 28, 170–176
    objectives 28, 152–160
    reduction targets 28, 161–169
Finland 20
fiscal
    impacts 27, 105–108
    incentives 172
fit-for-purpose process 14
flora impacts 27, 103–104
follow-up 11, 31, 33
formalized SEA 144
    attitudes towards 27, 126, 230
former East Germany 21
former West Germany 21
framework for comparing the
    consideration of sustainability
    aspects 28
framework principle 31
France 20

Gedeputeerde Staten (Provincial
    Executive) 41
Gemeenteraad (Municipal Council) 41
Gemeinde (Municipality) 42
Gemeinsame Landesplanung (Common
    Land Planning, GL) 21
General Administrative Act (The
    Netherlands) 54
German federal transport infrastructure
    planning 49
German spatial/land use planning 47
good practice 218, 221
Good Practice Guide (DoE) 109
government circular 41, 70
government expenditure plans 50
government offices for the regions
    (GOR) 41
Greece 20
guidance 49, 53, 78, 98, 186, 196, 213,
    226

Haarlem-IJmond 120
Habitats Directive 8
Havelland 89
highway agencies 44
Highways Act 53
Hilversum 66
House of Commons 40

housing impacts 27, 105–106

identifying suitable countries 19–21
identifying suitable regions 21–22
impacts 184
    coverage 8, 102, 115
    prediction 116
        see also methods
    types of 107–108
    wider consideration 185
    see also air; climate; cultural
        heritage; fauna; flora; noise;
        soil, waste; water
indirect assessment 112
influence of SEA 27, 128–135, 230–231
information and education 172
infrastructure charging 172
infrastructure investment 172
Institute for European Environment
    Policy (IEEP) 6
integrated
    procedure 11
    SEA 7
    spatial/land use planning and
        landscape planning 49
    Transport Plan (IVP) 65
    transport strategy 50
    Transport Vision (IPVR) 65
integration of SEA into PPP 137
interaction process 6
interactive communication 172, 261
inter-administrative tiering structure 91
inter-modal alternatives 116
    see also methods
International Association for Impact
    Assessment (IAIA) 15
interpretation of results 224
Inter-provincial Administrative
    Committee (IPO) 260
Inter-provincial Urbanization Vision 65
interviews 24
intra-modal alternatives 116
    see also methods
Ireland 20
Italy 20

Ketzin 66
Knooppunt Arnhem-Nijmegen 260
Kreis (county) 42
Kreis- und Stadttage (parliaments of
    counties and municipalities) 42

kreisfreie Stadt (self administering city) 42

Labour government 260
Lancashire 23, 89
Land Compensation Act 53
land development programme (LEPro) 65
Land Planning Convention 55, 85, 119
land suitability 113, 116, 186
land use planning 172–173, 180–181
Landesregierungen (*Länder* governments) 42
Landscape Framework Plan Havelland-Fläming 86
landscape planning system 49
landscape plans 49, 62, 87
landscape programmes 98
Landtage (*Länder* parliaments) 42
legal certainty 45
legislation 53–57
legislative environmental assessment 262
Local Agenda 21 64, 80, 261
Local Authority Circular 196
Local Authority Regulations 53
Local Government Act 41, 53
local land use PPPs 23, 130, 140, 153
local plans 50
local transport plans 50
long-range infrastructure and transport programme (MIT) 65
Luxemburg 20

Manchester 22–23
mapping 27, 119, 136
matrices 27, 119
Merseyside 22–23
meten=weten (to measure is to know) 98
methodological differences xiii
methodological requirements xiii
methods 14, 117, 136
  compensation 27, 116, 166, 259
  evaluation 120
  impact prediction 116
  inter-modal alternatives 116
  intra-modal alternatives 116
  mitigation 31, 116
  objectives setting 119
  scenarios 116

metropolitan county council 41
Ministry of Housing, Spatial Planning and the Environment (VROM) 9, 196
Ministry of Transport, Public Works and Water Management (MVW) 46
mitigation 31, 116
  see also compensation; methods
monitoring 11, 31
  see also meten=weten
motorways 44
multi-criteria analysis (MCA) 112
multi-modal 94

National Environmental Policy Act (NEPA) (US) 4–5
National Environmental Policy Plan (NMP) 169
National Spatial Plan (VINEX) 60
Nationale Spoorwegen (NS) (Dutch national railways) 46
nature 156–160, 175, 180, 233, 258, 261–162,
Nature Protection Law 49
negotiation process 6
Netherlands, The
  national transport infrastructure planning 47
  spatial/land use planning 45
NIMBYism 100, 184–186, 234
nitrous oxides (NO$_x$) 28
noise impacts 27, 103 104
Noord-Holland 21, 22, 23, 61
North Atlantic Treaty Organization (NATO) 15
North West England 21–22, 23, 59
not in my back yard (NIMBY) 13, 94, 100, 139, 147, 158, 184–186, 200, 207, 214, 234

objectives of the book 17
objectives setting 119
objectives-led SEA 7
  see also methods
Oldham 89
open process 100
  see also fit-for-purpose process; planning; strategic environmental assessment
operational choices 12
opinions on existing SEA 126, 230

organizational support 14

participation 13, 32, 44–45, 77, 197
plan-SEA
    application 95, 108, 113
    scores 5, 96, 212–241
planning
    approach 123, 218
    assumptions 106, 109
    cycle 87
    goals 106
    instruments 50–52
    policy guidance (PPG) 40
    systems 42
    see also collaborative planning;
        communicative planning; land
        use planning
policies, plans and programmes (PPP)
    58–84
    accountability 71
    formulation delay 138
    inter-modality 77
    policy orientation 67
    preparation delay 184
    procedure 78
    project orientation 67
    relevance 67
policy impact matrix 9
policy orientation 87
policy-SEA
    application 95, 108, 113
    non-project oriented character 100
    scores 5, 96, 212–241
population impacts 105–106
Portugal 20
postal questionnaire 24, 34, 66, 86, 125
potential SEA benefits 9–12, 182–206,
    234
precautionary principle 10, 47, 49, 86,
    116, 190, 193, 205
preparation times 122
principal roads 44–45
pro-active assessment 10, 188–190, 234
procedural coverage of SEA 95
procedural principle 31
process *see* fit-for-purpose process;
    open process; planning; strategic
    environmental assessment
programme-SEA
    application 95, 108, 113
    scores 5, 96, 212–241

project acceleration 141
project EIA 193
    orientation 87
    prioritization 112
    strengthening 191
    substitution 147
provinciale staten (provincial council)
    41
public administration, consensus-led,
    counter-current approach 4, 7, 56–
    57, 126, 181
public consultation 13, 29, 197–200,
    234
public opposition 13, 200, 234
public participation 13, 29, 197–200,
    234
public service impacts 105–108
public transport 172, 180
    growth 163
    measures 176
    service 78–79
Public Transport Regionalization Act
    57
publicly accountable decision making
    6

qualitative assessment 109
quality of SEA 129–145
quantitative assessment 109
quasi-statutory plans 69

Railtrack 44, 50, 260
Randstad 88
raw material consumption 28, 152–160,
    232
regering (government) 41
Regio Twente 260
Regio Utrecht 260
Regional Body of Amsterdam (ROA)
    22–23
regional development agency (RDA) 41
Regional Development Plan Berlin-
    Brandenburg 65
Regional Economic Strategy 79
regional level administration 42
Regional Plan 86
regional plans 51
    environmental appraisal 8
Regional Planning Act (Germany) 55
regional planning bodies 53
regional planning conferences 54

regional planning guidance (RPG) (UK) 40, 51, 54
Regional Planning Guidance Note for Manchester 54
regional planning system 51
regions 3
 baseline data 22–23
 choice of 19
 EU 17
 evaluating SEA practice 7
 identification of 21
regulation changes 172
research questions 16
review package 14
Rhône Transport Corridor 9
rijkswegen (national roads) 45
road and rail extension acts (Germany) 85
Road Development Plan Brandenburg 91
route determination procedure 46

scenarios 116
scoping 11, 31, 97
screening 11, 31, 97
SEA Directive 32–34, 142, 150
Second Transport Structure Plan (SVVII) 64
Secretary of State for Transport, Local Environment and the Regions 54
sectoral coverage 26
simulation techniques 119
site alternatives 118
Skeleton Law Changing Administration 54
slip roads 44
small-scale projects 10
social impacts 27, 105–107
society consensus-led, quasi top-down approach 45, 56–57, 140
socio-economic
Spain 20
 aspects 11, 27, 29
 impacts 25, 30, 103–104
soil impacts 103–104
spatial administration 65
Spatial Planning Act (Germany) 85
Spatial Planning Act (The Netherlands) 54
Stadsgewest Haaglanden 260
Stadsregio Eindhoven 260

Stadsregio Rotterdam 260
staten generaal (parliament) 41
statistical analysis 26, 36
statutory local land use plan 54
strategic decision making xiii, 5
strategic environmental assessment (SEA)
 background 4
 categorization 7–8
 classification 228
 context 25, 93, 95
 documentation 116
 EC Directive 202
 effectiveness 13
 extent of application 86, 228
 interpretation 224–227
 literature xiii, 15
 methods 117
 performance 219
 potential benefits 9, 182, 206, 234
 preparation times 122
 presentation aspects 95, 93
 principles 30
 procedure 95
 provisions 31
 quality 131
 report 205
 report review 13, 98
 requirements 31
 stages 97
  see also follow-up; monitoring; participation; scoping; screening
 structuring the PPP process 188
 techniques 119
 transport sector 20
 types of 87–90
strategic outlook plans 52
streamlining 12
Structural Funds 8
sulphur dioxide (SO_2) 28
sustainability 149–181, 262–263, 190, 212
 analysis 27
 appraisal 9
 aspects 27, 149, 206, 211–238
 measures 170, 232–234
 objectives 27–28, 152–161, 232–234
 scores 179, 226
 targets 27–28, 161–170, 232–234
 test 27
sustainability and the role of SEA 27, 233–234

sustainable development
  SEA as a supporting tool for 188
Sweden 20

techniques 119
  see also checklists; expert
    consultation; field research;
    mapping; matrices; simulation;
    workshops
terms of reference 5, 11
Town and Country Planning Act 53
Town and Country Planning
  Regulations 53
transnational comparative research 22
transport
Transport Act 53
  corridors 7
  networks 7
  regions 51
  see also motorways; public
    transport; waterways
Transport Infrastructure Planning
  Acceleration (Germany) 55
Transport Planning Act (The
  Netherlands) 54
Triangle Hamburg–Hannover–Berlin
  250

UK
  trunk roads planning 45
  spatial/land use planning 43
uncertainty 10
uni-modal 94
unitary development plan (UDP) 32,
  51, 59
United Nations Economic Commission
  for Europe (UNECE) 9
Upper Land Environment Authority
  (*Landesumweltamt*) 196
urban environment 28, 149–180, 232–
  233

VERDI 260
vertical integration 44
views of local authorities 131
visions 186

Warrington 41
waste 28, 154
water impacts 27, 103–104
waterways 44, 52
work load of local authorities 141
workshops 15, 27, 118–119

zero alternative 185–186

Also available from Earthscan

THE PRACTICE OF STRATEGIC ENVIRONMENTAL ASSESSMENT
Edited by Riki Therivel and Maria Rosario Partidario

'Essential reading for those with a practical or academic interest in SEA. The diversity of SEA applications revealed by the book is of great interest and the fast pace of development in SEA methodologies is impressive' Town Planning Review

This unique selection of case studies will be particularly suitable for anyone commissioning, carrying out or reviewing SEAs, as well as students of environmental assessment and management.
Pb 1 85383 373 8

CITY-REGION 2020
Integrated Planning for a Sustainable Environment
Joe Ravetz

'This book is a revelation... It gives clarity to many of the frustrations we routinely face, and provides inspirational pointers for the future... It clearly illustrates the universal principles and issues that cause concern among urban planners, city politicians and city inhabitants... an essential read' Landscape Design

This leading publication sets a standard for the integrated strategic management of cities and regions, with methods and tools such as sustainability indicators and appraisals that can be applied anywhere in the western world.
Pb 1 85383 606 0 ▪ Hb 1 85383 607 9

ENVIRONMENTAL POLICY IN THE EUROPEAN UNION
Actors, Institutions and Processes
Edited by Andrew Jordan

This highly useful guide and course book incorporates a range of detailed case studies, drawing out the links between levels of governance and the role of the environment in other policy areas such as transport. Jordan examines whether the EU is fully prepared or even able to respond to the new sustainability agenda of EU policy. An essential reference and course book for all those involved in or studying environmental politics and policy, not just in Europe but also worldwide.
Pb 1 85383 795 4 ▪ Hb 1 85383 755 5

ENVIRONMENTAL POLICY INTEGRATION
Greening Sectoral Policies in Europe
Edited by Andrea Lenschow

The European Union has made the principle of environmental policy integration (EPI) a core policy objective and this volume explores the success with which EPI has been implemented, and analyses the problems encountered. This is the first book to systematically study of the practical issues EPI throws up and the difficulties for policy formulation, decision-making and implementation. Essential reading for those studying or working on environmental and other sectoral policies.
Pb 1 85383 709 1 ▪ Hb 1 85383 708 3

SUSTAINABLE COMMUNITIES IN EUROPE
Edited by William M Lafferty

This book presents detailed research into the implementation in 11 European countries of Local Agenda 21 (LA 21), the action plan for sustainable development at community level. The most broad-based and systematic study of LA 21 ever produced, it has invaluable case studies and analysis for the future on achieving sustainability from Scandinavia, UK, Ireland, The Netherlands, Spain, Italy and Austria.
Pb 1 85383 791 1 ▪ Hb 1 85383 790 3

GREENING THE BUILT ENVIRONMENT
Maf Smith, John Whitelegg and Nick Williams

'Timely, engaging, far-ranging and insightful. This book should be on every reading list of courses on environmental politics as well as urban planning. It is also the first of a series of books on the Built Environment to be published by Earthscan. If all of these match this one in quality and content, the series promises to be one of classics' Environmental Politics
Hb 1 85383 404 1

THE TRANSITION TO SUSTAINABILITY
The Politics of Agenda 21 in Europe
Edited by Timothy O'Riordan and Heather Voisey

'Details how all nations are repositioning their economies, their societies and their collective purpose to maintain all life on Earth, peacefully, healthily, equitably and with sufficient wealth to ensure that all are content in their survival'
From the Preface
Hb 1 85383 469 6

TOMORROW'S WORLD
Britain's Share in a Sustainable Future
Duncan McLaren, Simon Bullock and Nusrat Yousuf for Friends of the Earth

'Goes straight on to the "must read" list for businesses. If you want to understand the agenda for the 21st century, this book is packed with clues' John Elkington, SustainAbility

Tomorrow's World argues that Britain must make deep cuts in resource consumption in order to allow developing countries to escape from poverty, and to prevent further breaches of environmental limits. It sets targets for reduced consumption levels, and shows how these can be met.
Pb 1 85383 511 0 ▪ Hb 1 85383 510 2

URBAN TRANSPORT, ENVIRONMENT AND EQUITY
The Case for Developing Countries
Eduardo Alcântara Vasconcellos

This book highlights the importance of the social and political aspects of transport policy and provides a methodology to support this approach. It emphasizes the importance of coordinating urban transport and traffic planning, and addresses the major challenge of modifying the building and use of roads. The author makes valuable suggestions for innovative and radical new measures aimed at an equitable and sustainable urban environment.
Pb 1 85383 727 X ▪ Hb 1 85383 726 1

www.earthscan.co.uk